A PORTRAIT OF MANCHESTER

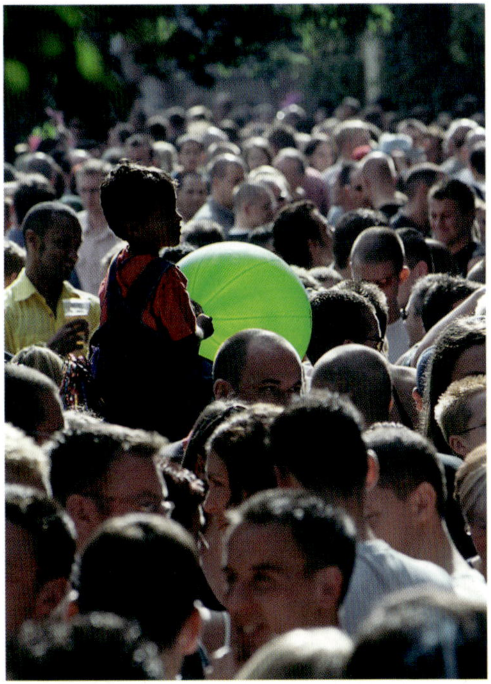

LEN GRANT

HALSGROVE

First published in Great Britain in 2004

British Library Cataloguing-in-Publication Data
A CIP record for this title is available from the British Library

ISBN 1 84114 380 4

HALSGROVE
Halsgrove House
Lower Moor Way
Tiverton, Devon EX16 6SS
Tel: 01884 243242
Fax: 01884 243325
email: sales@halsgrove.com
website: www.halsgrove.com

Printed and bound by D'Auria Industrie Grafiche Spa, Italy

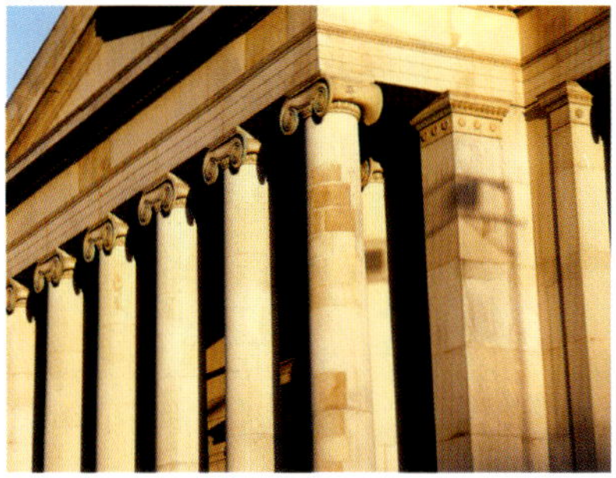

Preface

Some months ago a man stopped me in the street and asked directions. We got chatting – it's that kind of city – and he told me he'd grown up in Manchester before emigrating in his early thirties. Twenty-five years later, he was back in the city on one of his infrequent visits to see relatives ... and he was lost.

He was astonished at all the changes: familiar landmarks had disappeared with shiny new buildings in their place; new public spaces where there had been none before; trendy new shops and pavement cafés. The place had been transformed – and he liked what he saw.

I have been a photographer for about fifteen years, a time during which Manchester has seen unprecedented change. I have recorded the construction of many new landmark buildings, followed regeneration projects in the inner city and, most significantly, documented the rebuilding of the city centre after the terrorist bomb of 1996.

Like any city, Manchester is forever changing, constantly opening up new opportunities to capture new images. I never tire of watching the light on the sandstone, terracotta or glass of the city's finest buildings.

I feel very fortunate to have been able to document Manchester's renaissance and am pleased to offer this book as a celebration of this wonderful city.

Len Grant, 2004

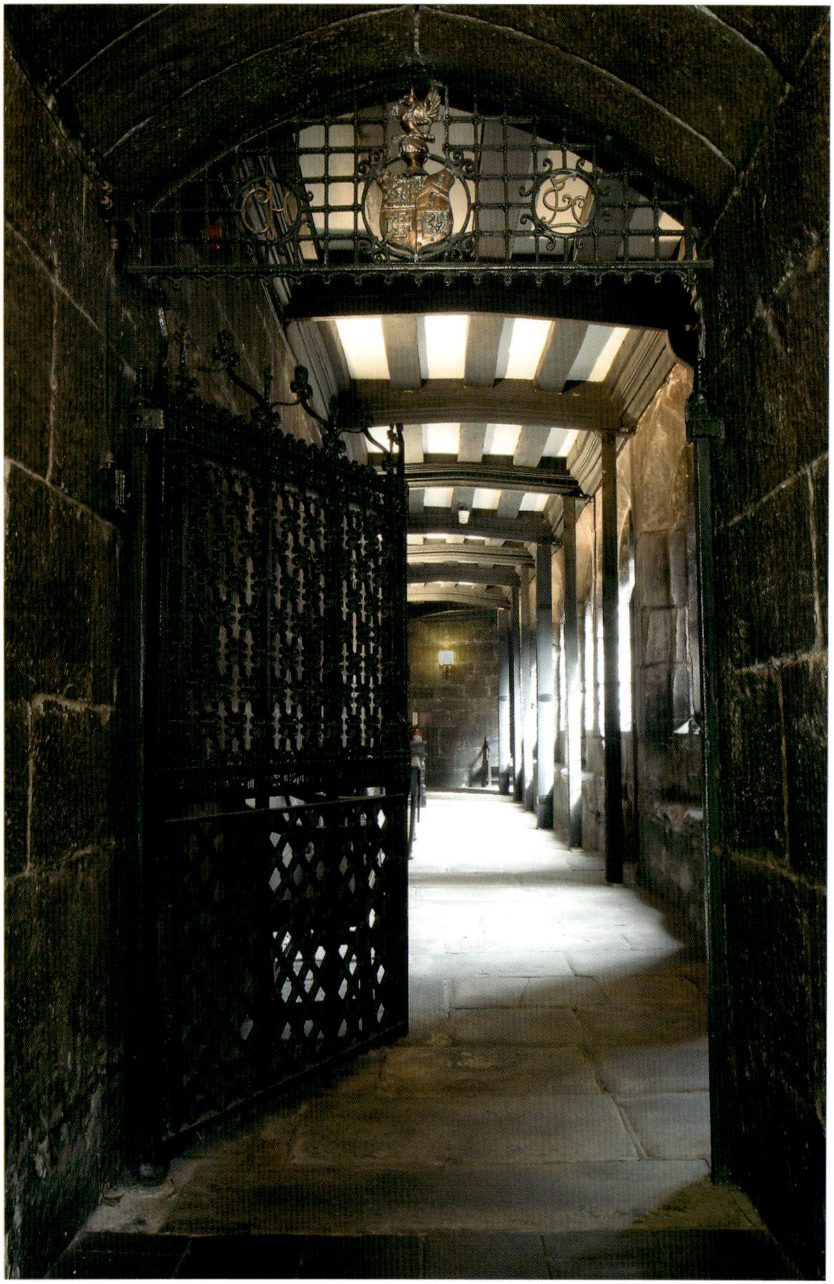

Chetham's Library is the oldest public library in the English-speaking world. It dates from 1422 when the buildings were home to the priests of the nearby collegiate college, now the cathedral.

The library itself was founded in 1653 by local merchant Humphrey Chetham. Visitors can sit in the bay window where Marx and Engels famously met.

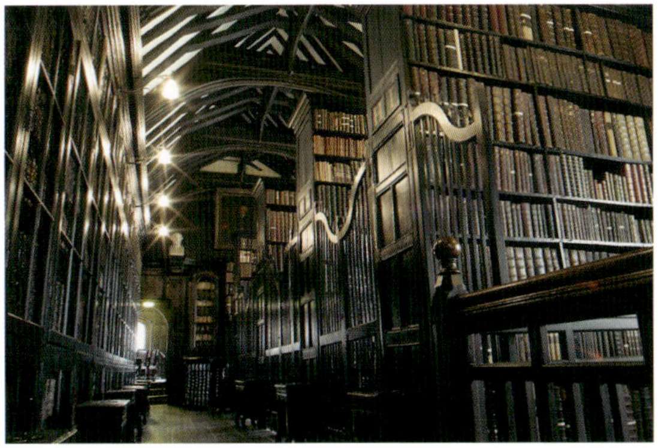

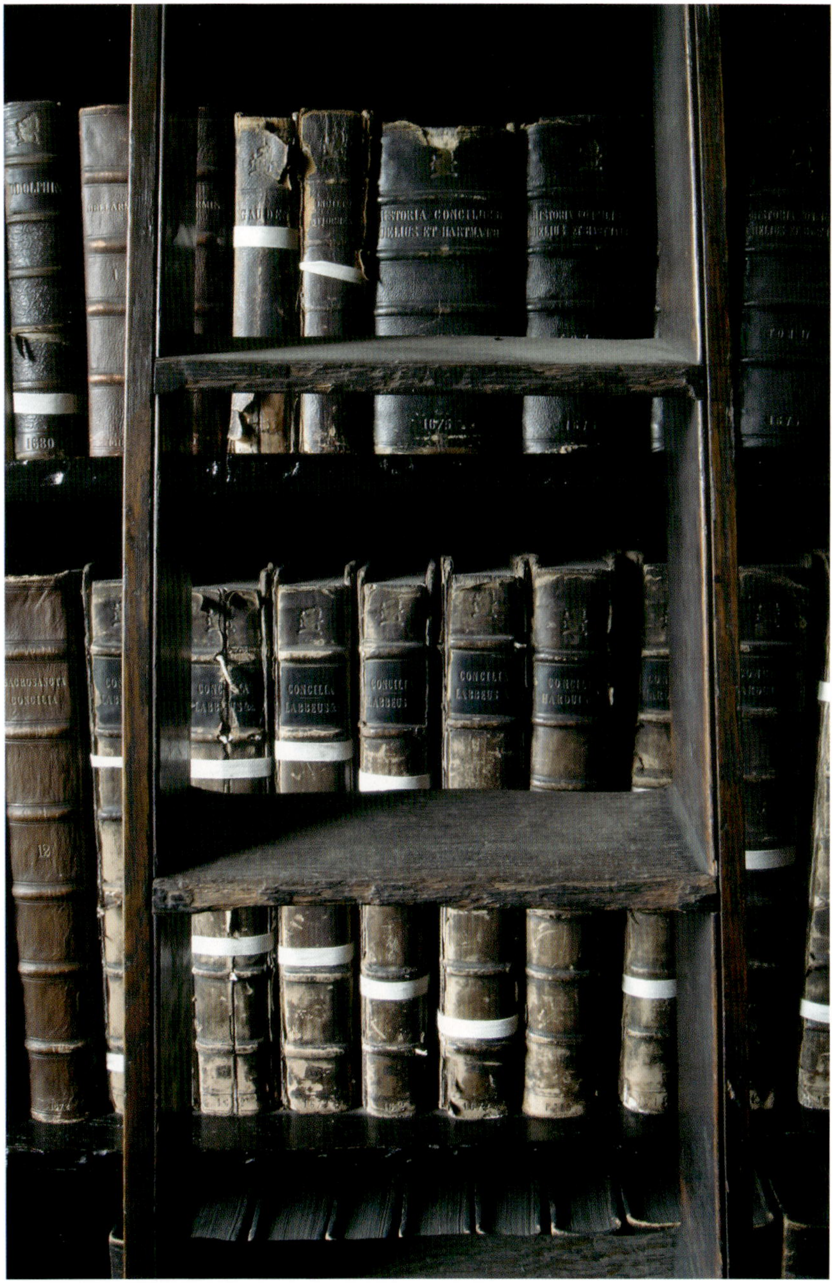

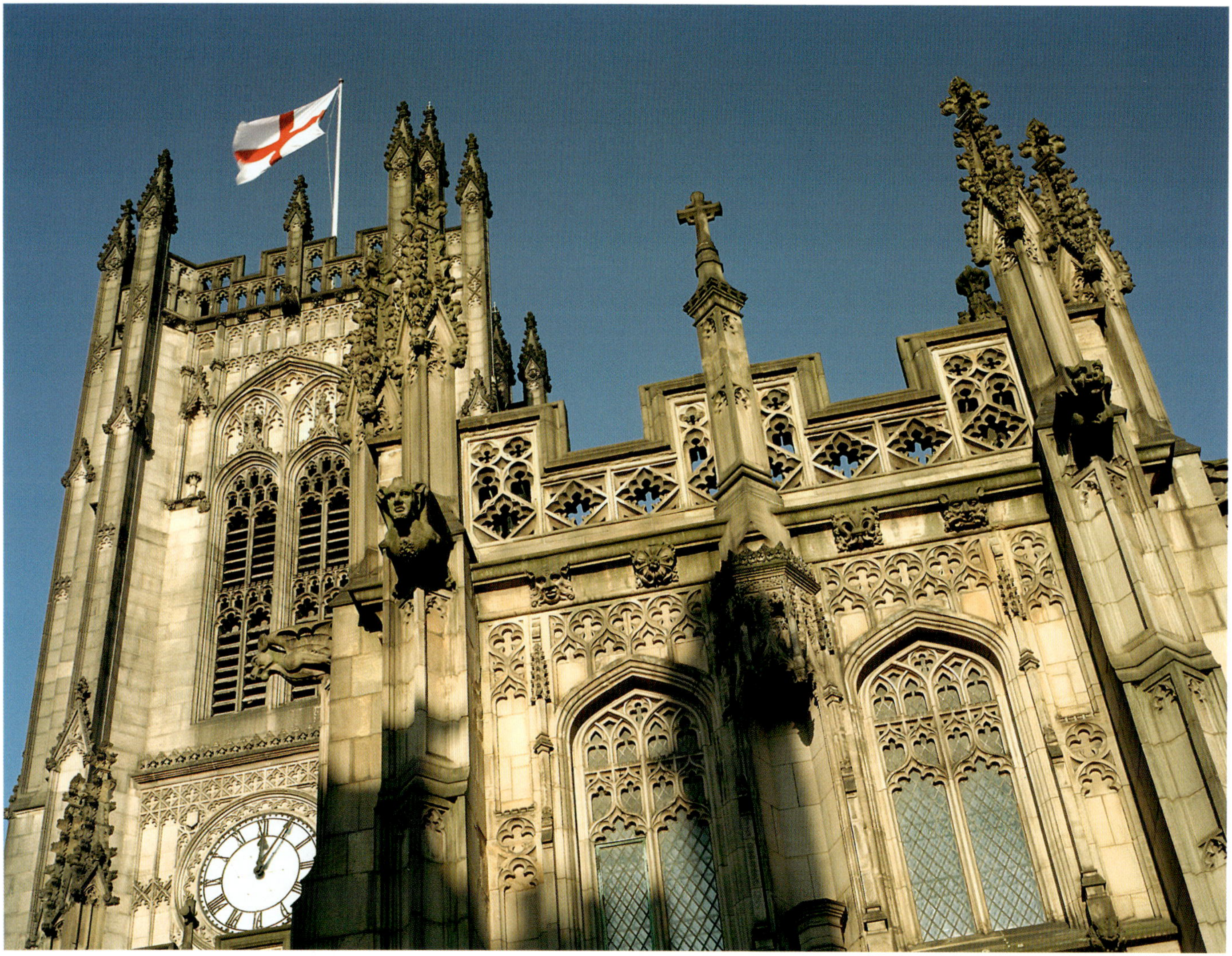

Reintegrated into the city centre with the creation of the Millennium Quarter in 1999, Manchester Cathedral has been extensively added to and altered since its origins in the fifteenth century.

In red sandstone and terracotta, Mynshull's House snuggles up to its neighbour on the corner of Cateaton Street, its wonderful carvings often overlooked by busy shoppers.

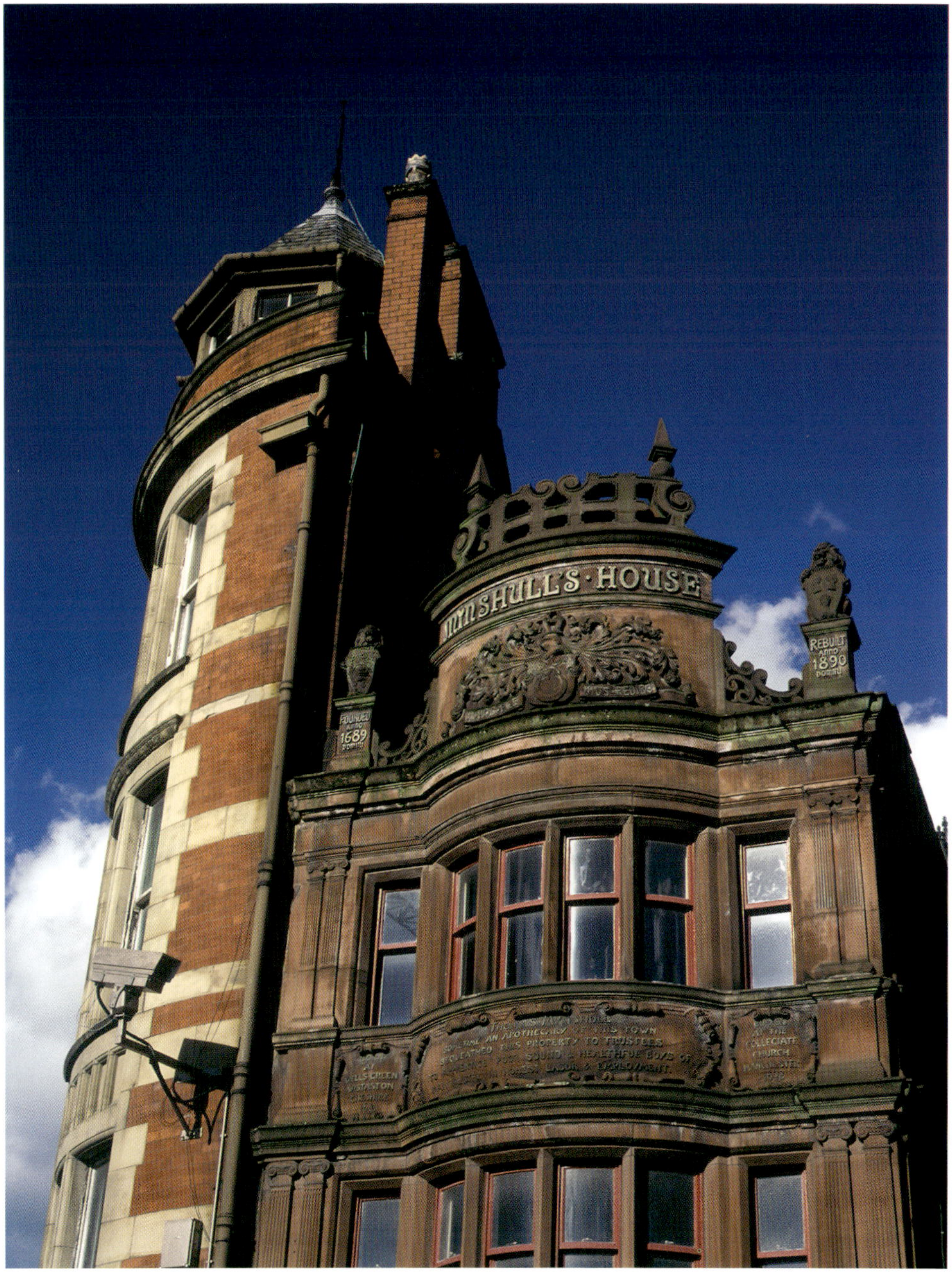

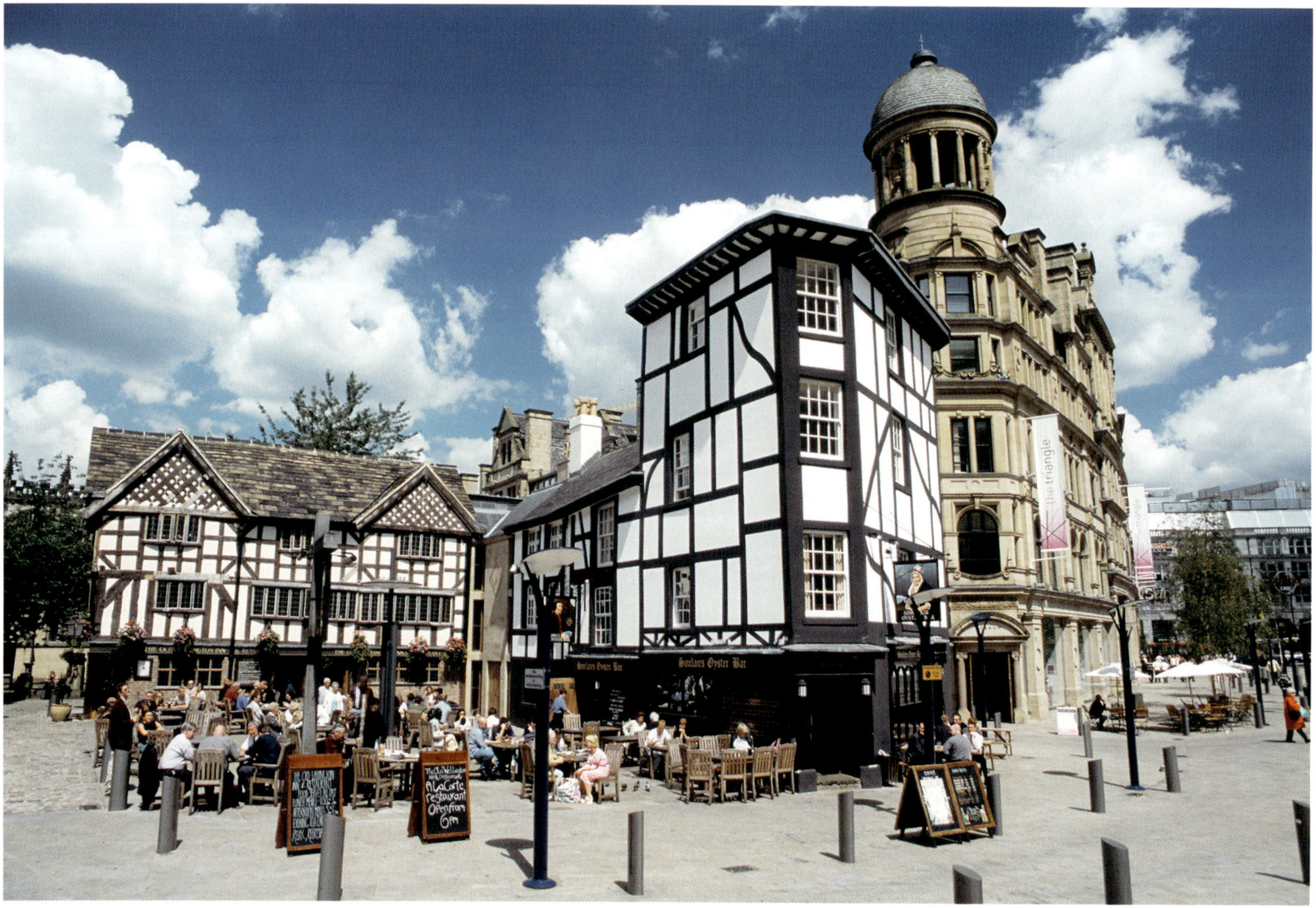

The Old Wellington Inn and Sinclair's Oyster Bar. Following the rebuilding after the terrorist bomb of 1996, these two historic pubs were dismantled and relocated in Exchange Square.

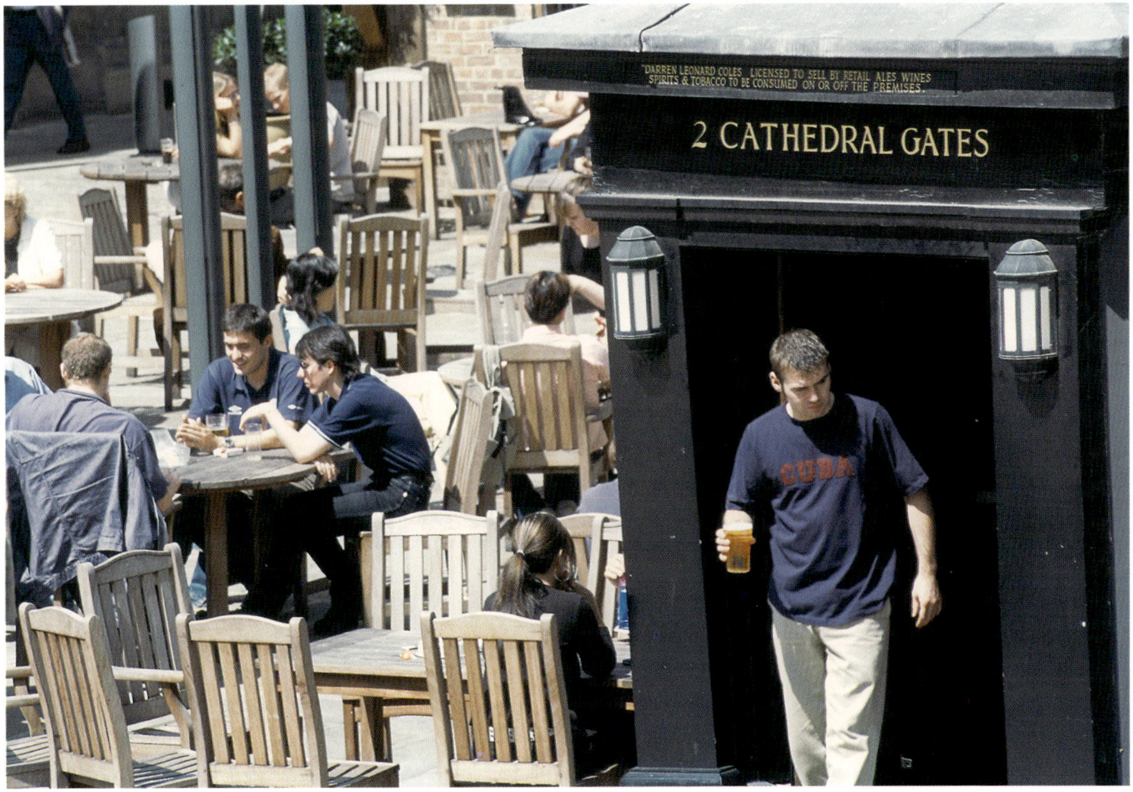

Emerging into the sunshine from Sinclair's. Apparently their beef and oyster pie is recommended.

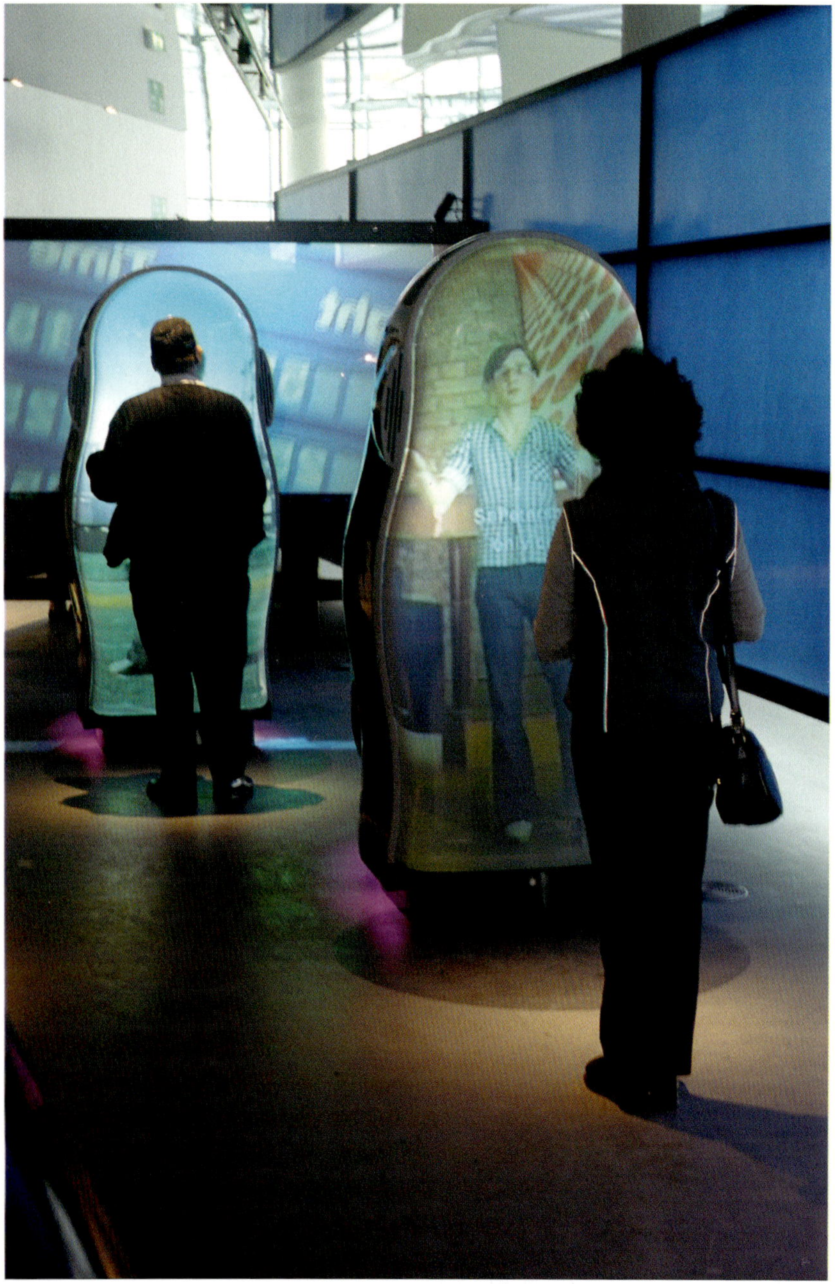

Urbis, one of Manchester's new signature buildings, dominates the Millennium Quarter with its façade of steel and glass (*opposite*).

Full of high tech displays, it explores urban life in the modern city.

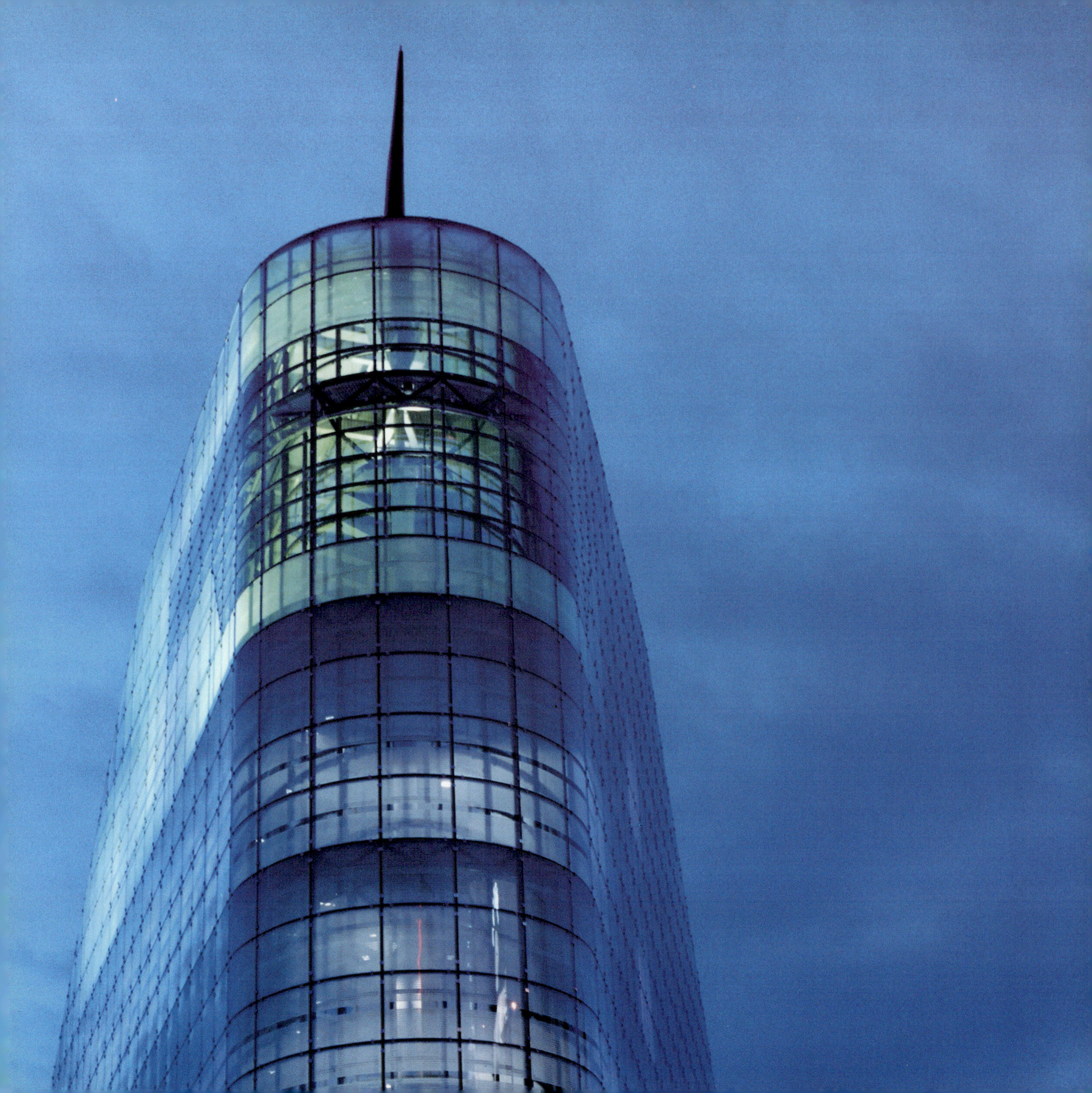

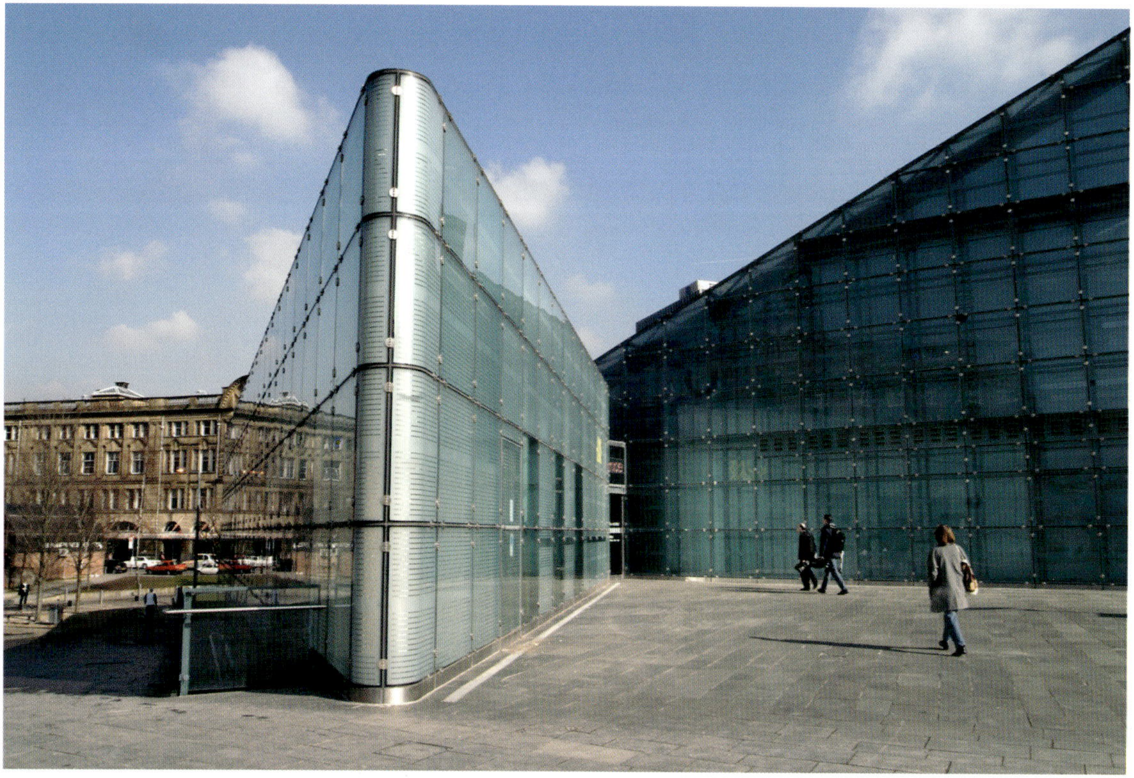

Designed by Manchester-based Ian Simpson Architects, the award-winning Urbis overlooks Victoria Station, built by George Stephenson 160 years earlier.

Together with Urbis came Cathedral Gardens, a much-needed new green space well used by shoppers and city workers.

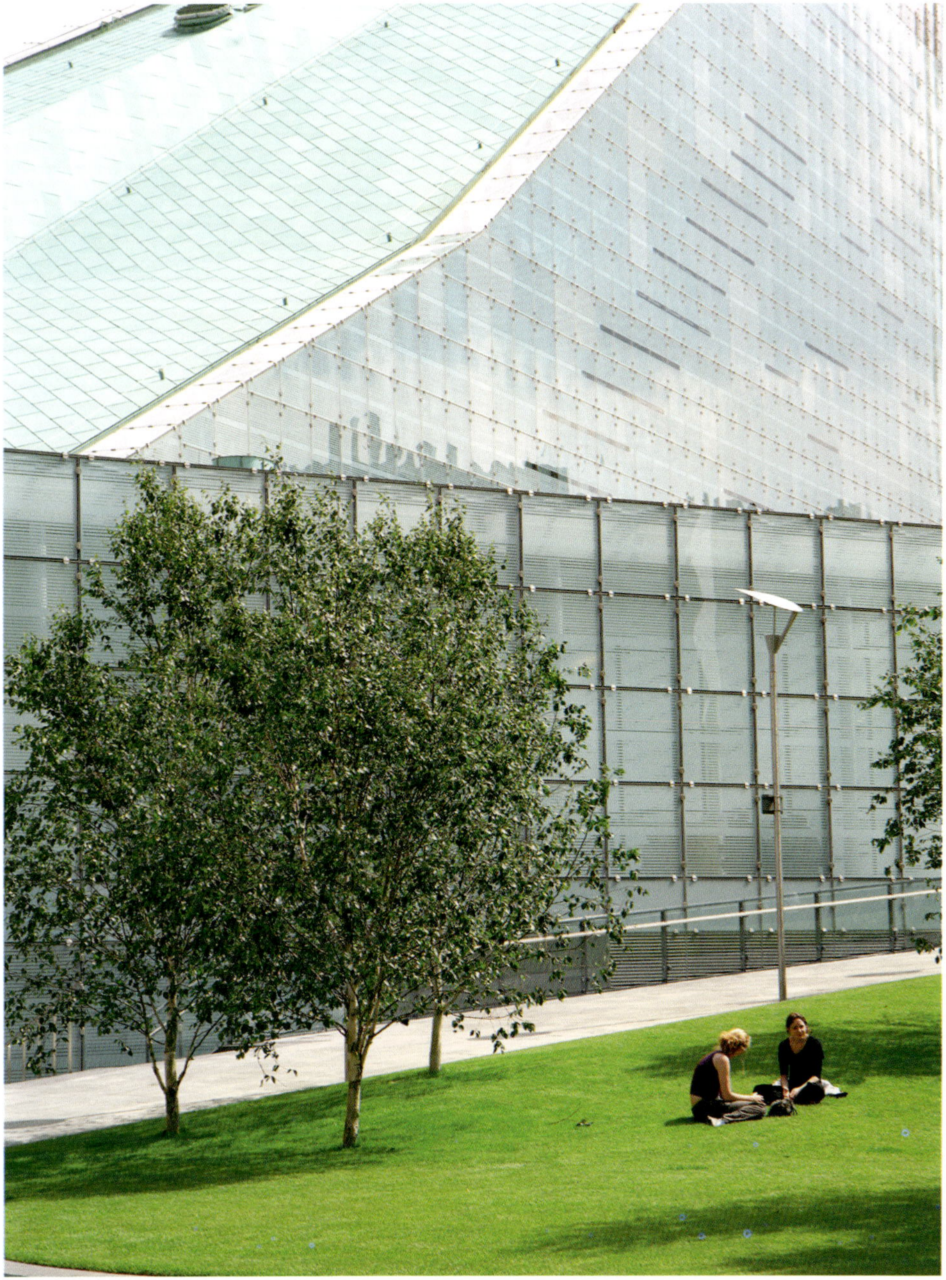

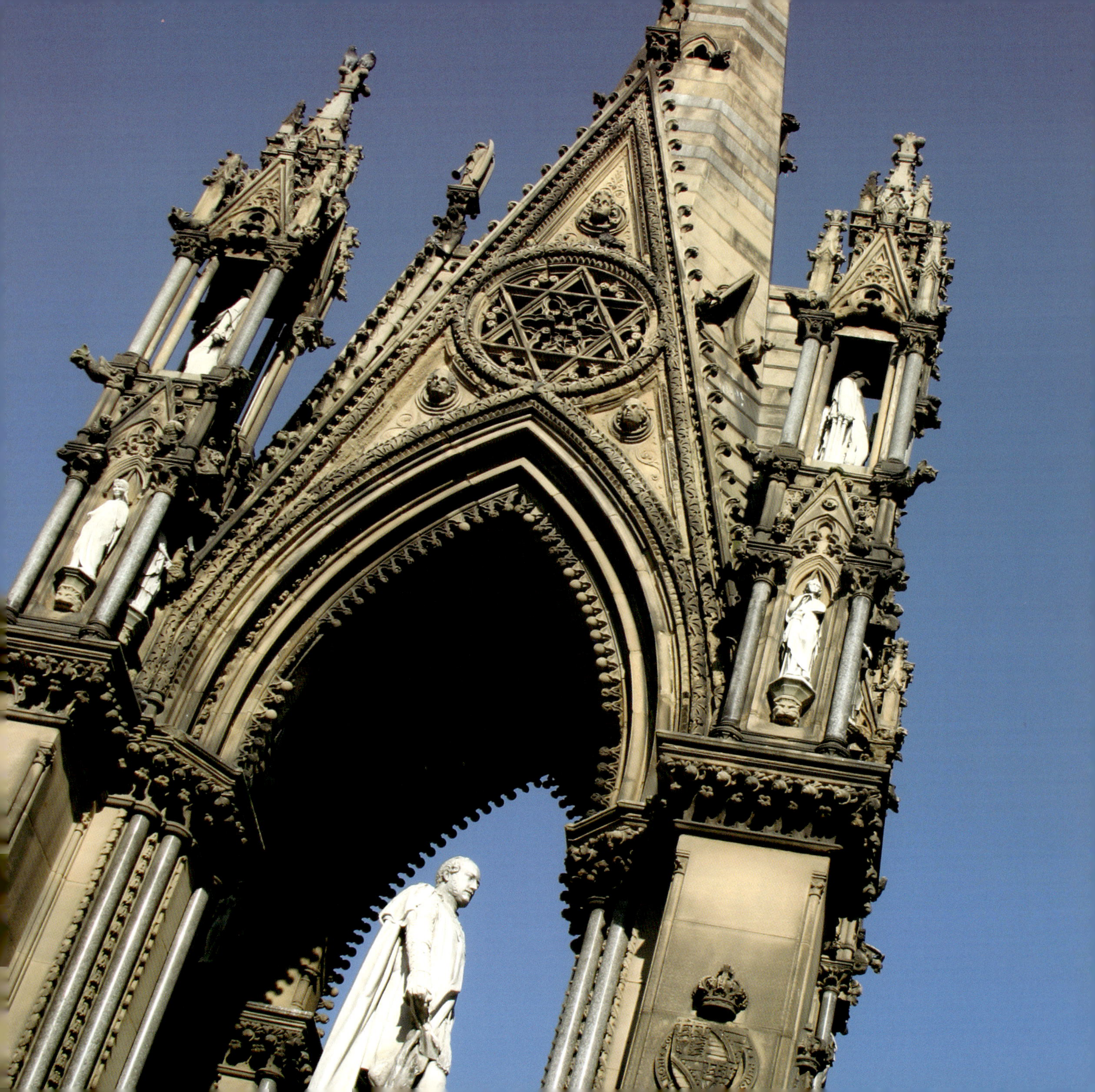

Albert Square: the Albert Memorial *(opposite)*, was funded by public subscription during national mourning for Victoria's Prince Consort. The fountain was built to celebrate the opening of the Thirlmere Aqueduct.

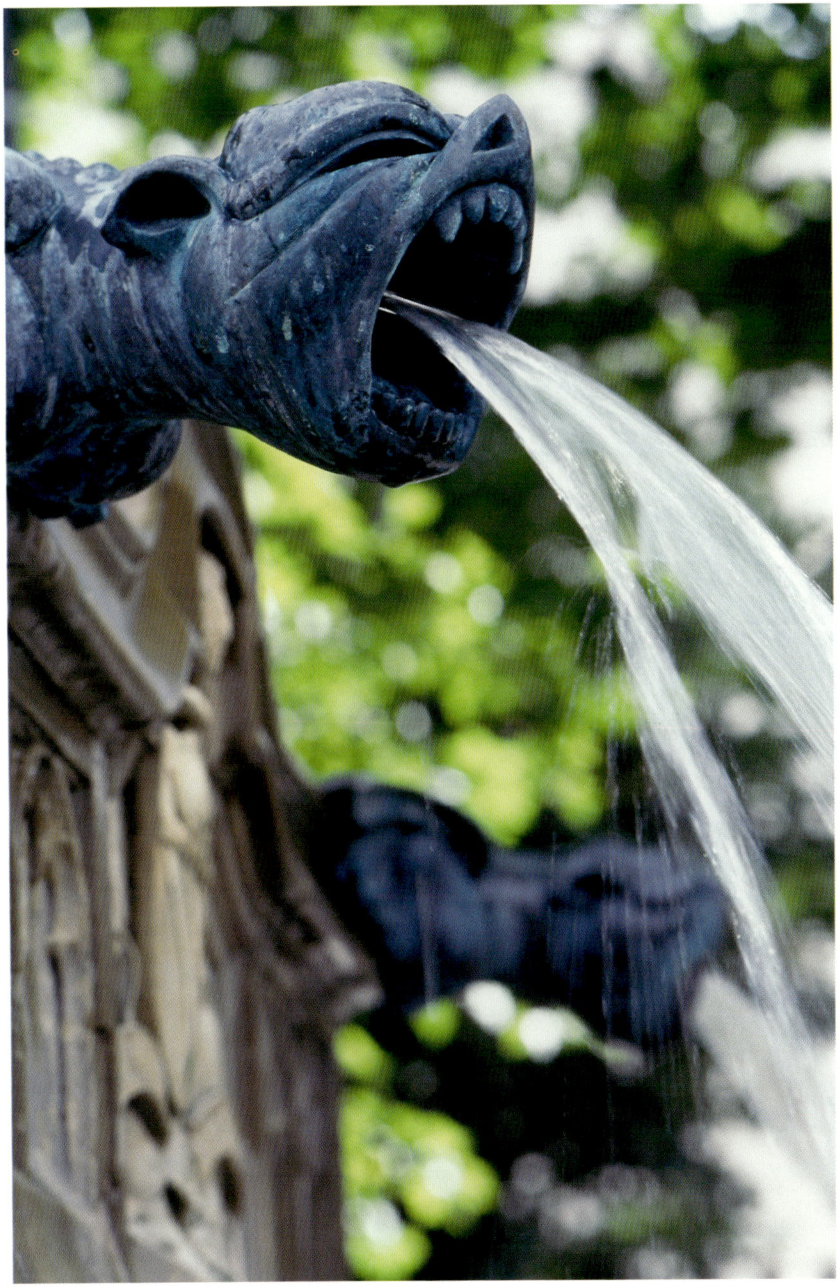

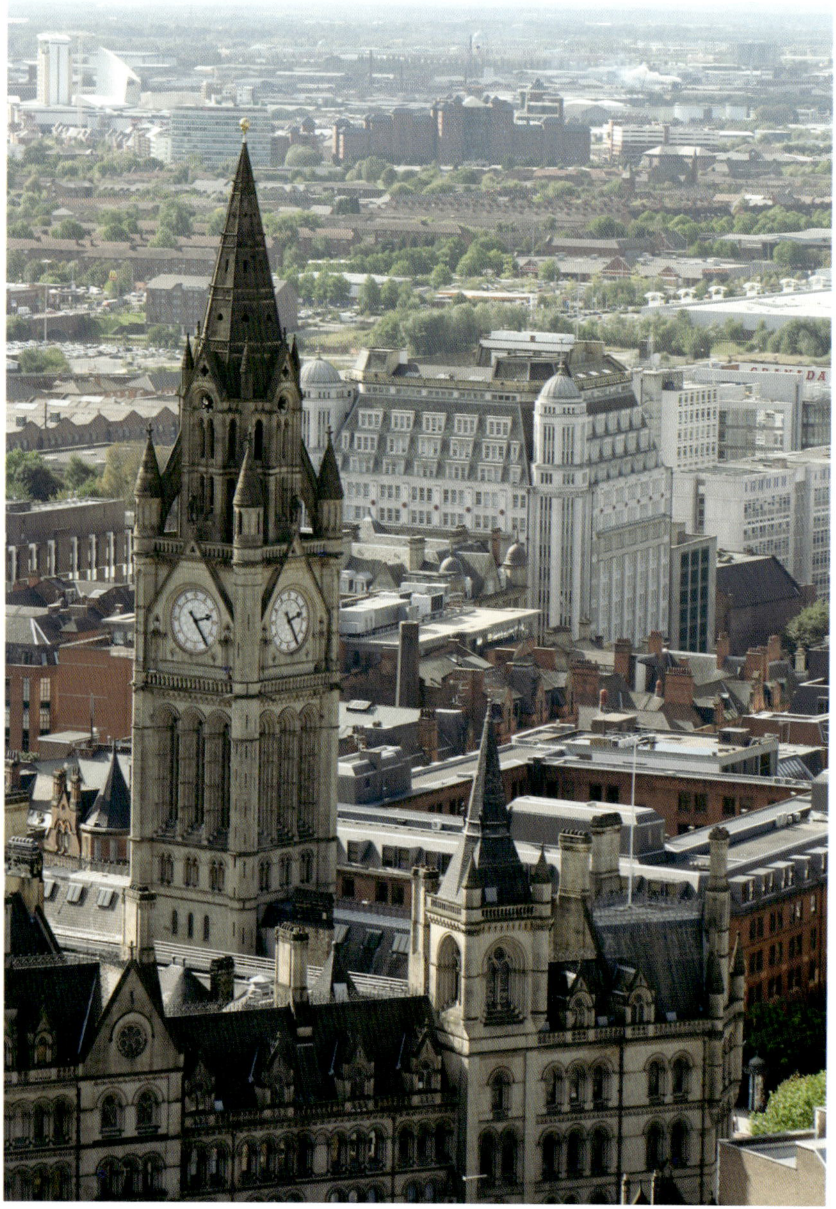

Built on a triangular site, the neo-Gothic Town Hall is thought to be architect Alfred Waterhouse's greatest work.

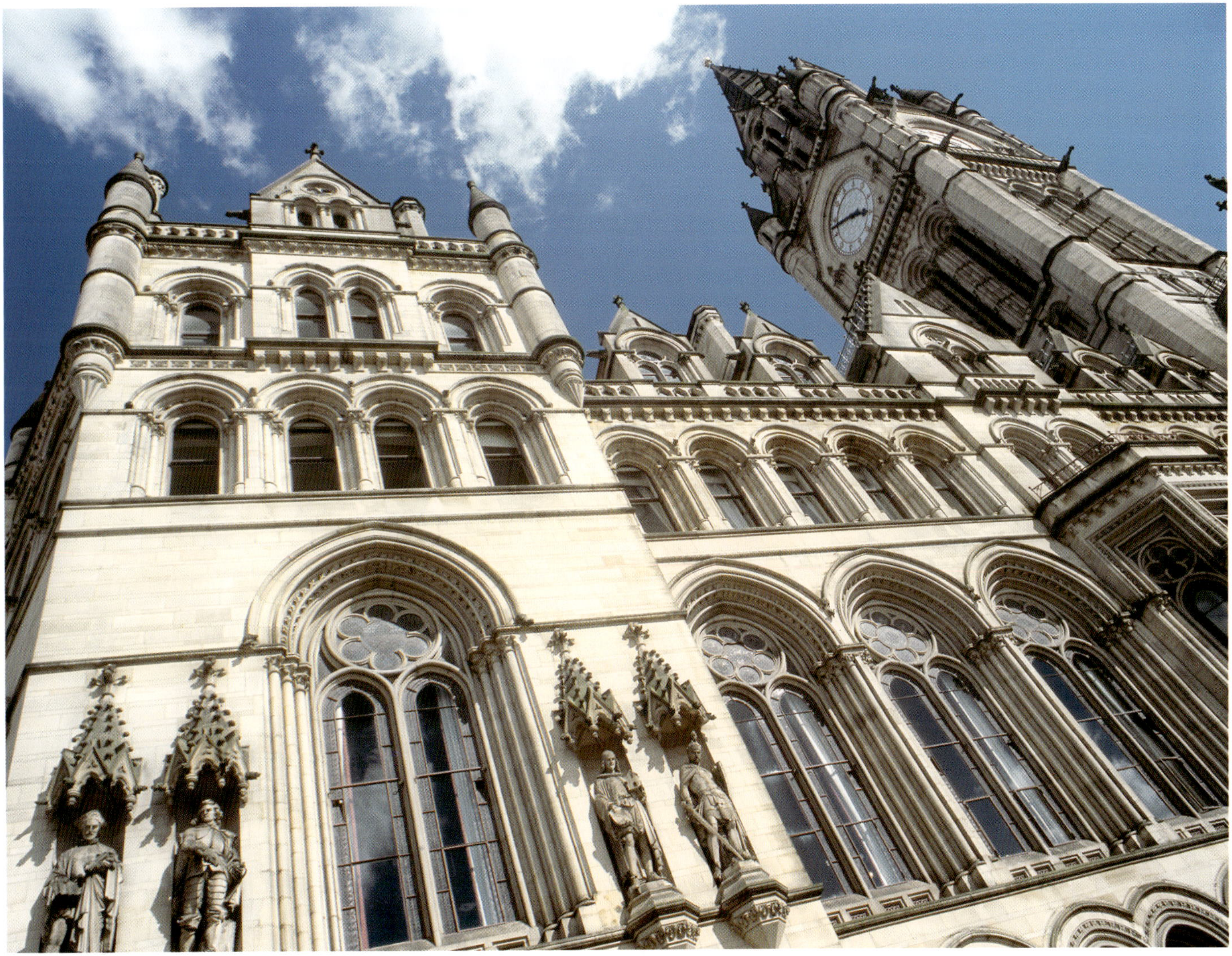

The clock tower rises 87 metres/285ft at the front of the building, while statues of prominent Mancunians adorn the first floor.

The Cooper Street entrance with the city coat of arms *(right)*, and stone masonry detail *(below)*, around the door.

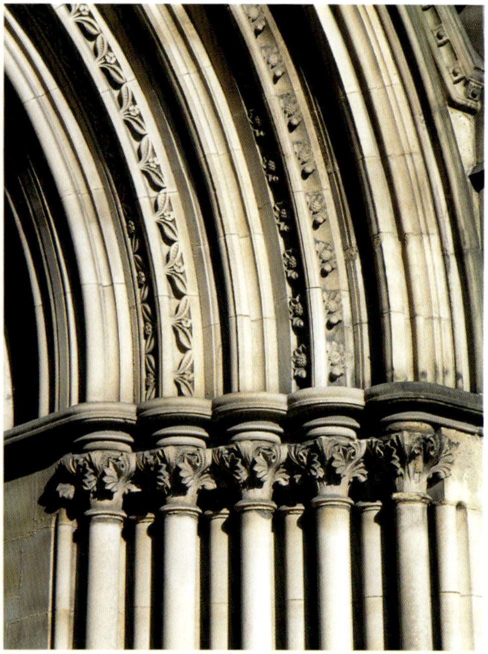

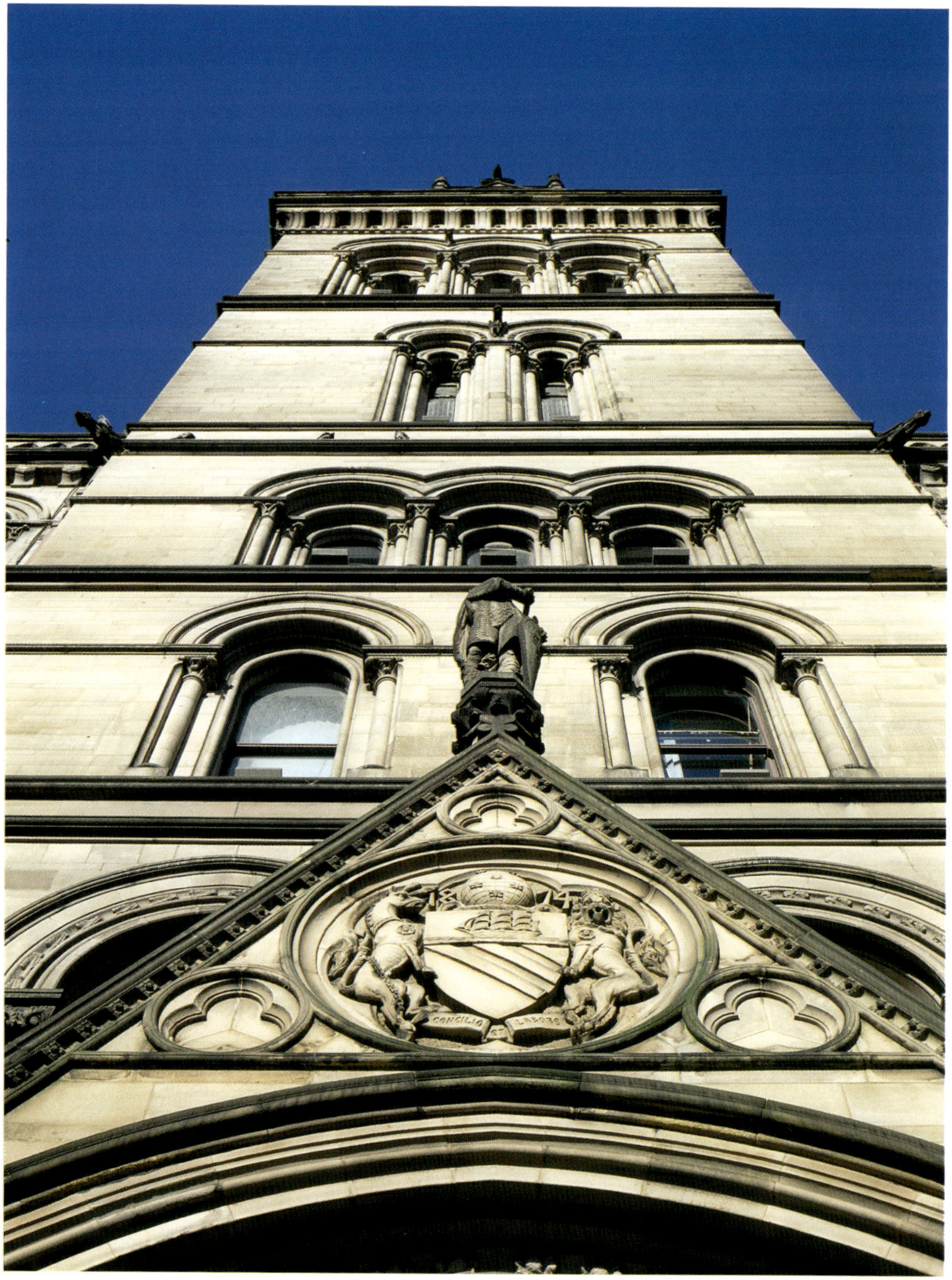

Small balconies in the centre of the building provide excellent views of the internal courtyard.

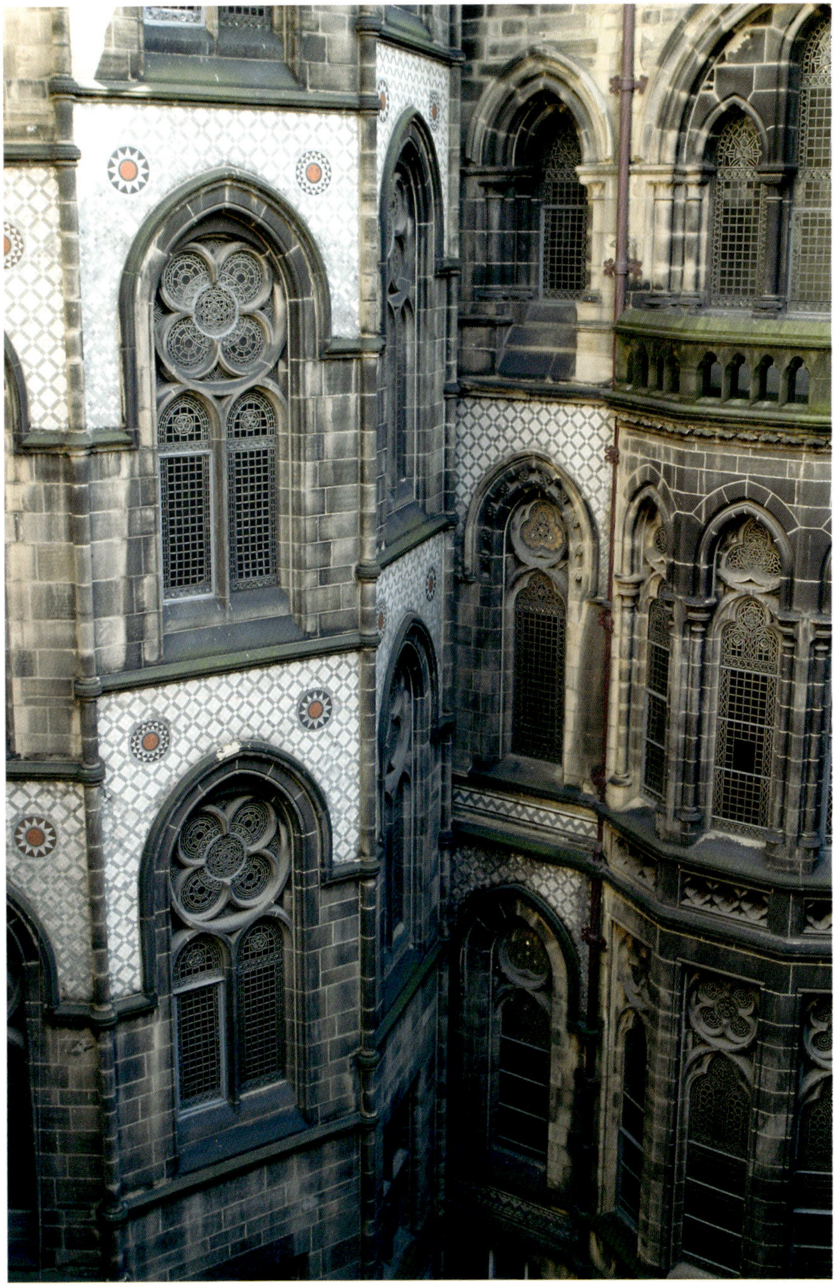

The landing in front of the Great Hall has a pattern of bees – symbolic of the industrious city – on its mosaic floor.

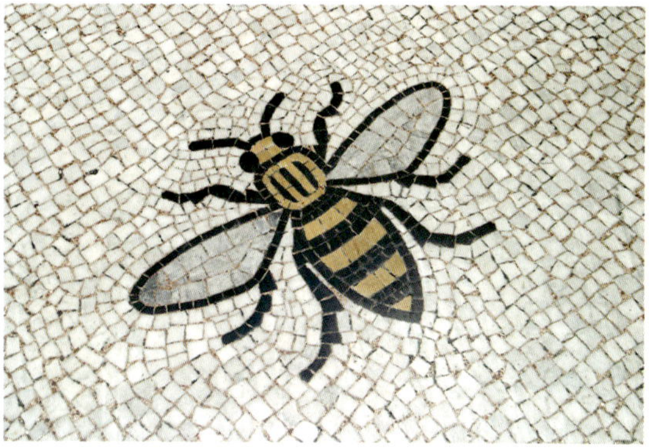

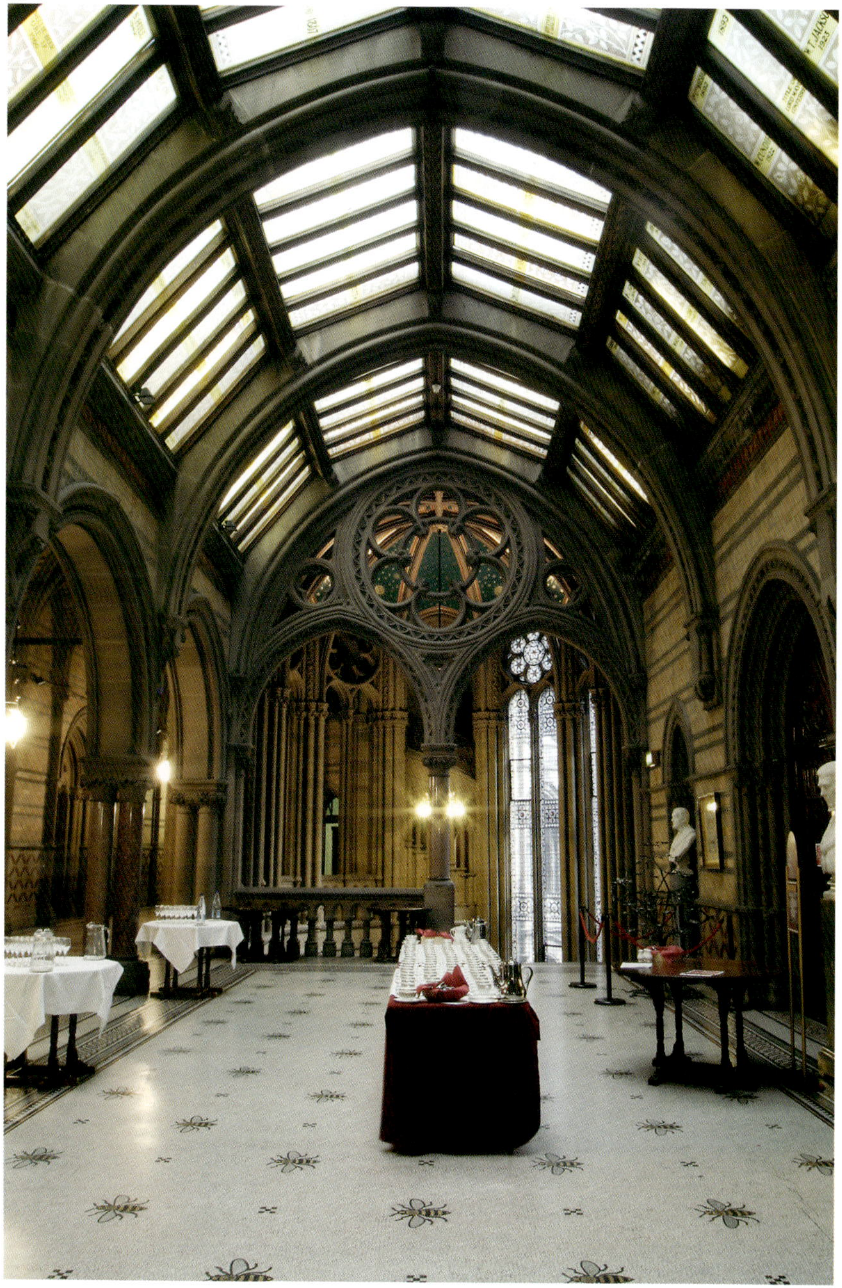

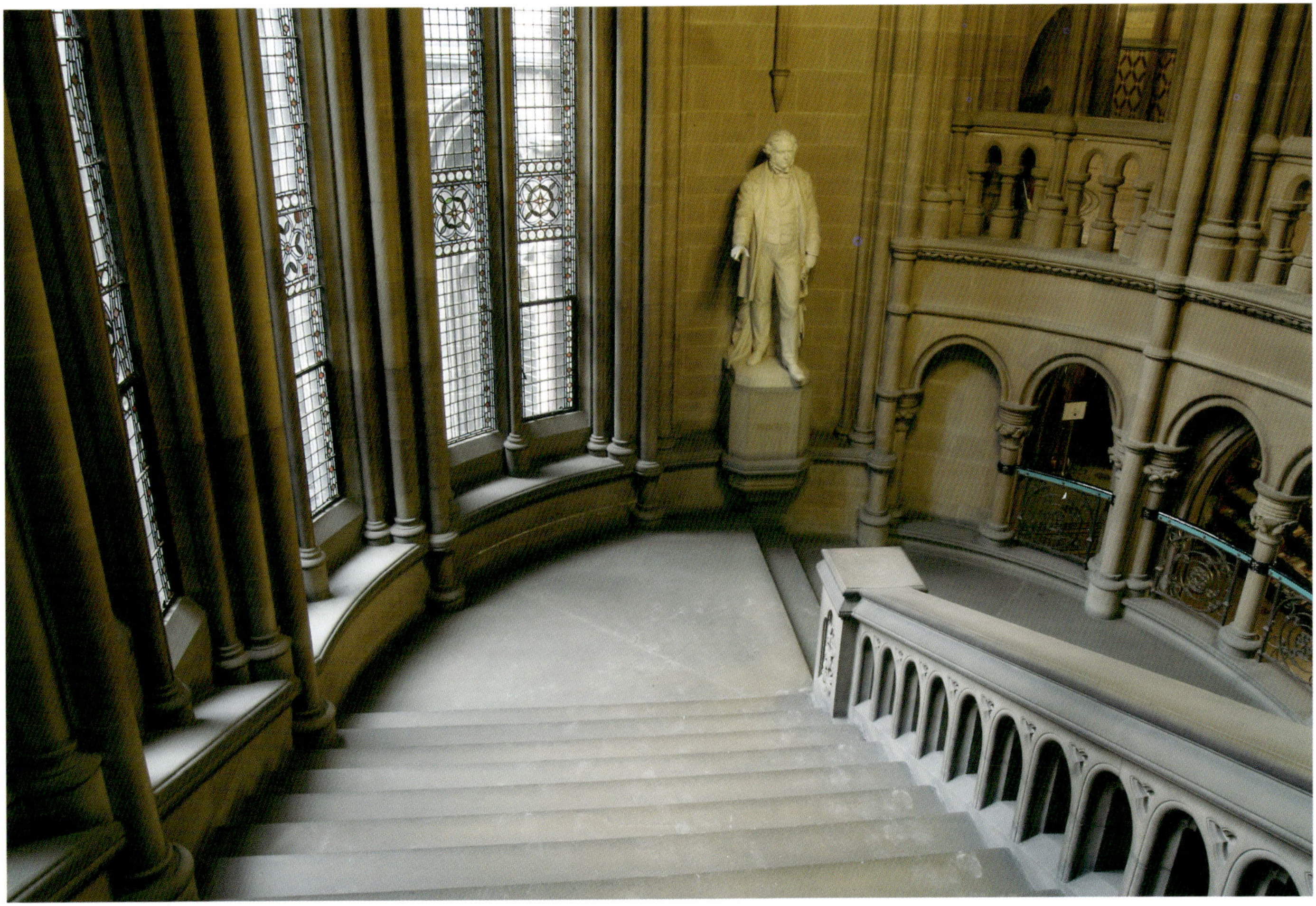

One of two ceremonial staircases which lead to the first floor.

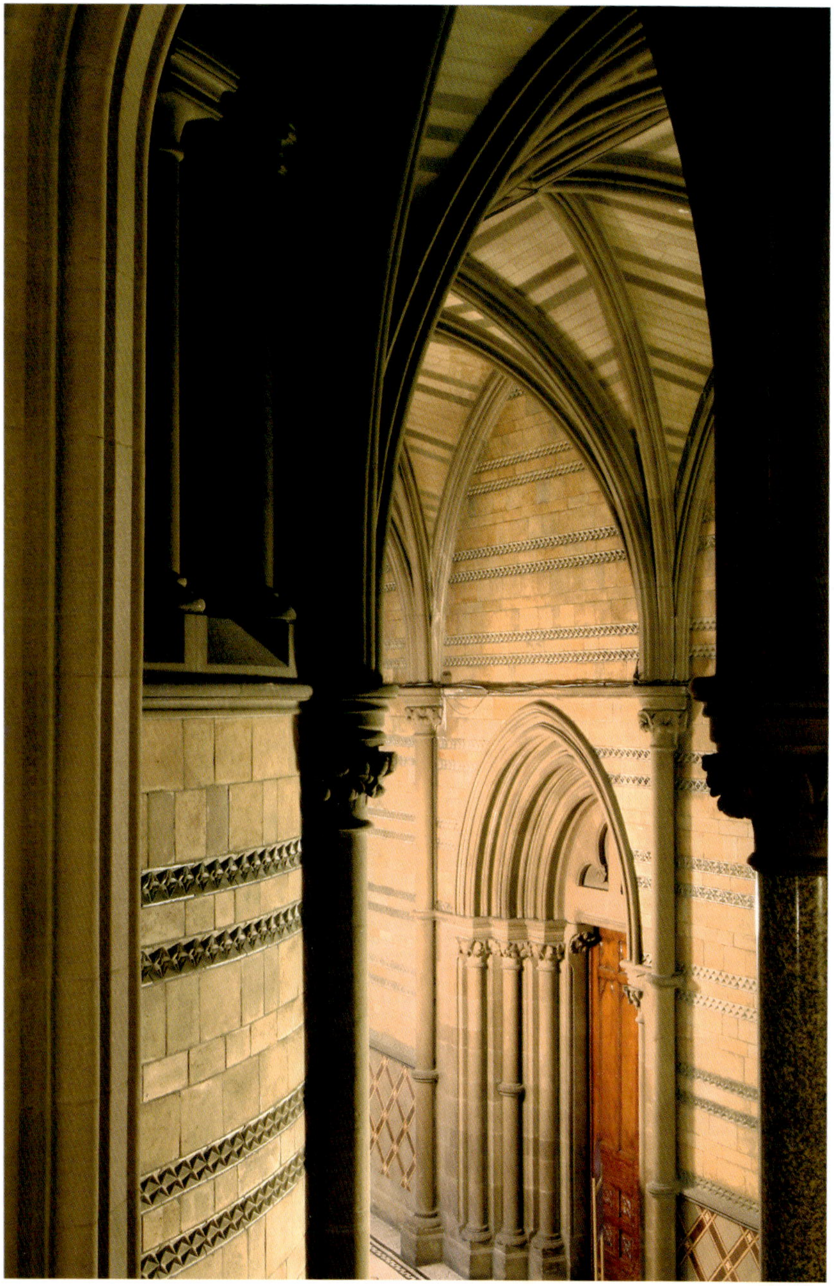

The entrance to the Reception Room on the first floor. Seven hundred stonemasons were employed during the construction of the Town Hall.

Stained glass and roof detail.

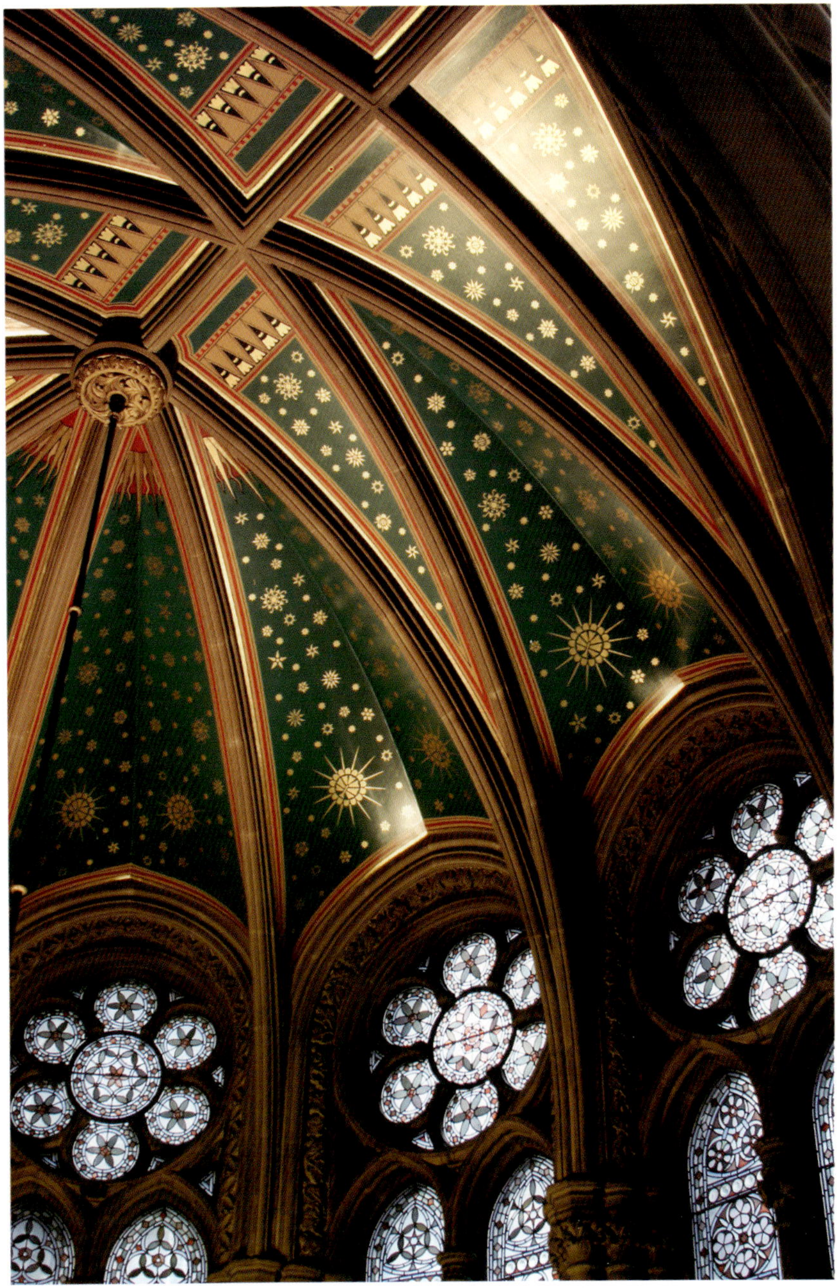

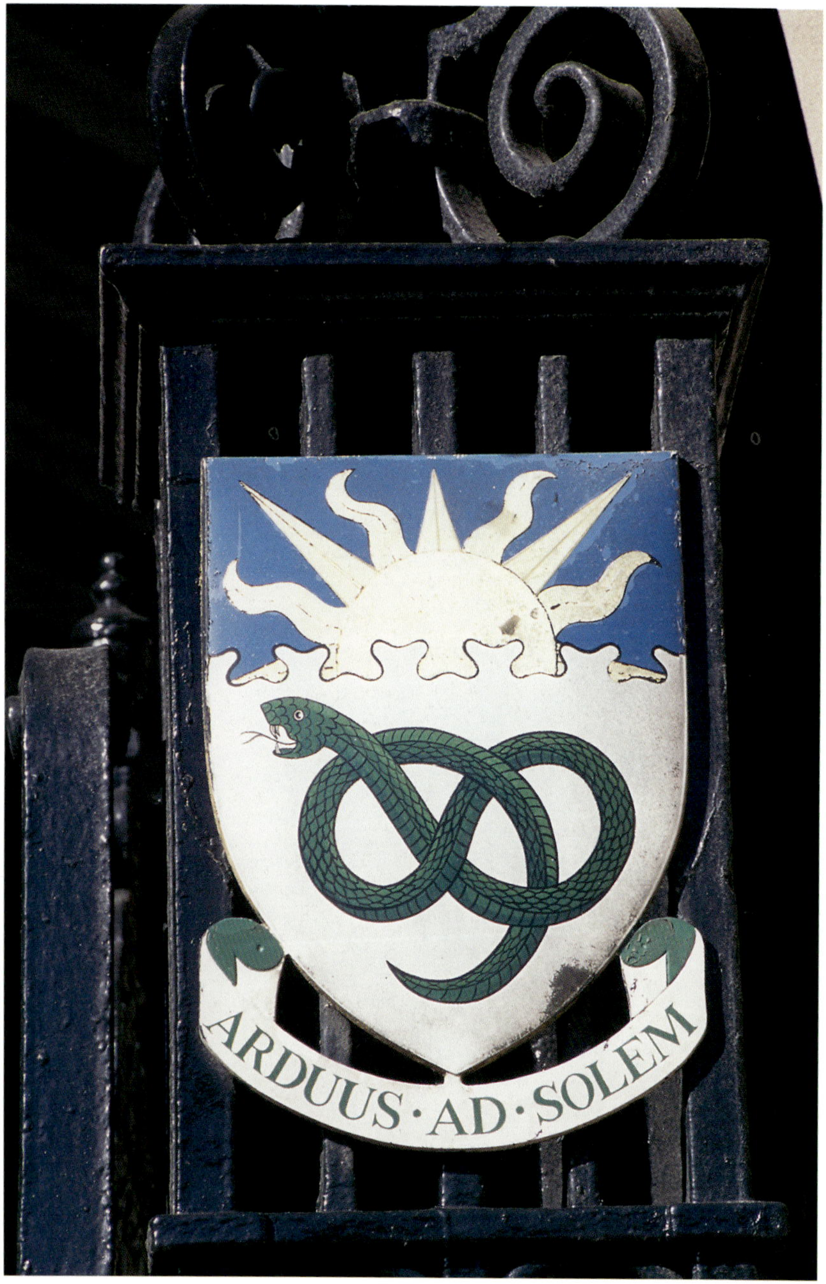

The University of Manchester's crest:
'The steep or difficult ascent to the sun'.

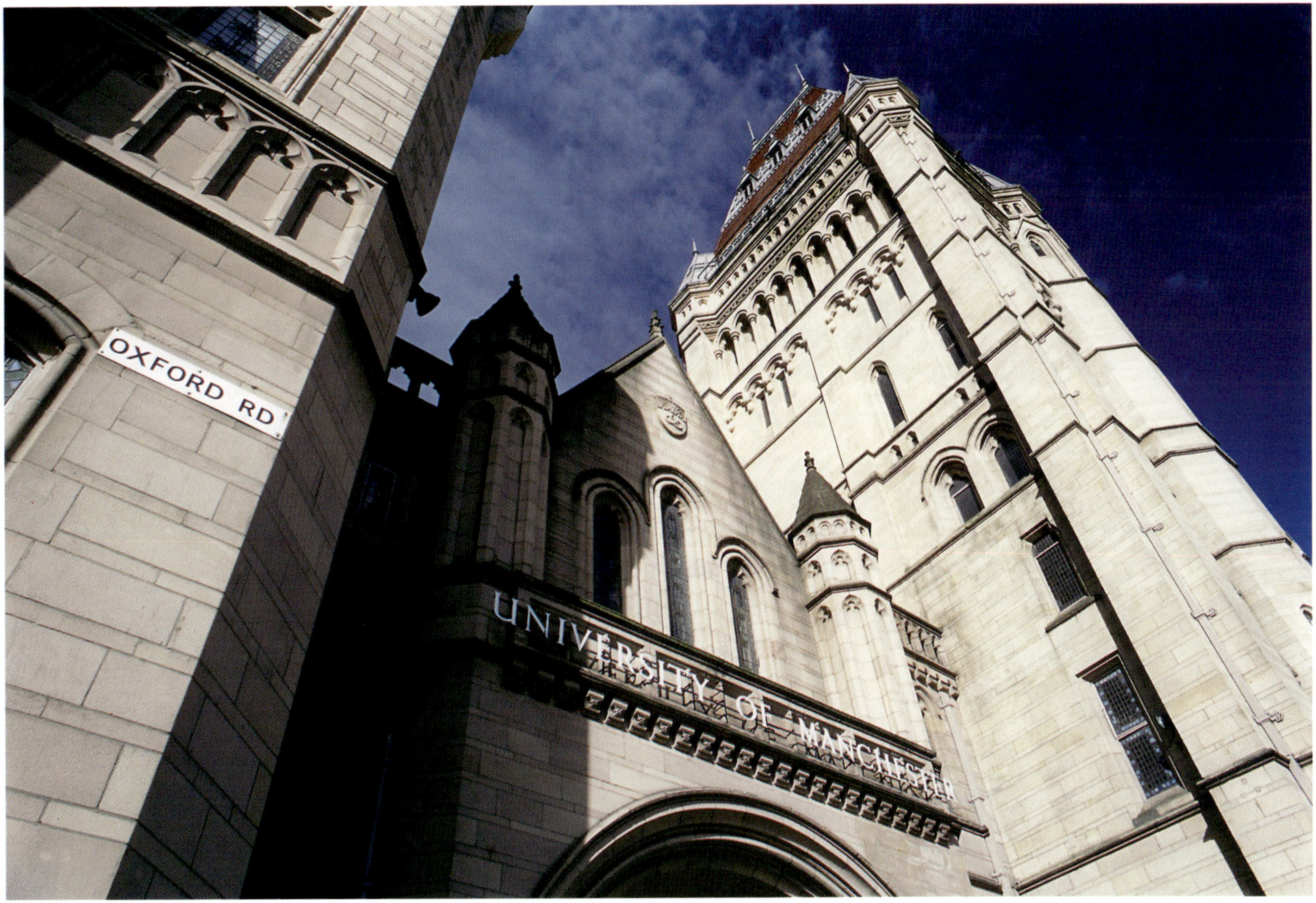

While working on Manchester's Town Hall, Alfred Waterhouse started on the impressive Owens College on Oxford Road, which later became the Victoria University of Manchester.

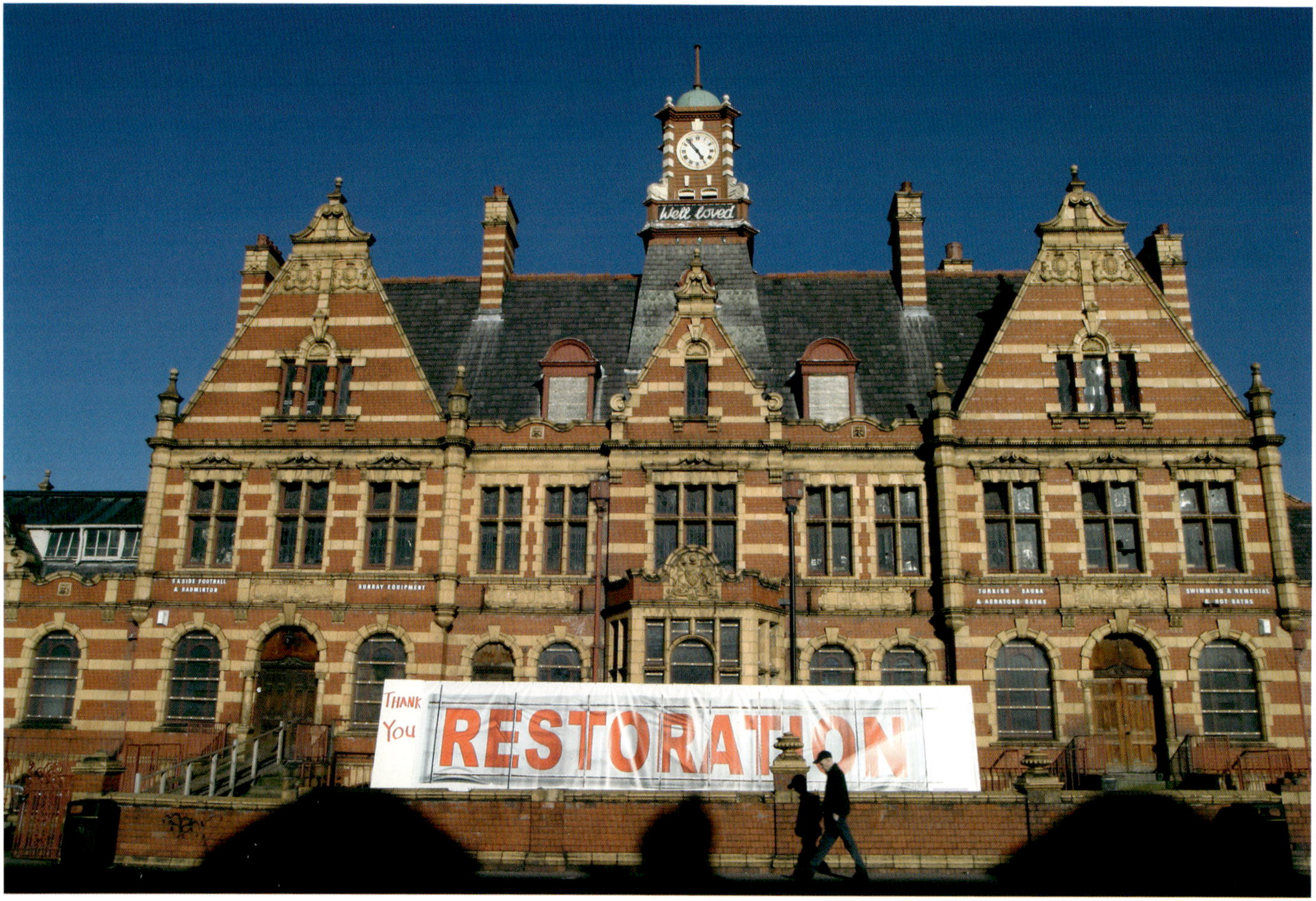

With glazed tiles from floor to ceiling and stained glass windows, no expense was spared when Victoria Baths opened in 1906. Nearly a century later, and after a decade of neglect, the baths won BBC 2's *Restoration* programme and will be partly renovated.

Victoria Baths has separate entrances for its three swimming pools: Males 1st Class, Males 2nd Class and Females.

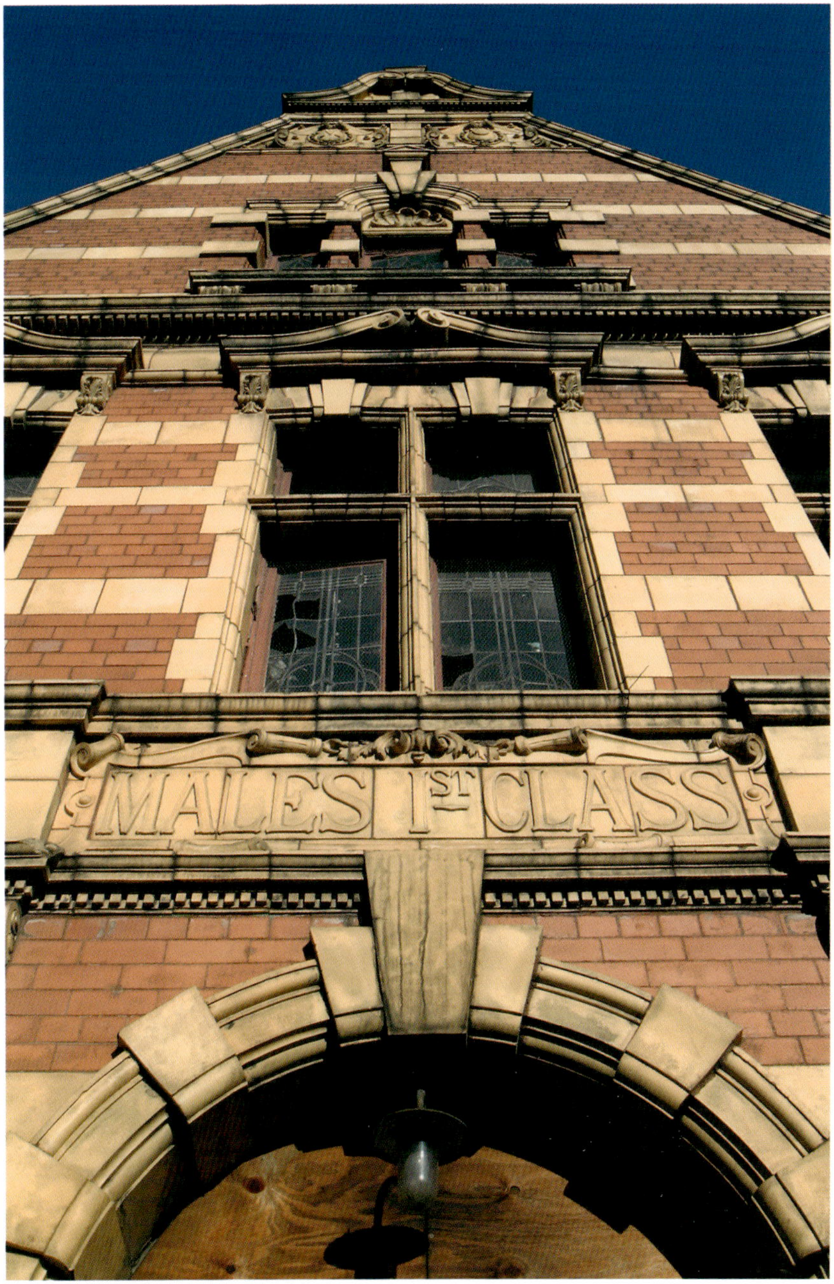

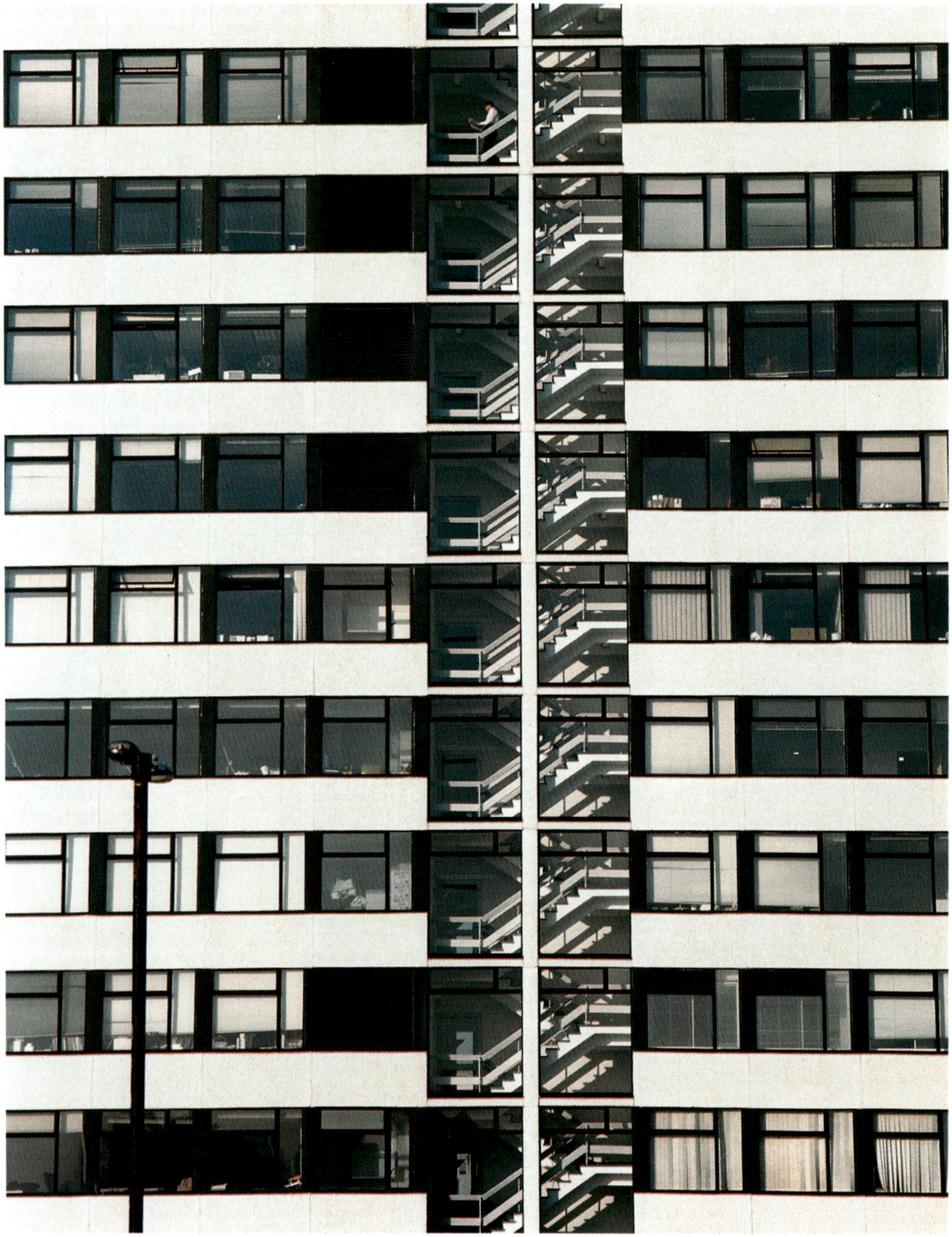

Portland Tower, formerly St Andrew's House, is one of several concrete office blocks constructed in the 1960s to replace those lost during the war.

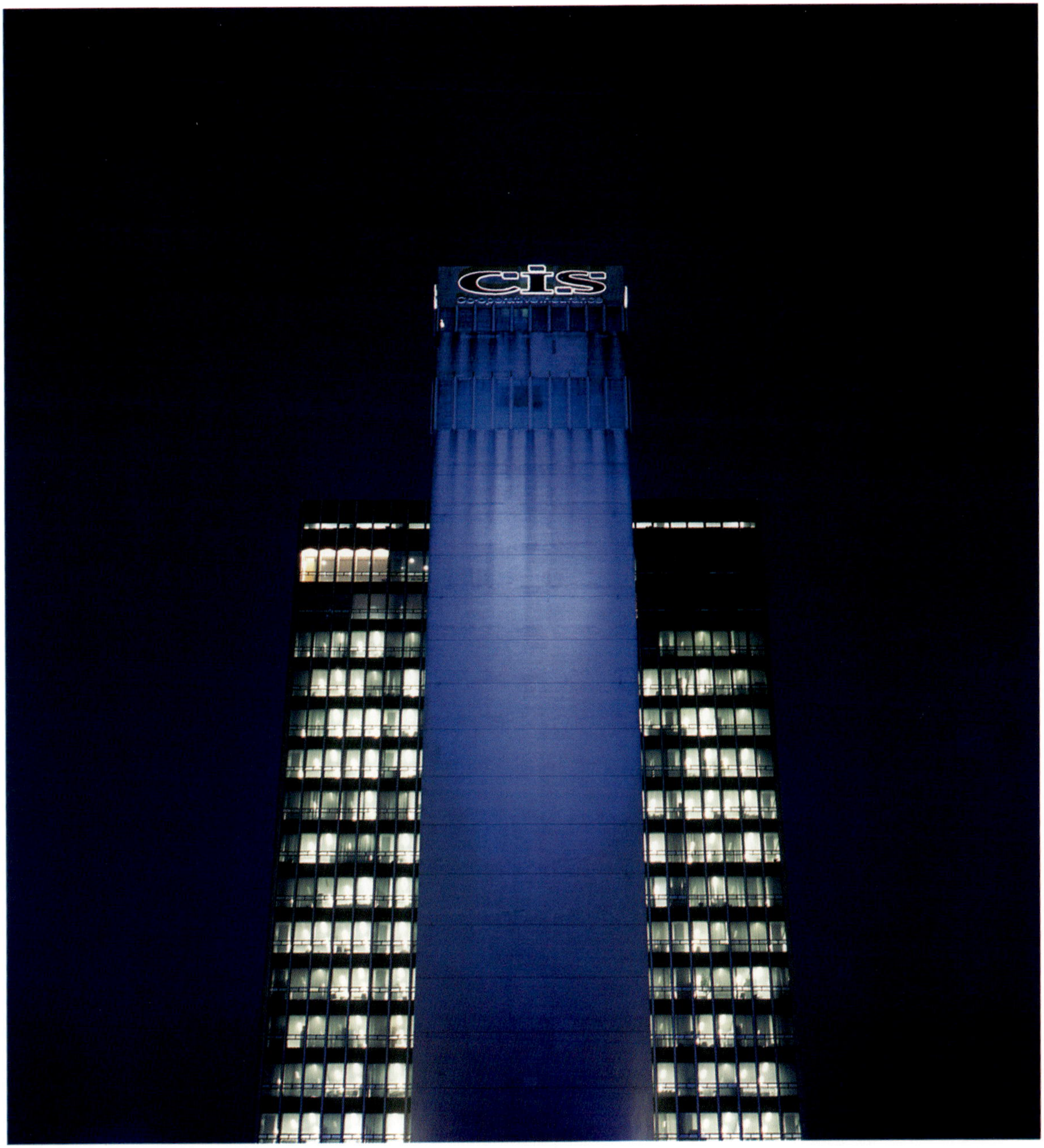

At 23 storeys, the CIS Tower dominates the city skyline. It is currently Manchester's tallest building.

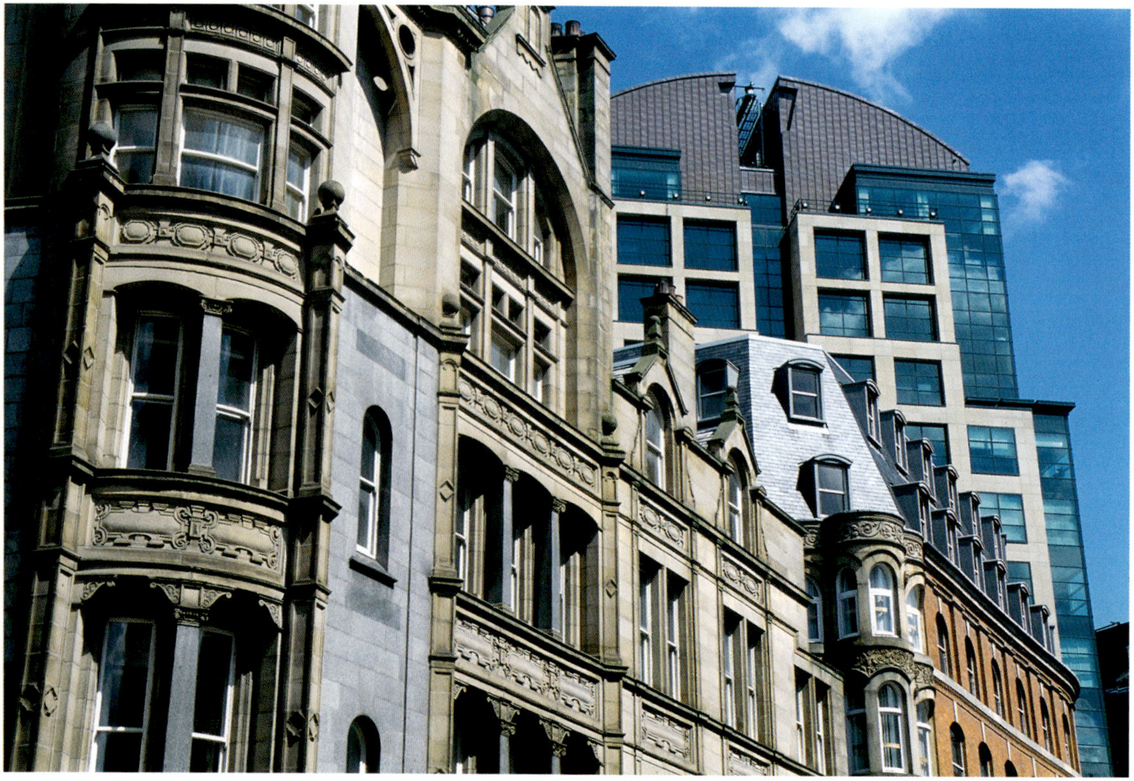

Old and new: the Northern Assurance Building on Princess Street with No 82 King Street, a new office block, over its shoulder.

The cool Sardinian grey granite of Barbirolli Square contrasts with the traditional red brick of Mendal's Warehouse, now Chepstow House.

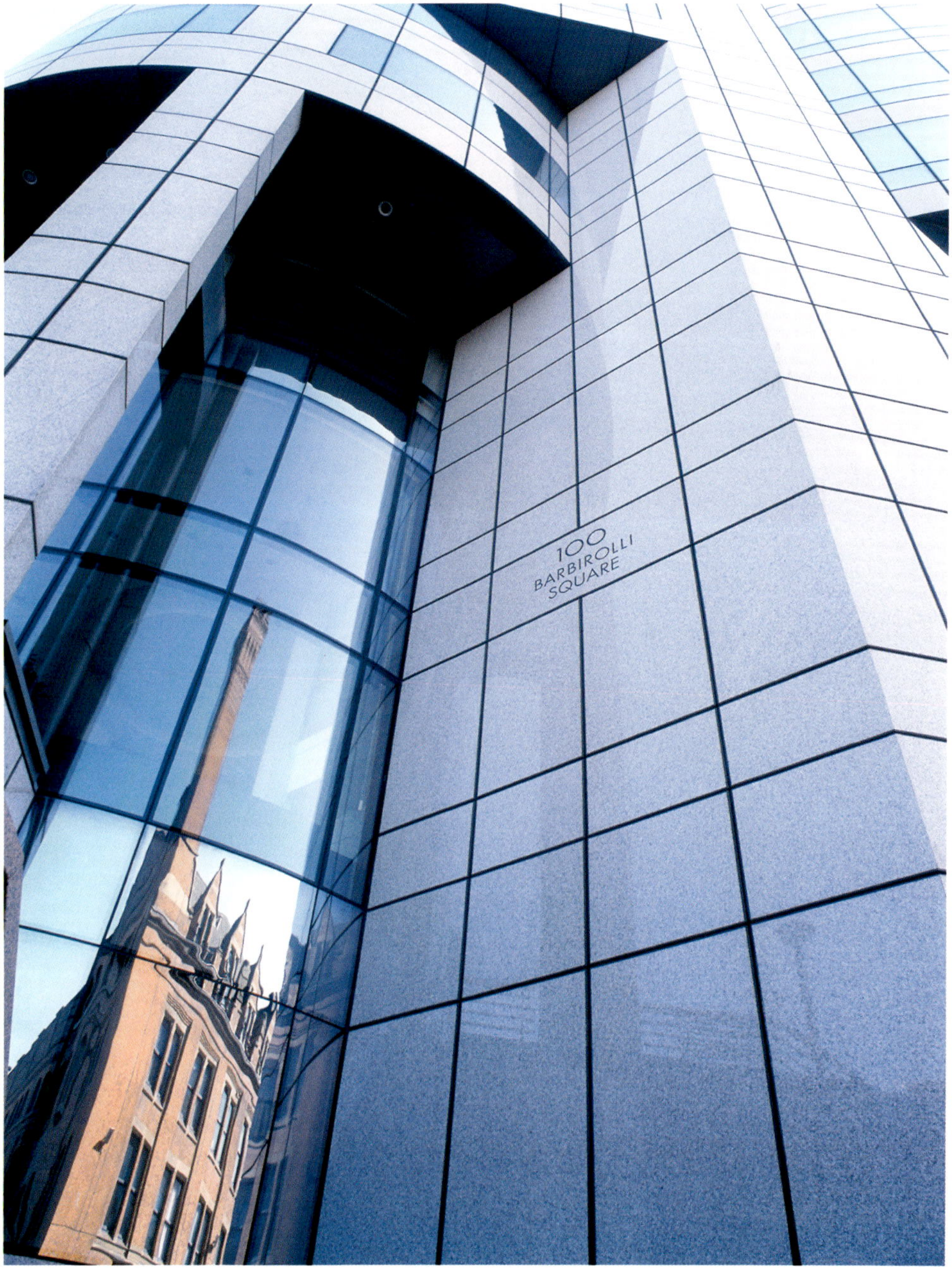

Overleaf Canada House, an architectural gem with its wonderful arched windows and buff terracotta.

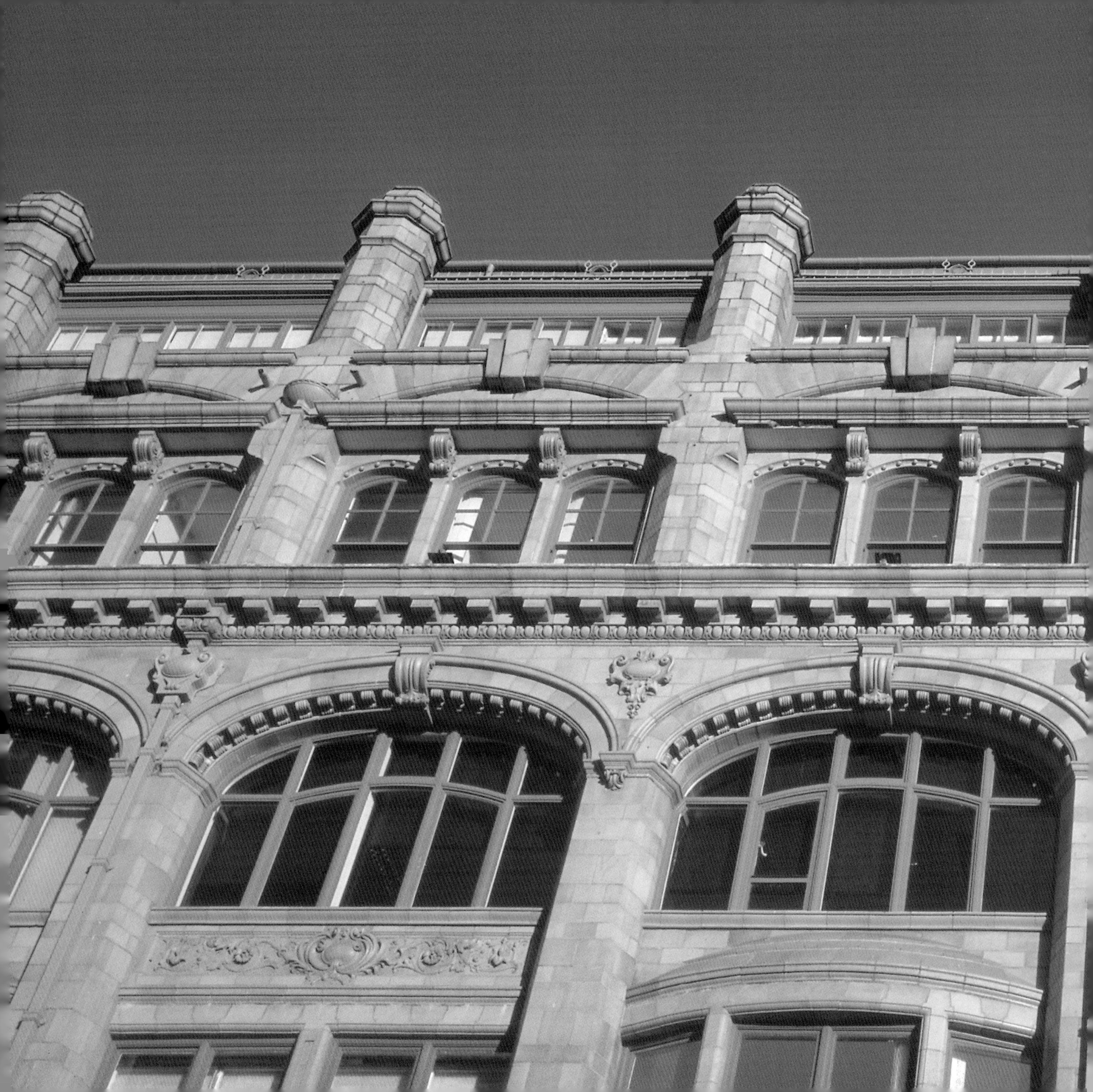

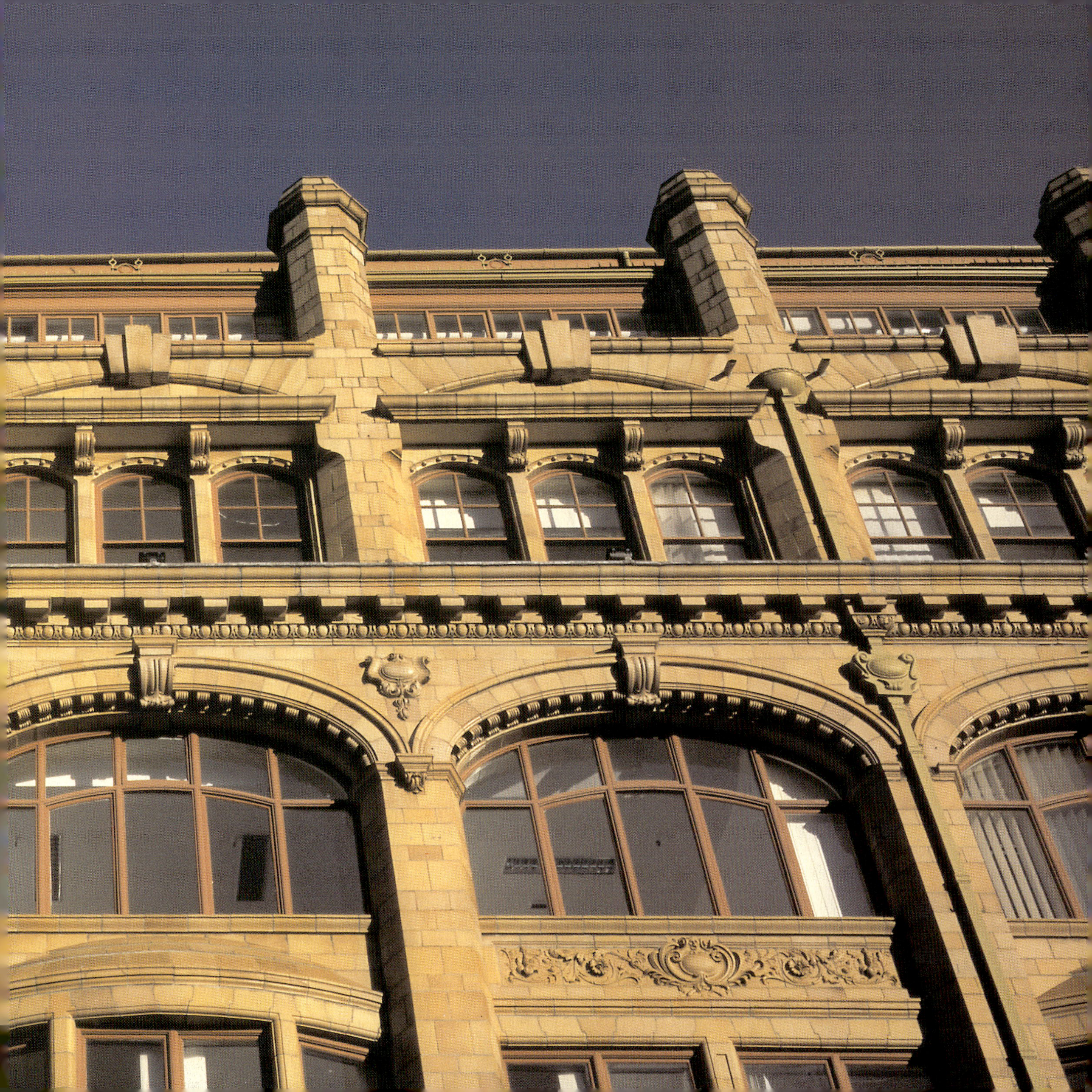

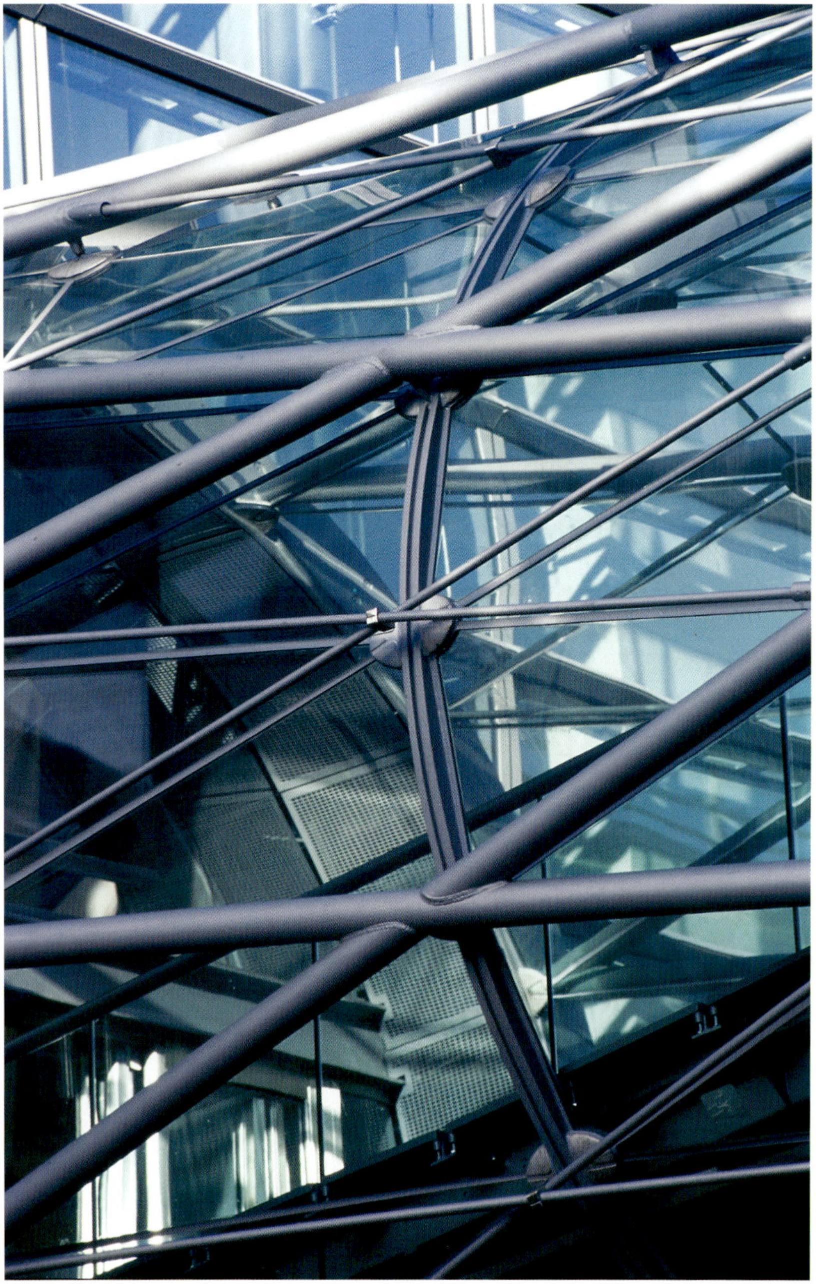

Many new footbridges have been built in Manchester in the past decade. This one, with its innovative twisted steel and glass, replaced its bomb-damaged predecessor across Corporation Street.

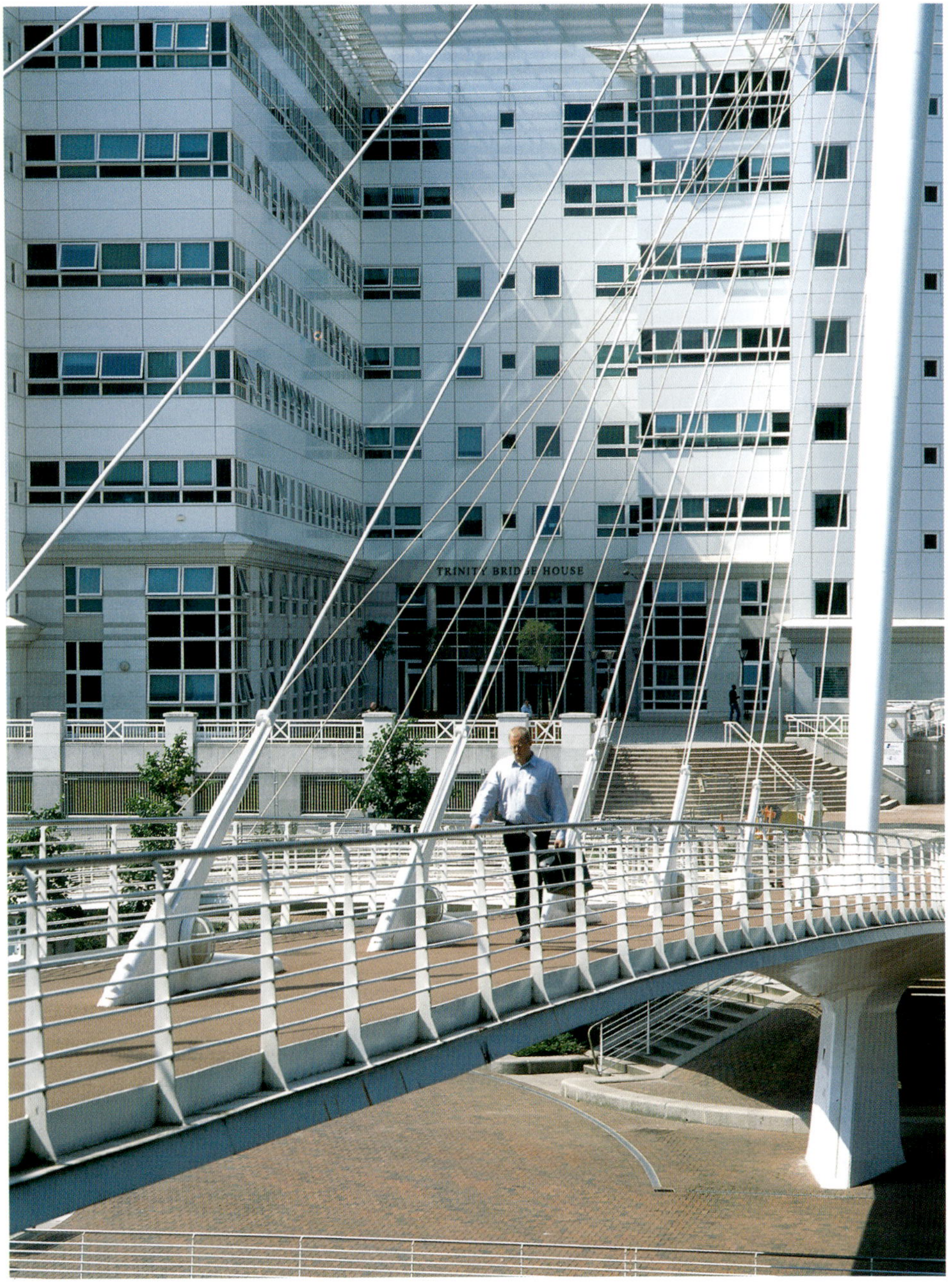

Santiago Calatrava's Trinity Bridge spans the River Irwell and links Salford to Manchester city centre.

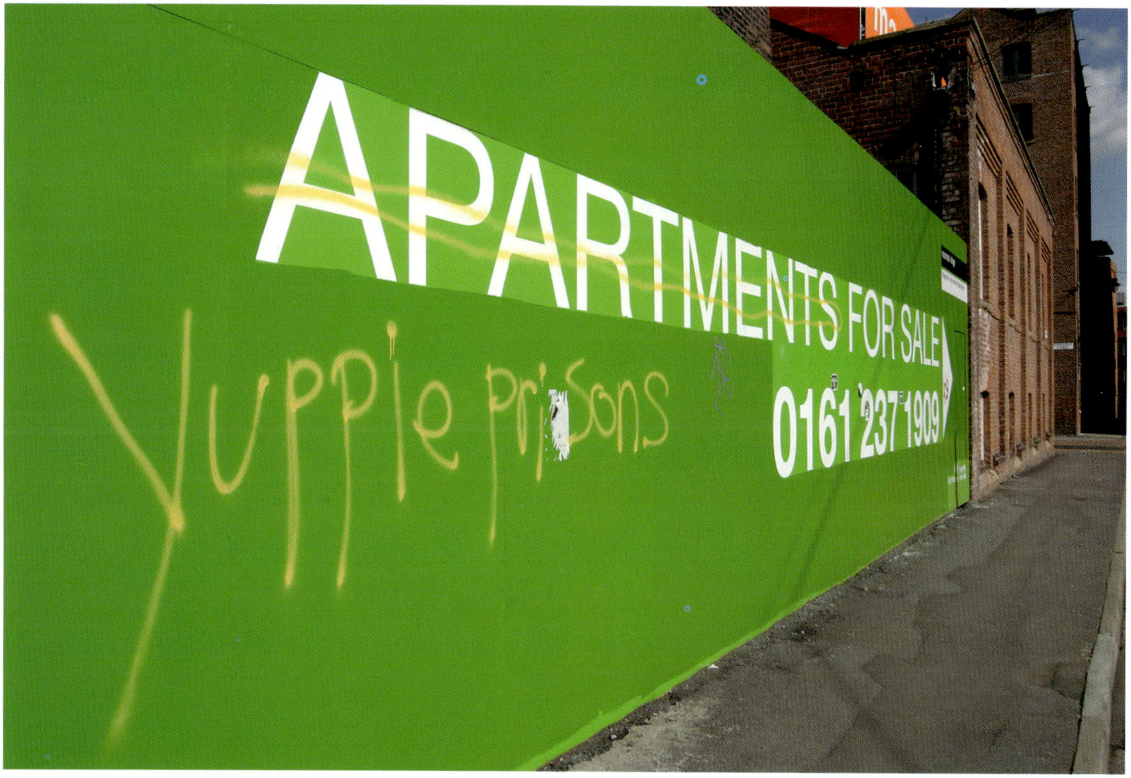

Although not universally appreciated, the city centre has seen a phenomenal boom in inner-city living. In 1991 only 800 people lived in the city; it is estimated that 20,000 will live there by 2007.

Raised above the trendy stores below, No 1 Deansgate is one of the more desirable new addresses in the city centre. With 14 floors of glass-clad apartments, it offers spectacular views across the city.

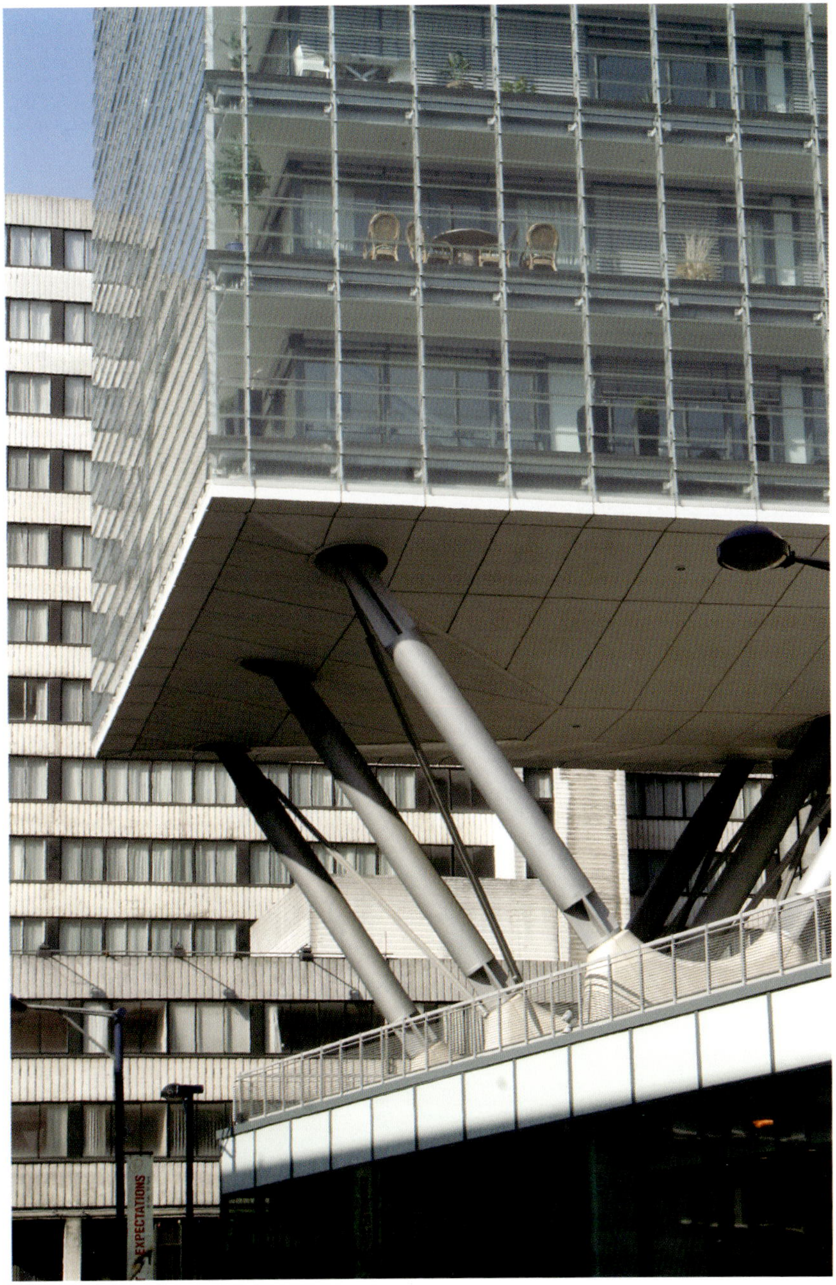

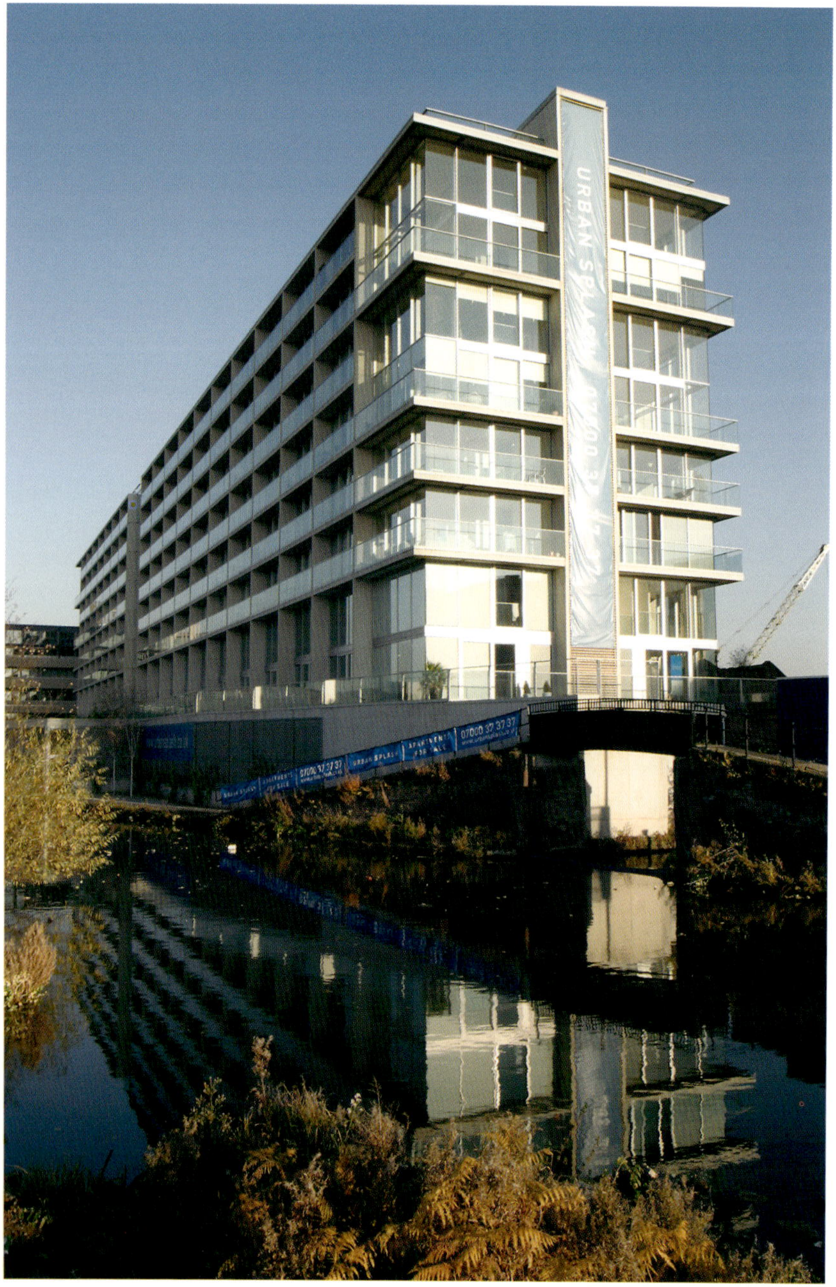

Widely credited as being the first to see the potential for city centre living, developers Urban Splash have many significant schemes in their portfolio. This is Timber Wharf on the banks of the Bridgewater Canal.

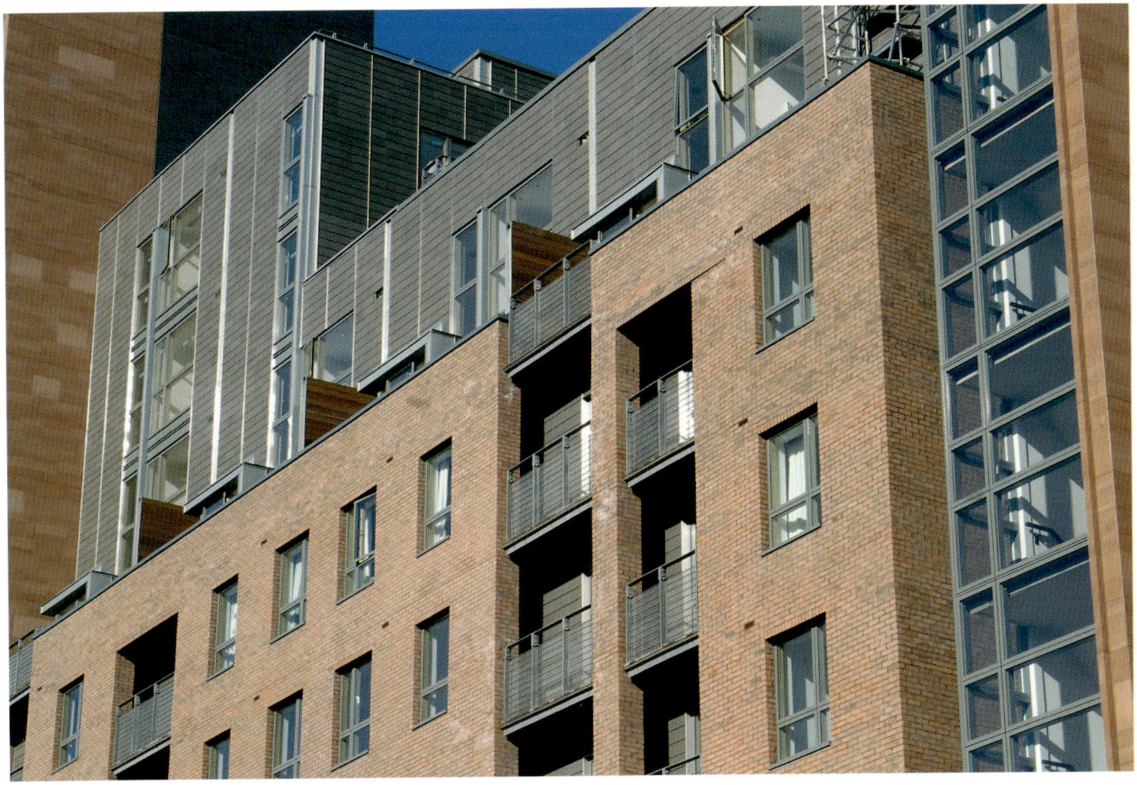

With mounting debts and drug-related problems, Manchester's most famous night club, The Haçienda, closed in 1997. It was later demolished to be replaced by 130 apartments in this development which bears its name.

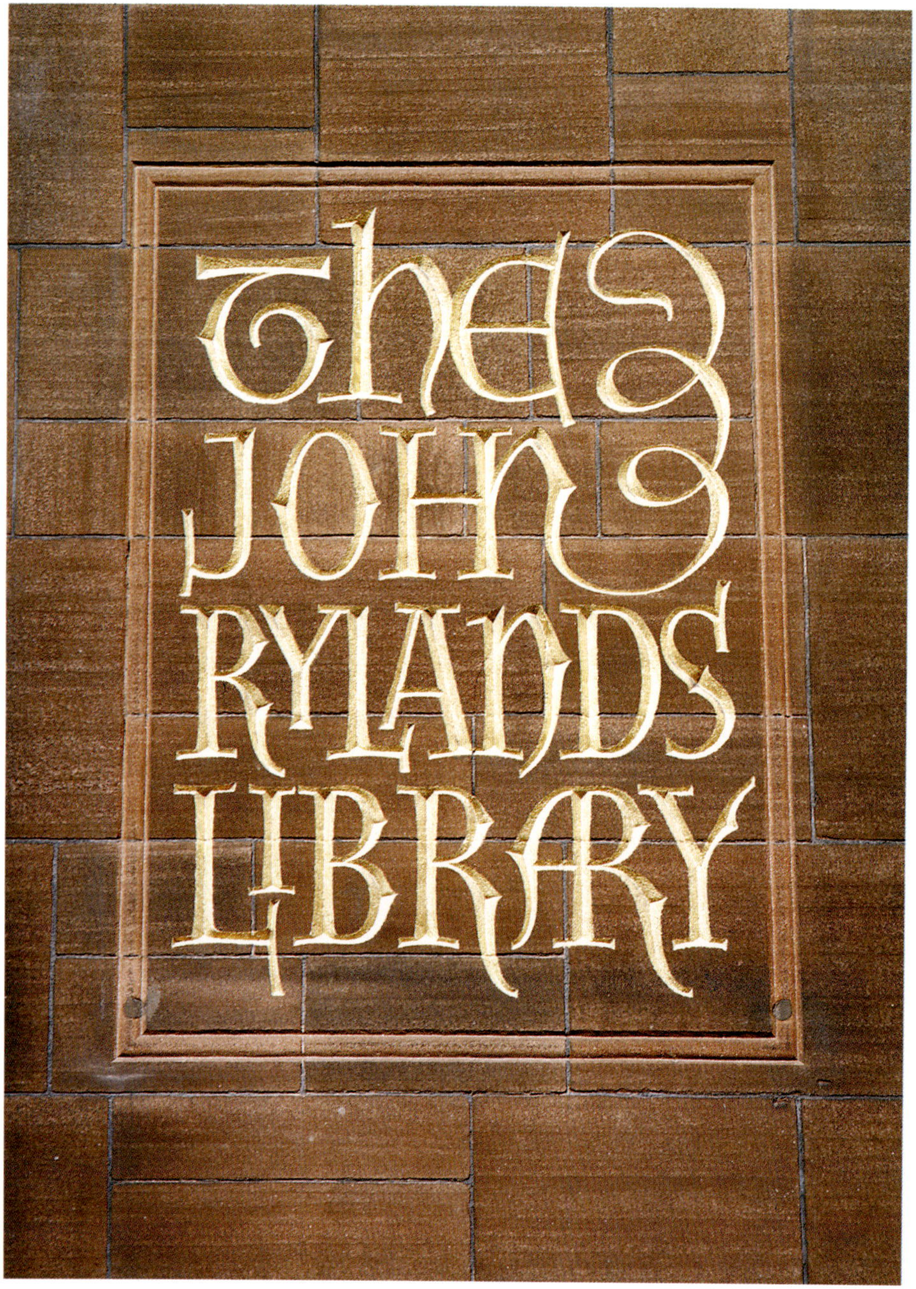

Built by Enriqueta Augusta Rylands as a memorial to her merchant husband, the John Rylands Library contains a world class collection of theological books and manuscripts.

Among its collection is a copy of the so-called 'Wicked Bible' where the word 'not' has been omitted from the seventh commandment: Thou shall not kill.

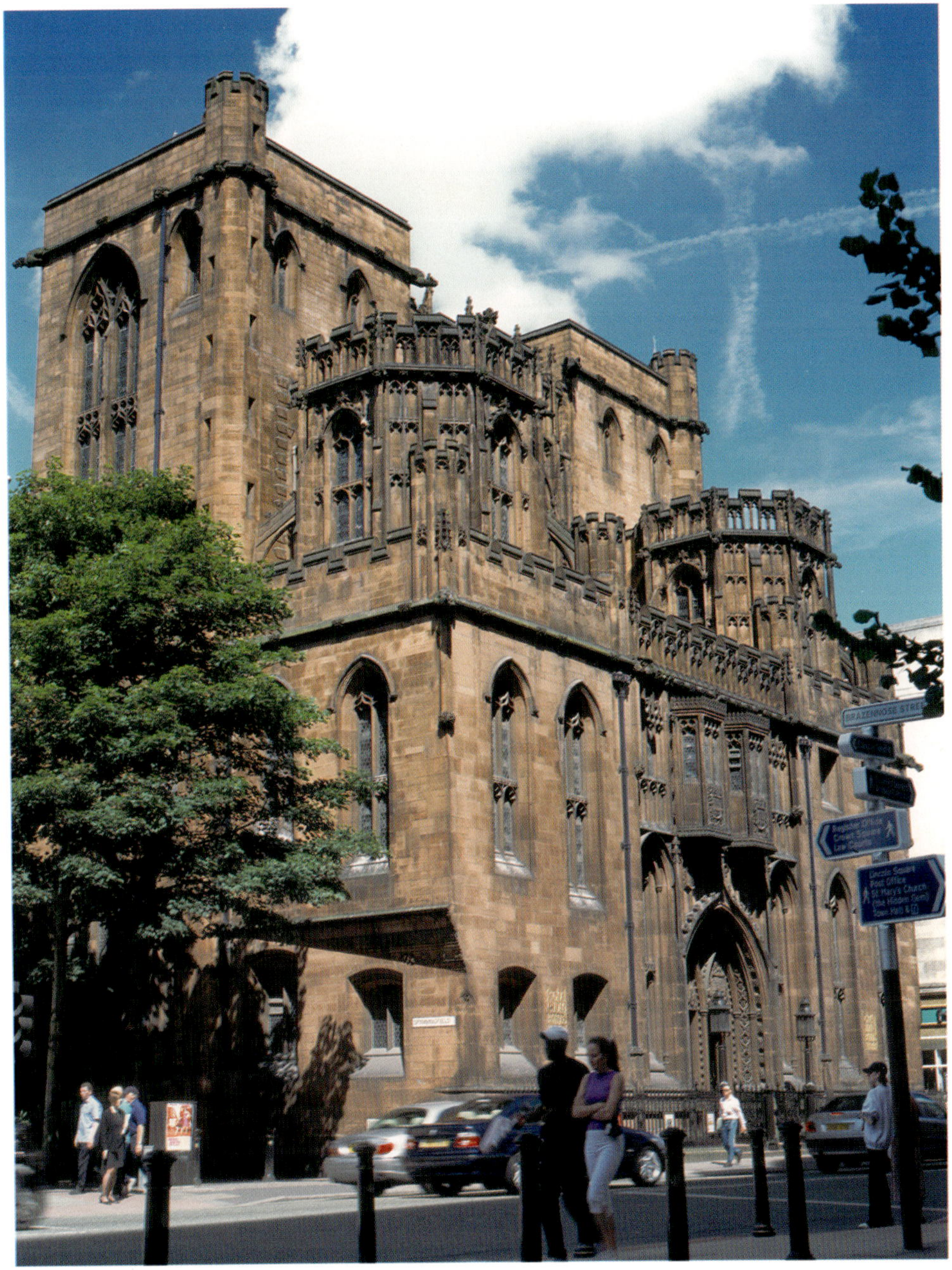

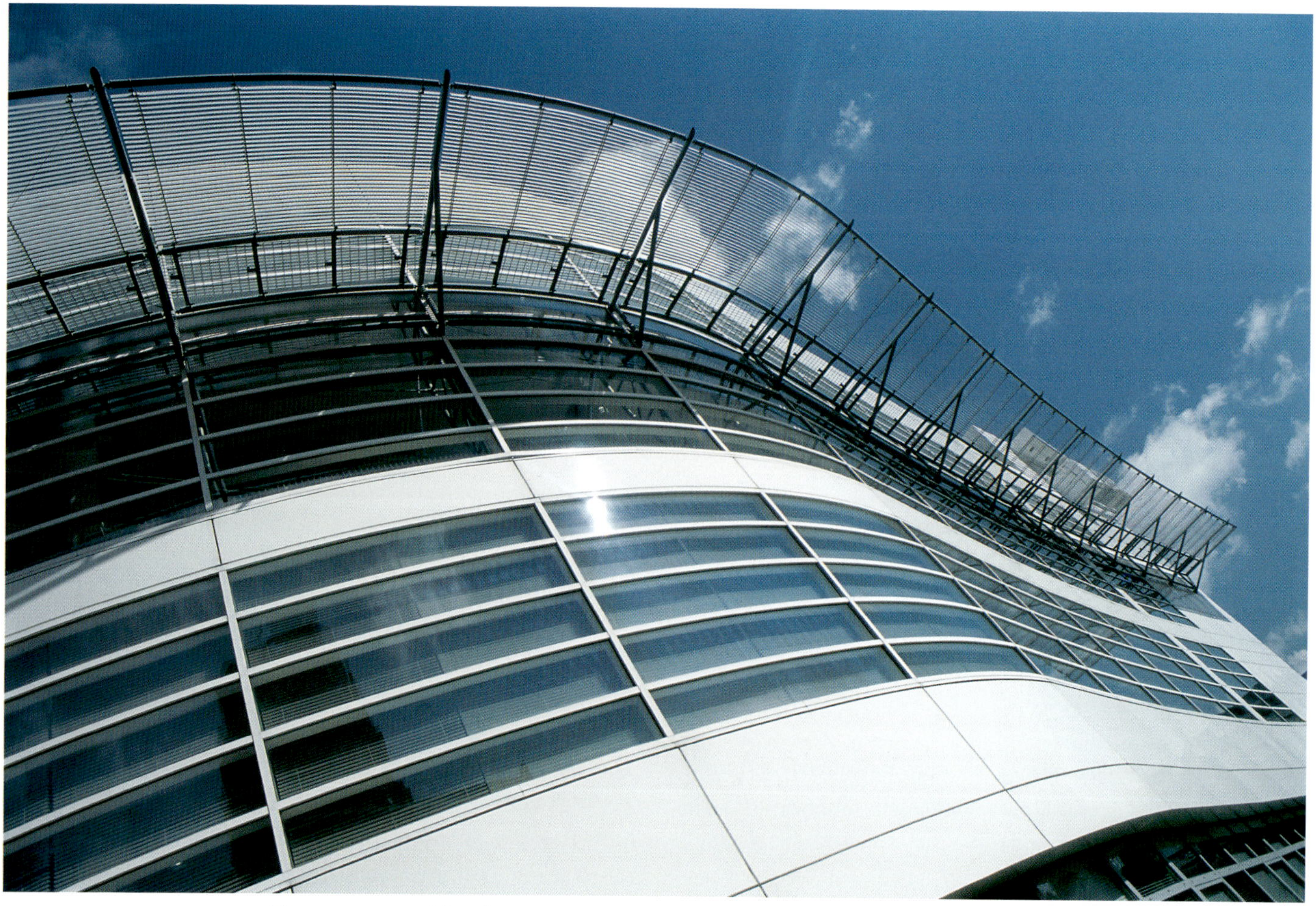

Elegant curves: Manchester Metropolitan University's Aytoun Library *(above)* and Central Reference Library with the Town Hall Extension *(opposite)*.

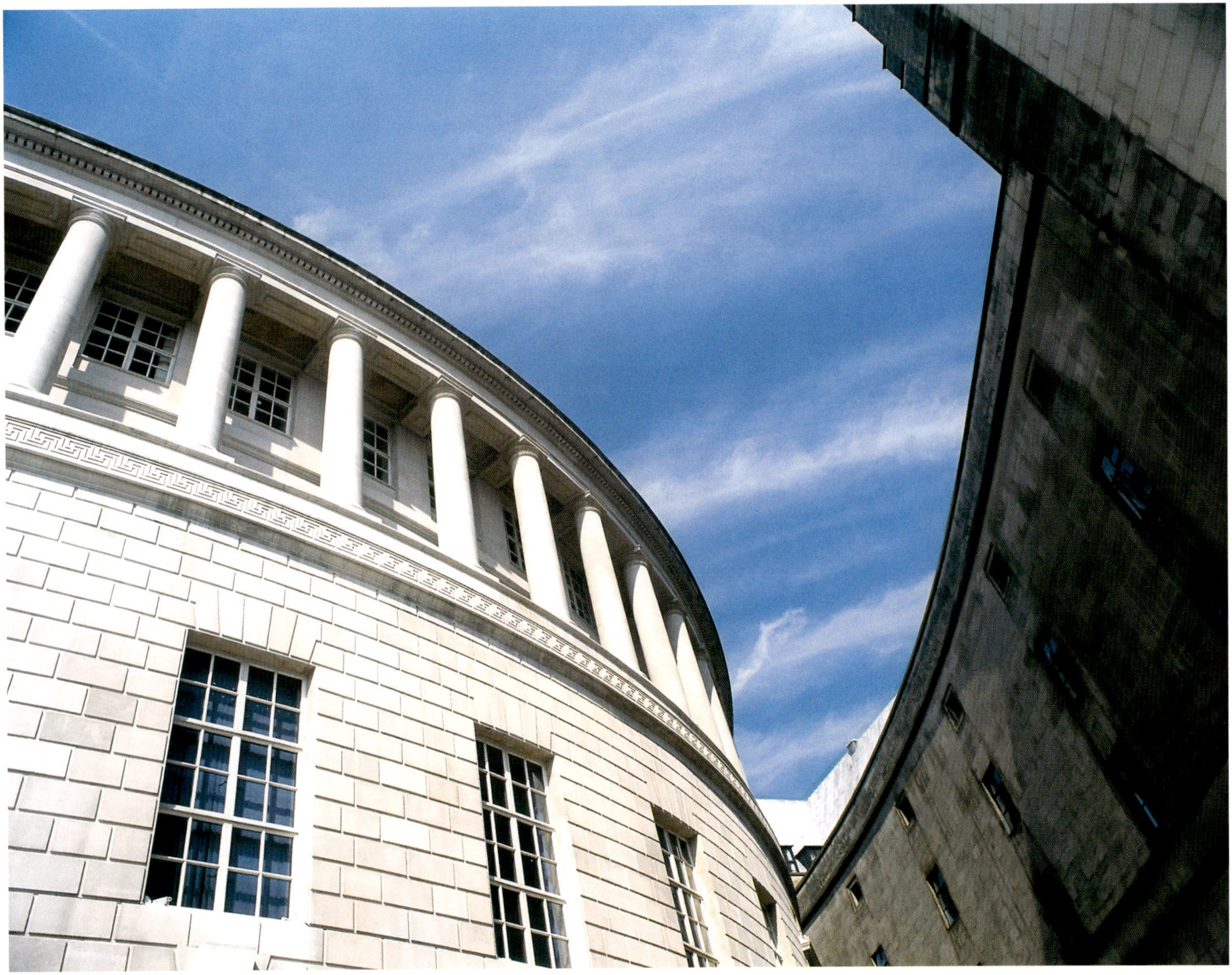

'Central Ref', *(above, left)* as it is known locally, boasts an impressive domed reading room on its first floor, complete with echoes that are far from conducive to quiet study.

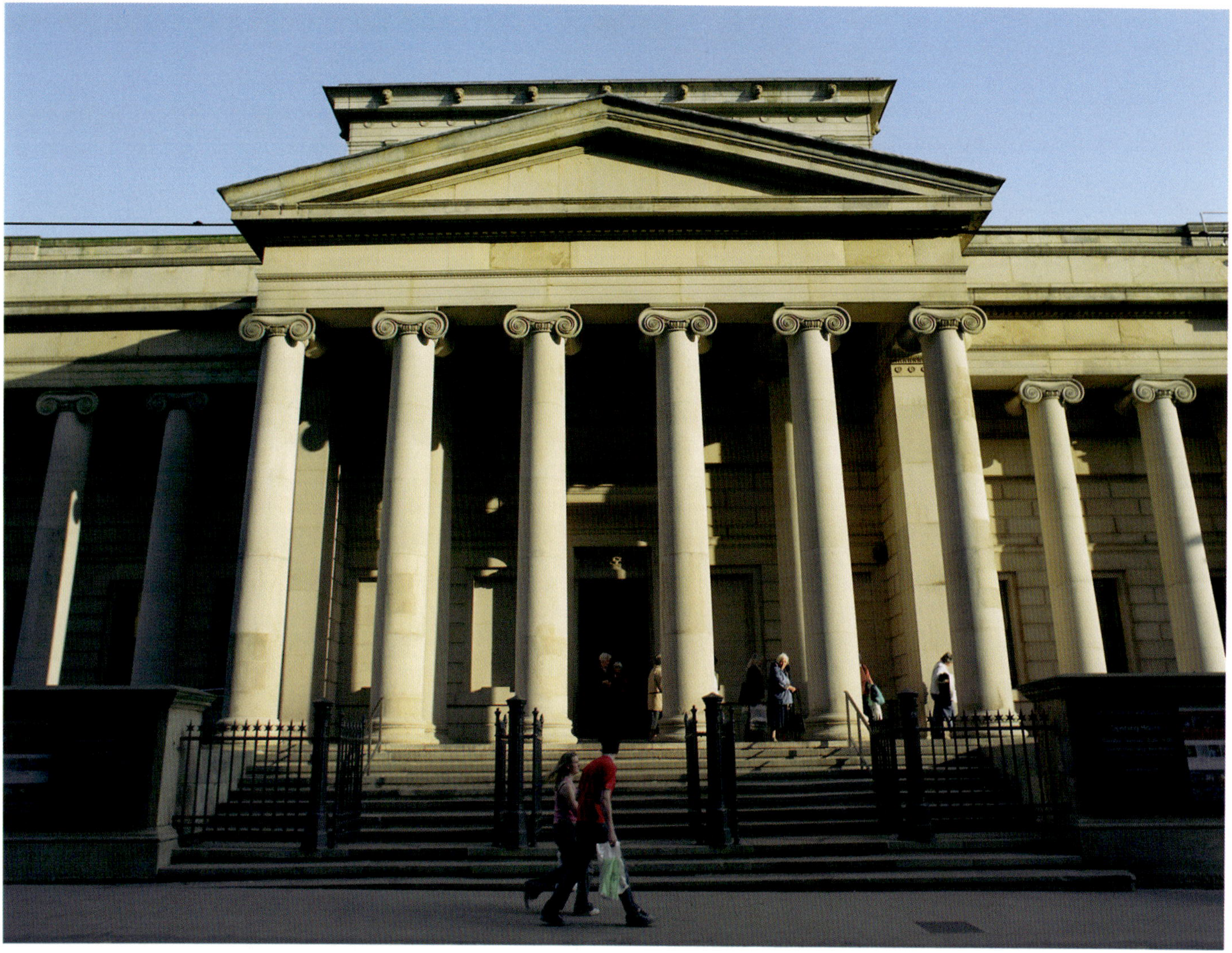

World renowned for its collection of Pre-Raphaelite paintings, the Manchester Art Gallery on Mosley Street has recently undergone an impressive expansion programme.

Architects Hopkins and Partners have created extensive new galleries and refurbished disused spaces, in addition to designing this wonderful glass link between the old and new.

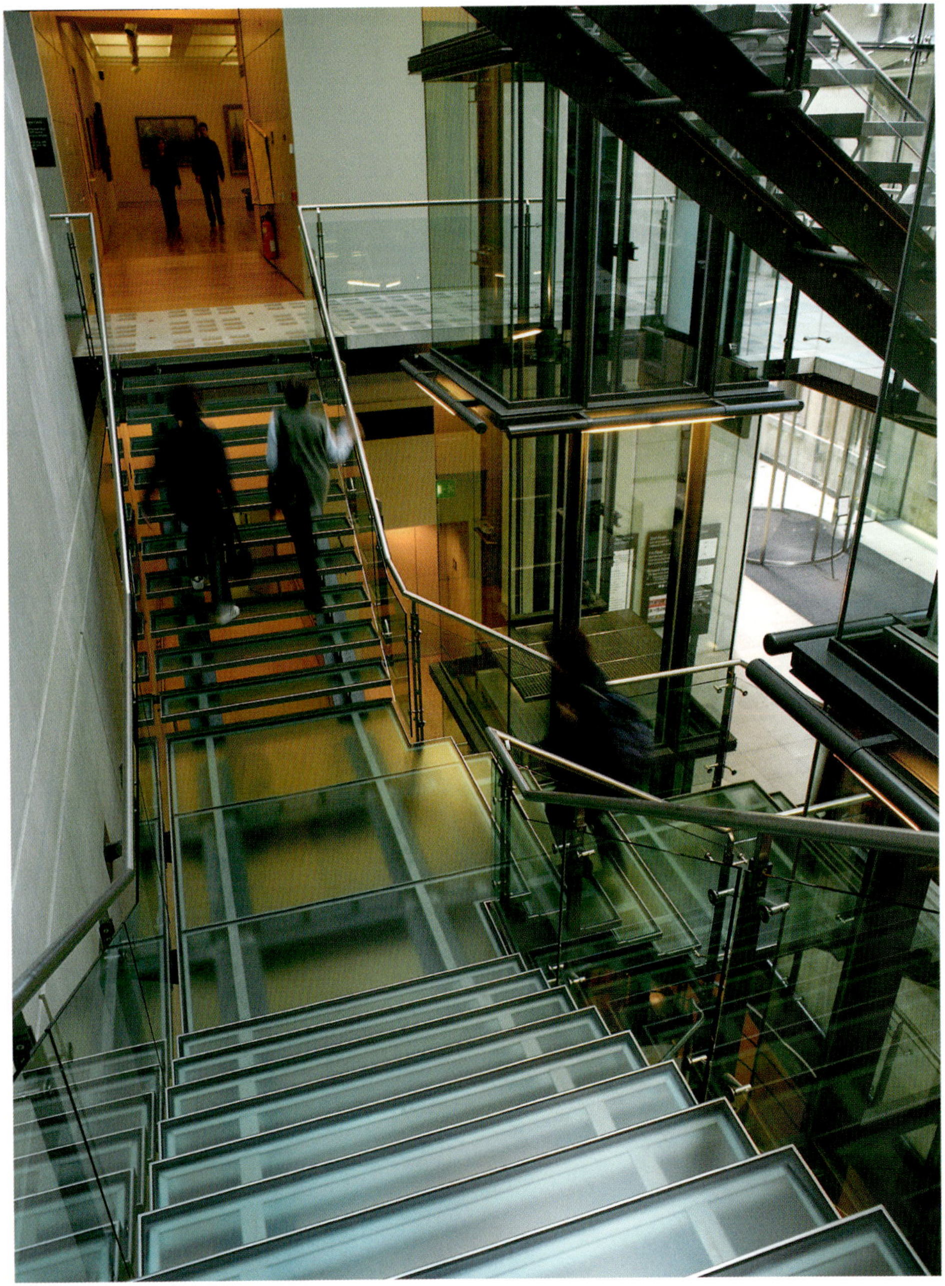

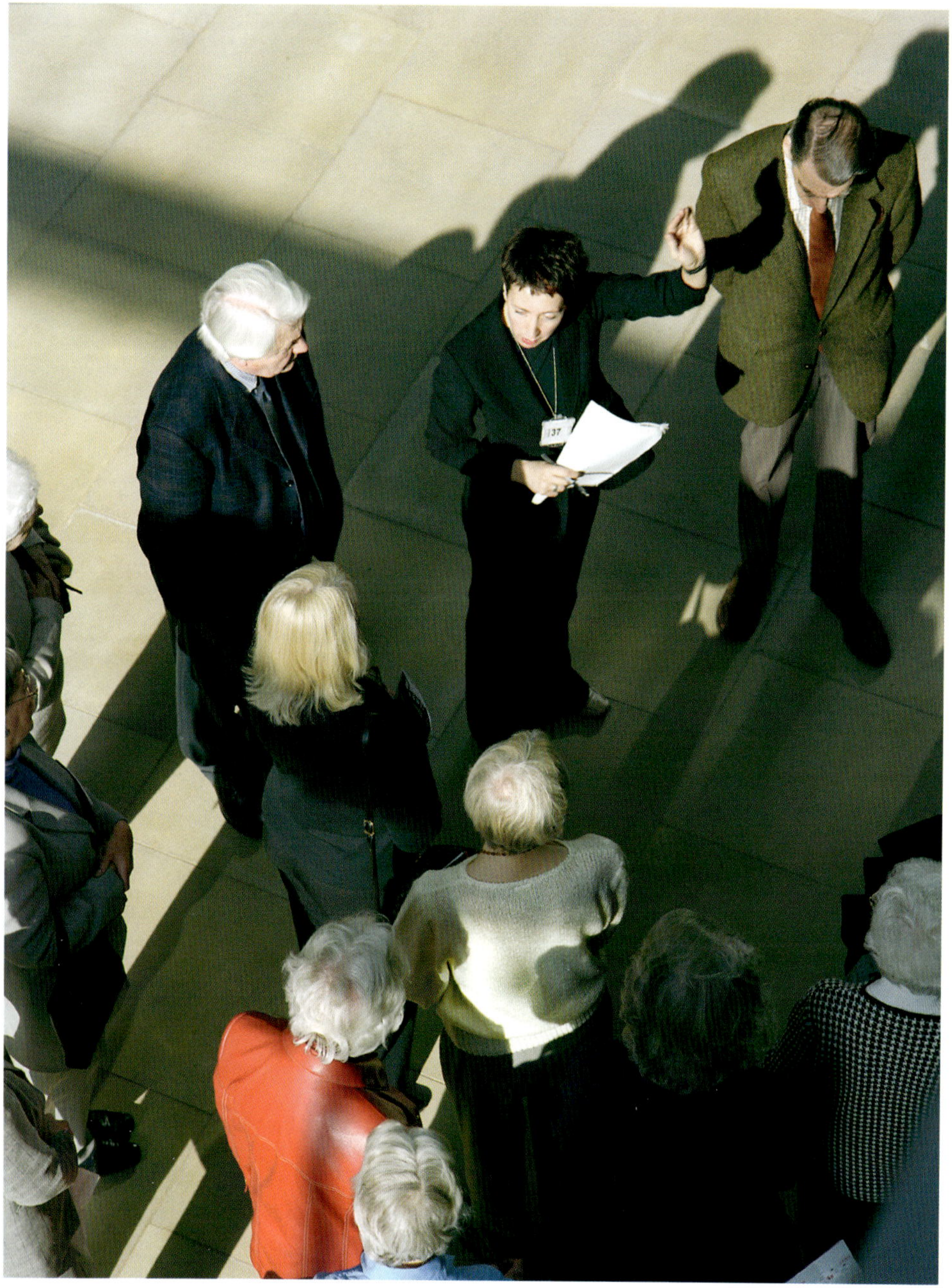

Manchester Art Gallery attracts around 250,000 visitors each year. Some come for formal tours...

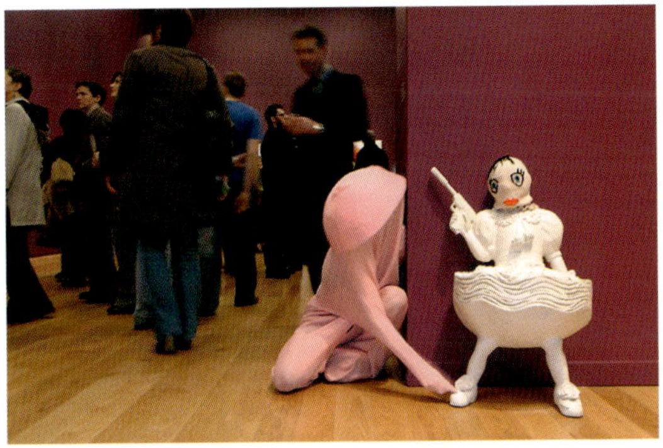
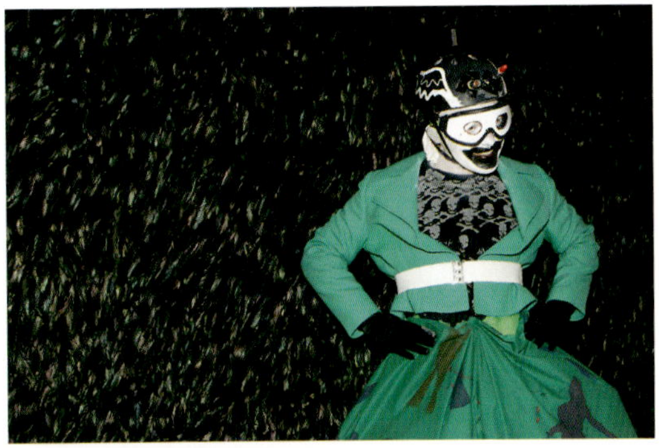
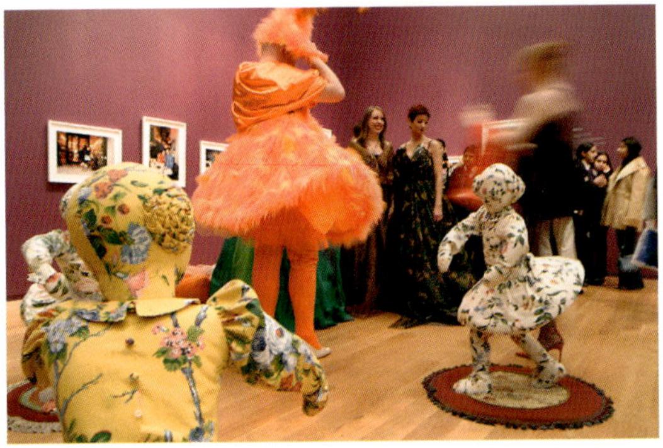
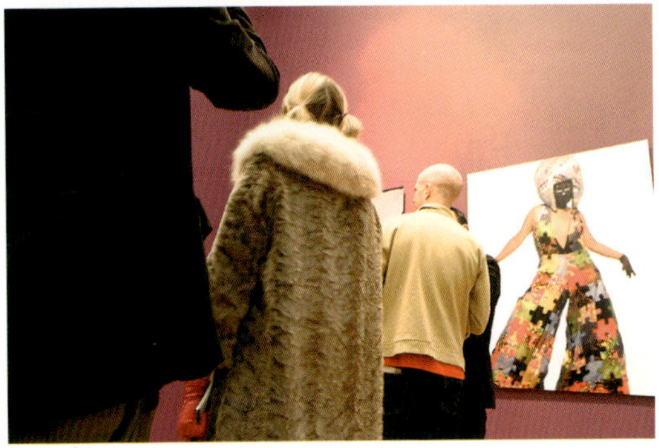

...while others have fun at the opening nights of new exhibitions.

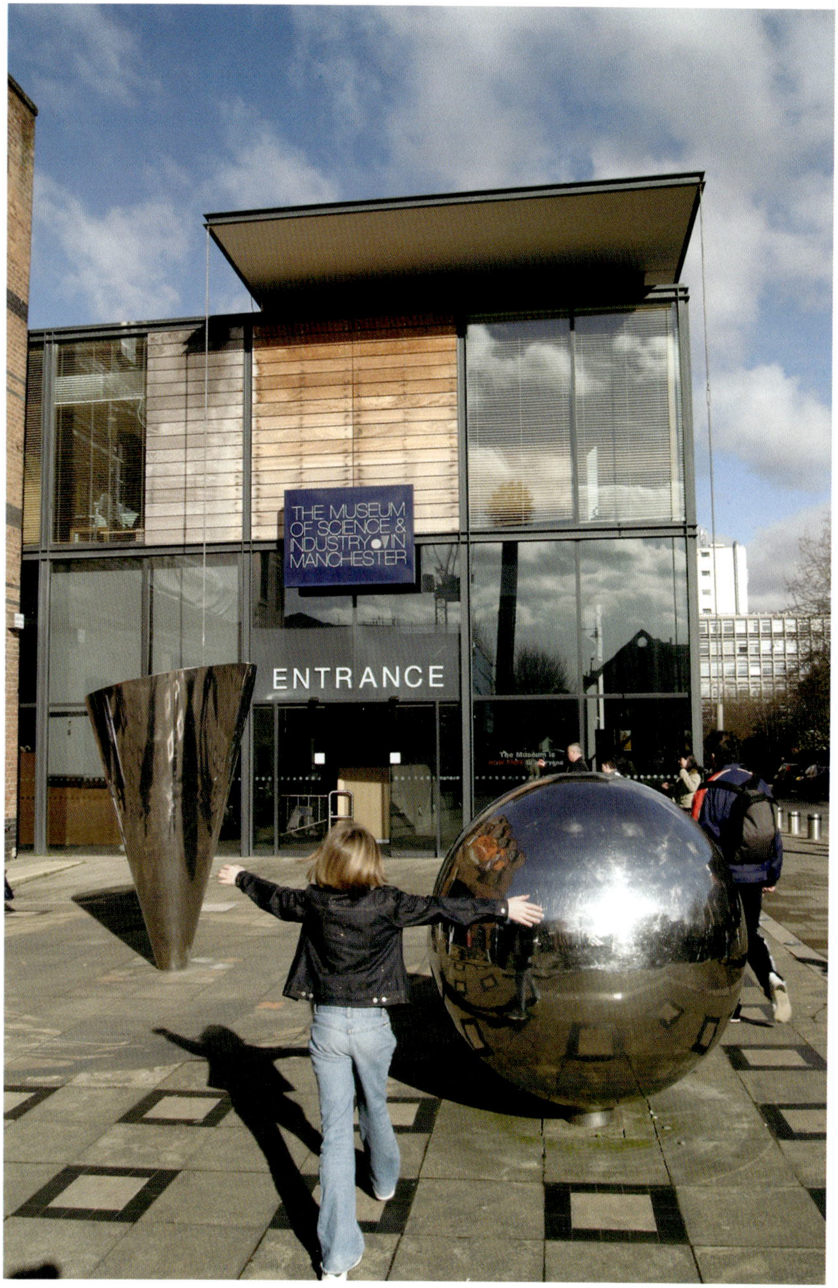

Mirror sculptures welcome visitors to the Museum of Science and Industry in Manchester, the site of the world's first passenger railway station.

The Wild Monkey theatre troupe *(below)* entertain at the Museum's Air and Space Gallery.

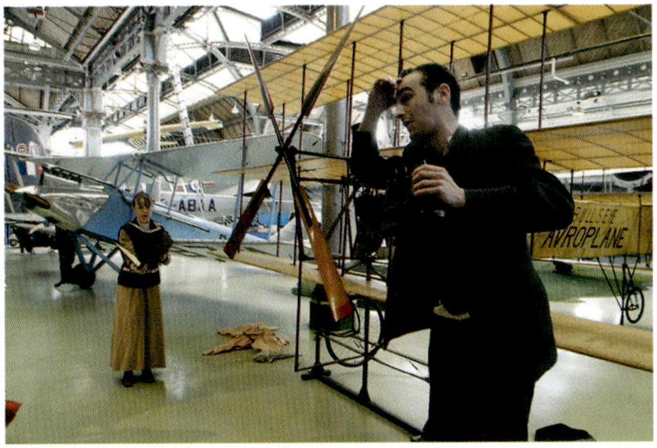

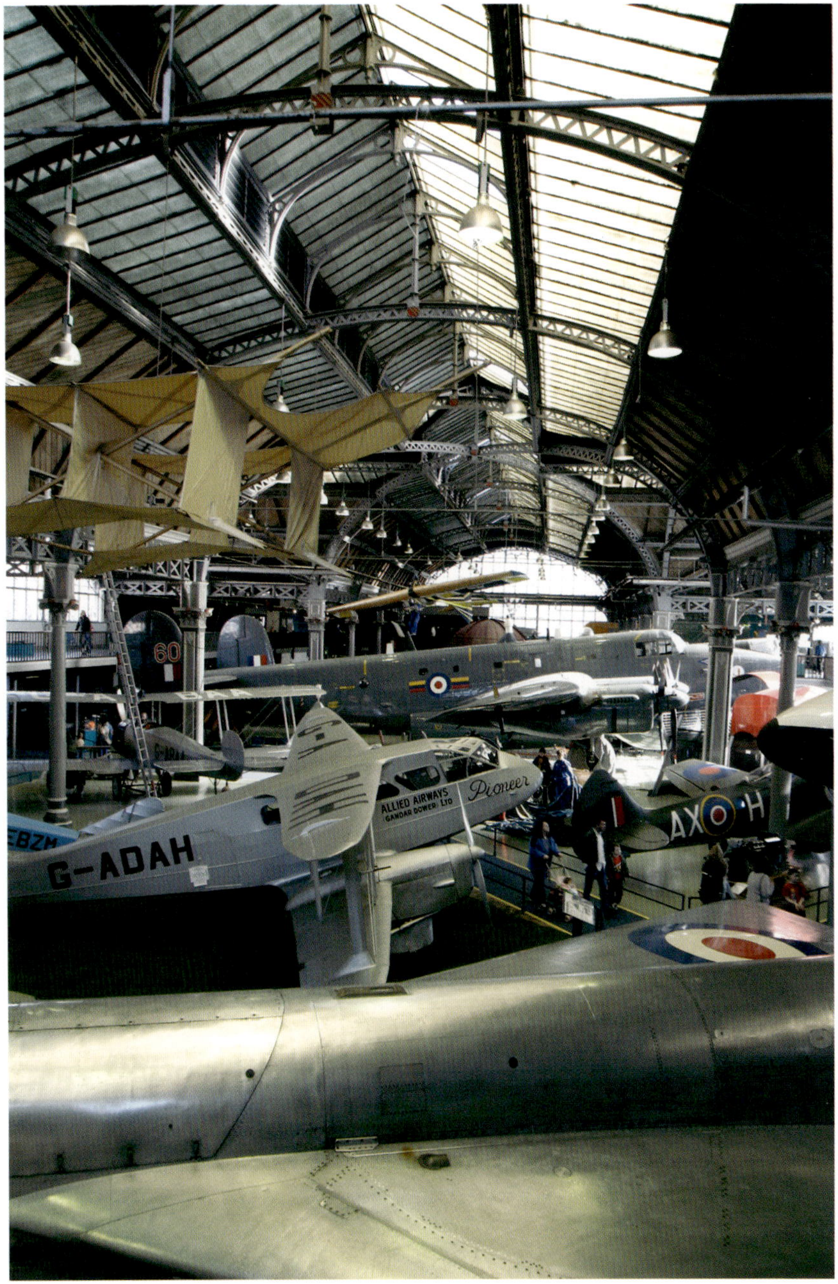

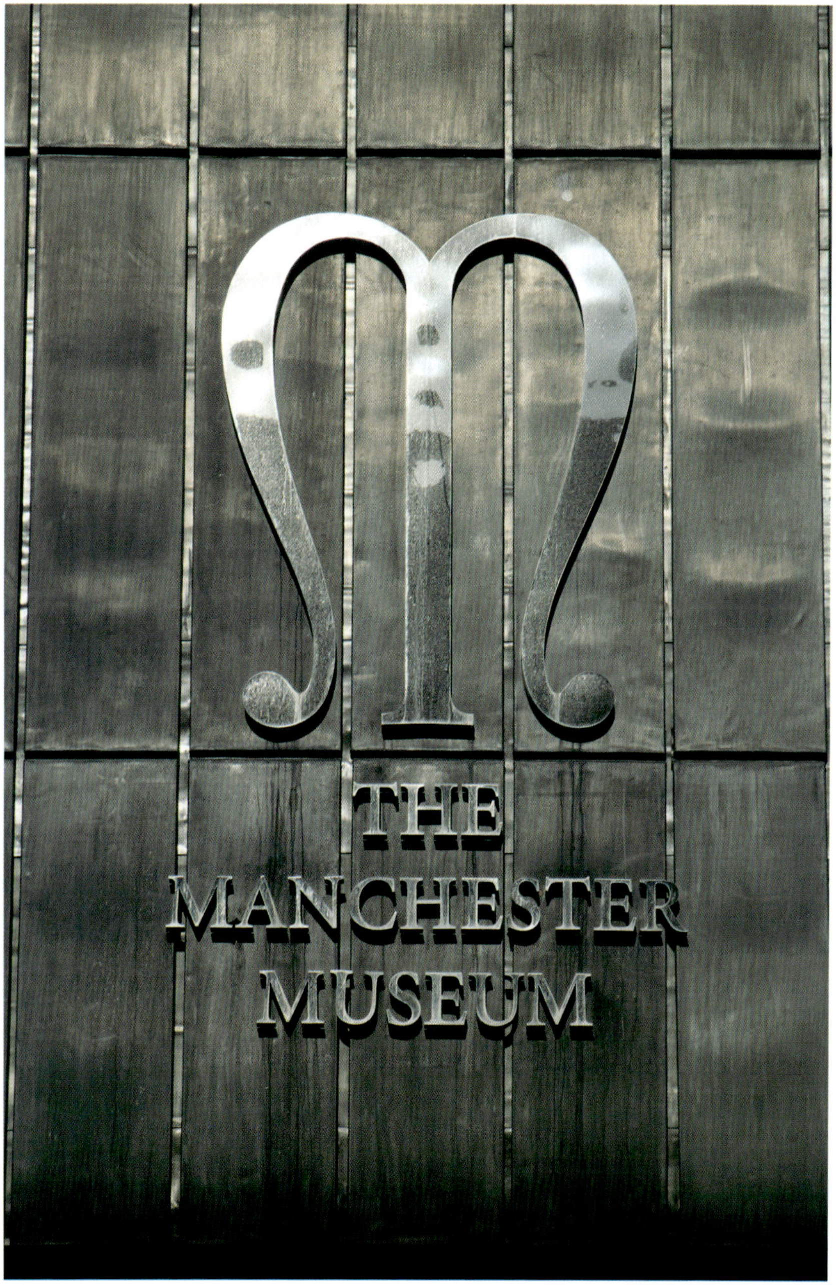

From Egyptian mummies to Henry Moore: The Manchester Museum *(left)* and the Whitworth Art Gallery *(opposite page)* are just two attractions on the University's Oxford Road campus.

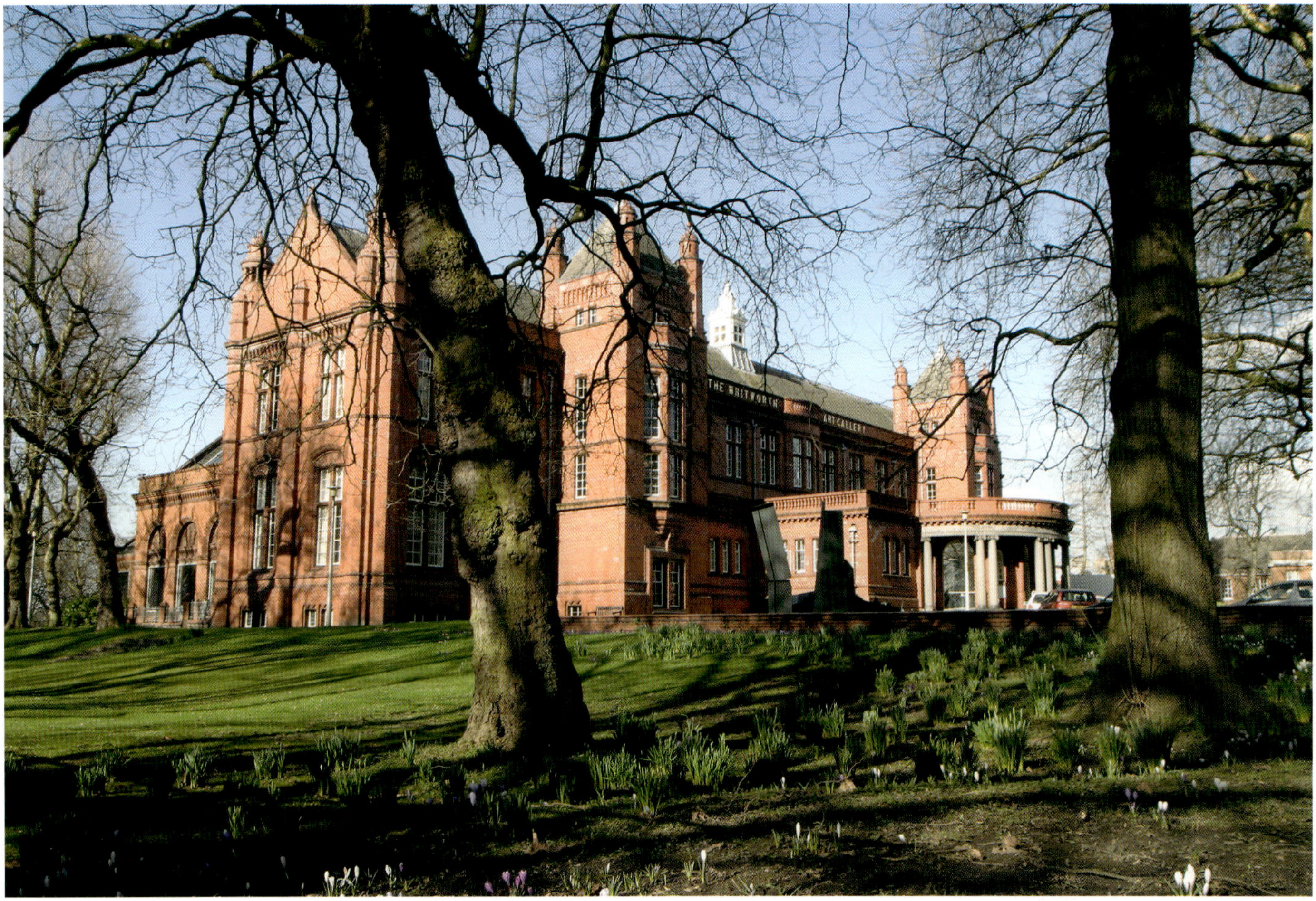

The Whitworth was founded in 1889 after Stockport-born engineer, Joseph Whitworth, left money in his will for the establishment of a number of charitable institutions.

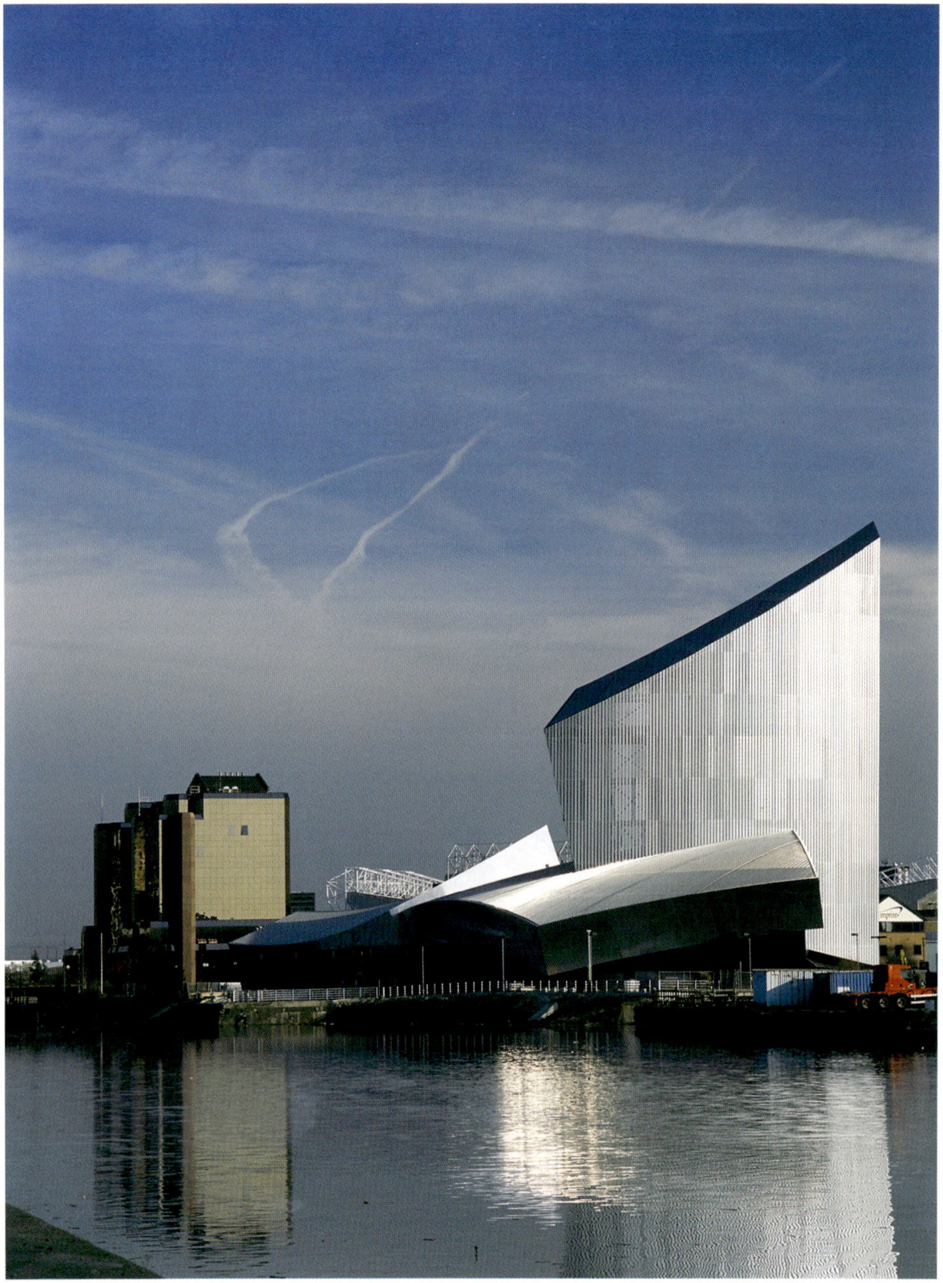

Completed in 2002, the Imperial War Museum North, designed by architect Daniel Libeskind, stands beside the Manchester Ship Canal in Trafford.

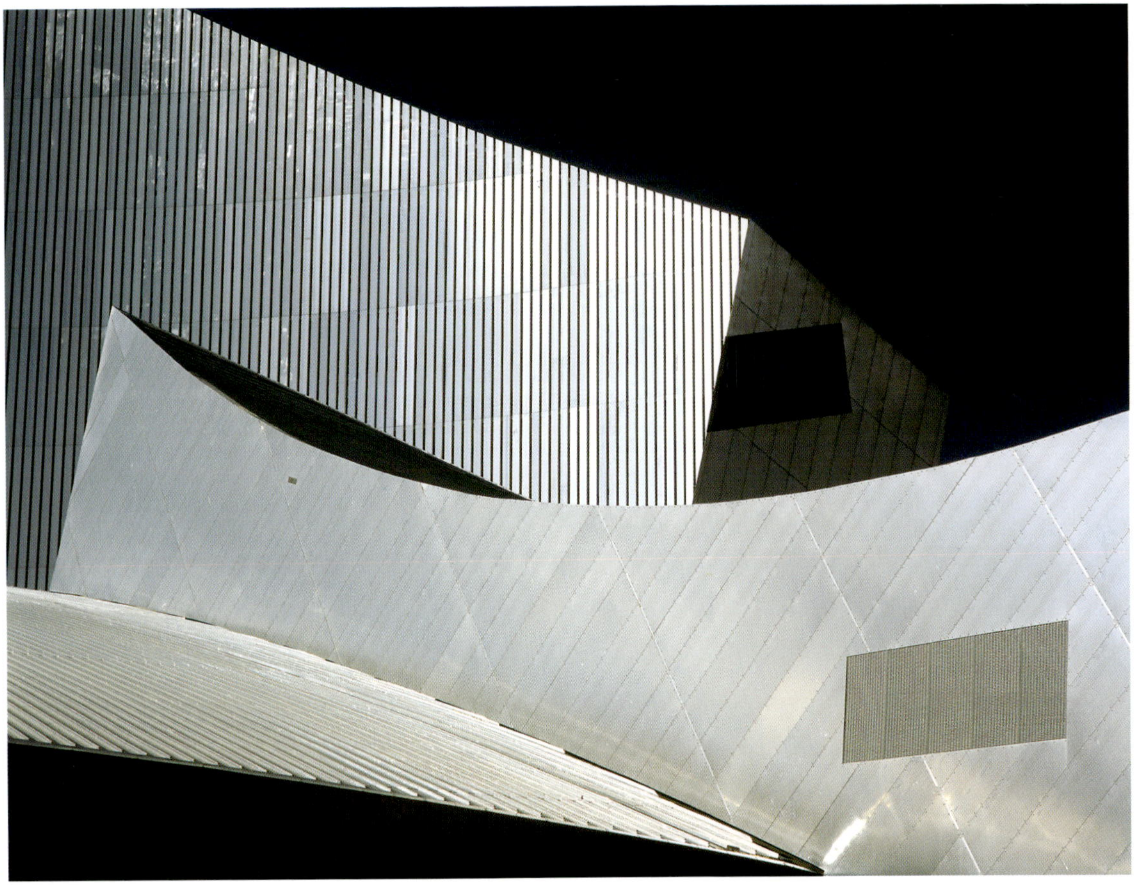

The three 'shards' of the IWM North represent conflict on land, in the air and on water.

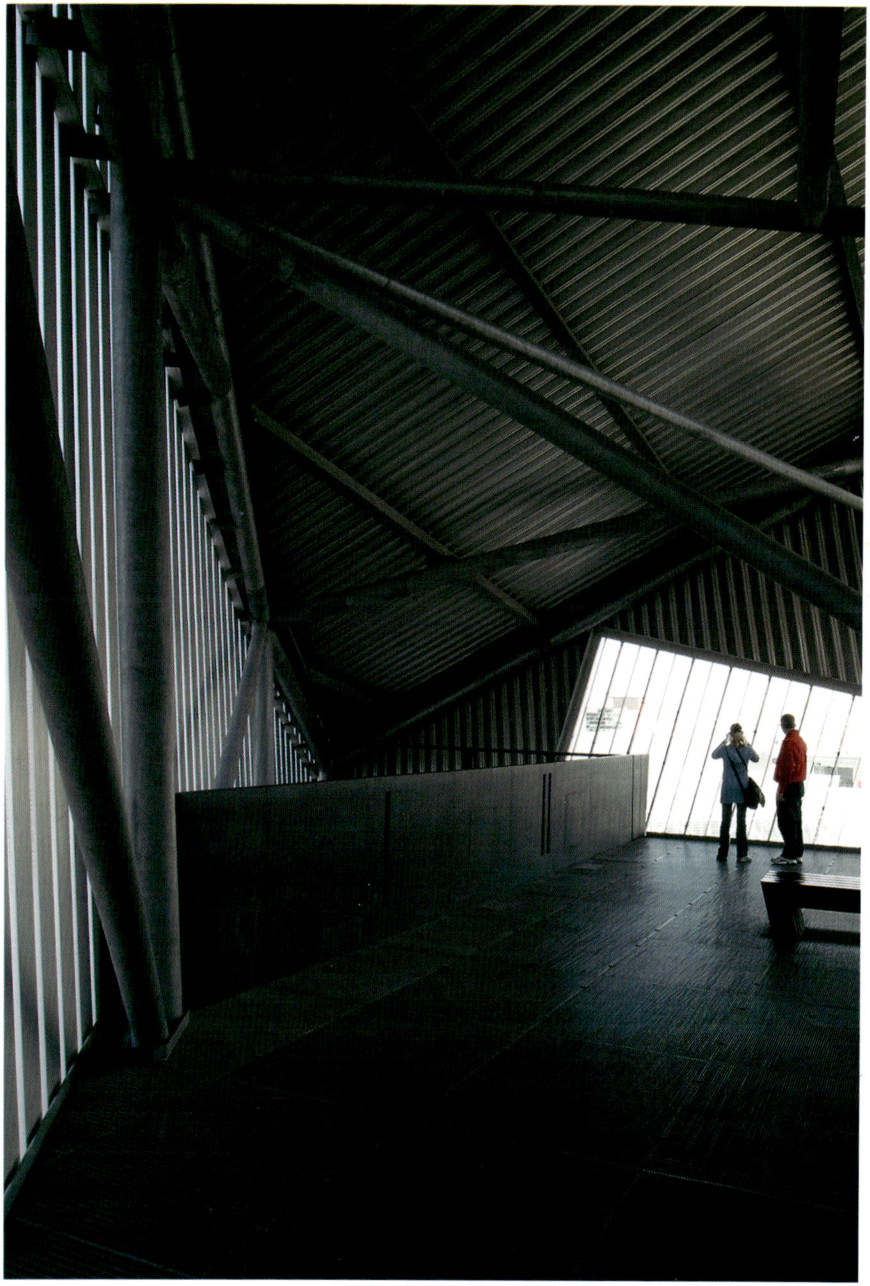

The viewing platform within the 'air shard' offers unrivalled views across Salford Quays and beyond. A truly emotive space.

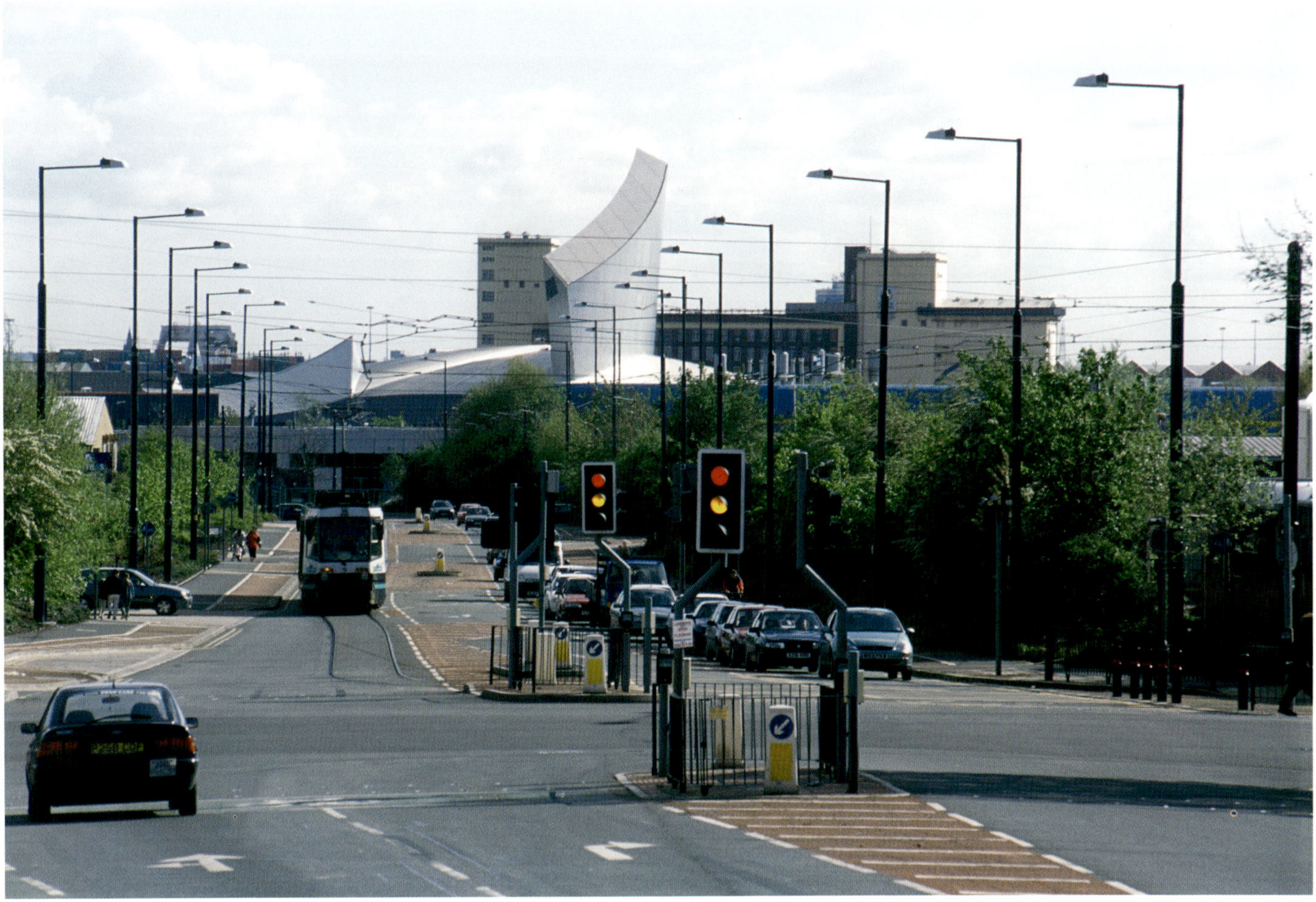

A landmark from every direction: the Imperial War Museum North from Langworthy Road in Salford.

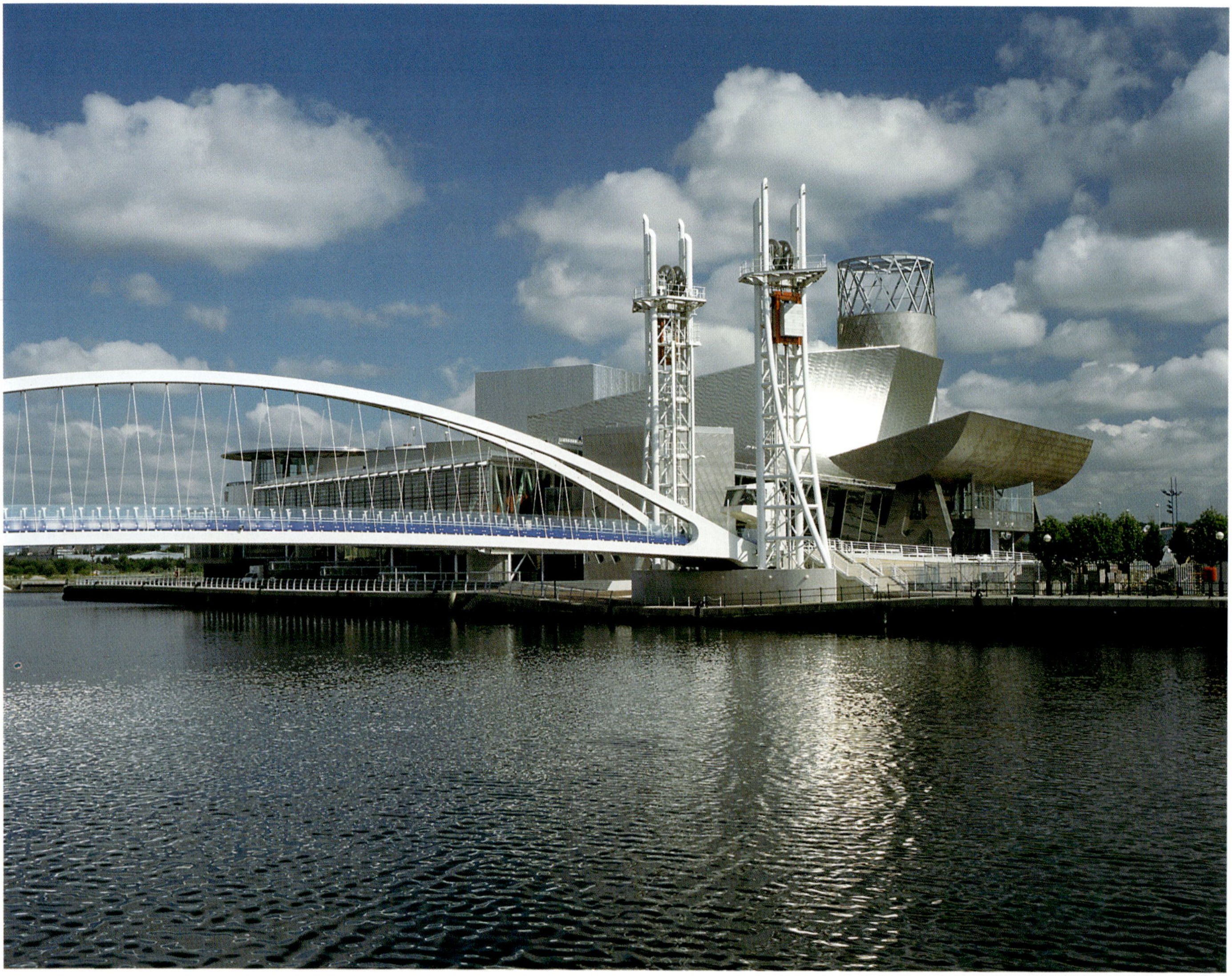

When it opened at the turn of the millennium, The Lowry sat in isolation at the end of Pier 9 but soon became the 'icing on the cake' in the ongoing regeneration of Salford Quays, the old Manchester Docks.

The Lowry stands on a triangular site beside the Manchester Ship Canal and with its galleries, two theatres, bars and restaurants, it is a popular venue for young and old.

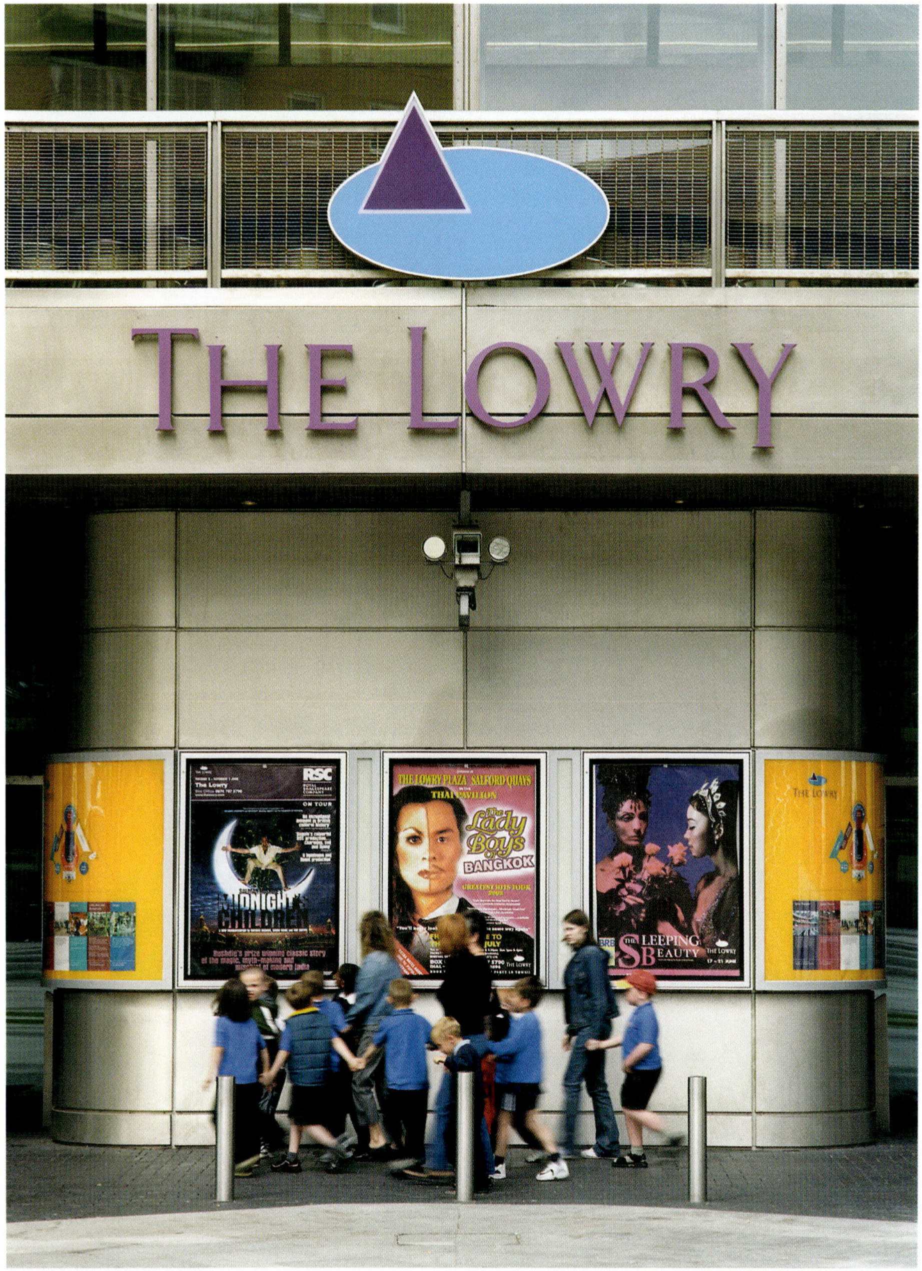

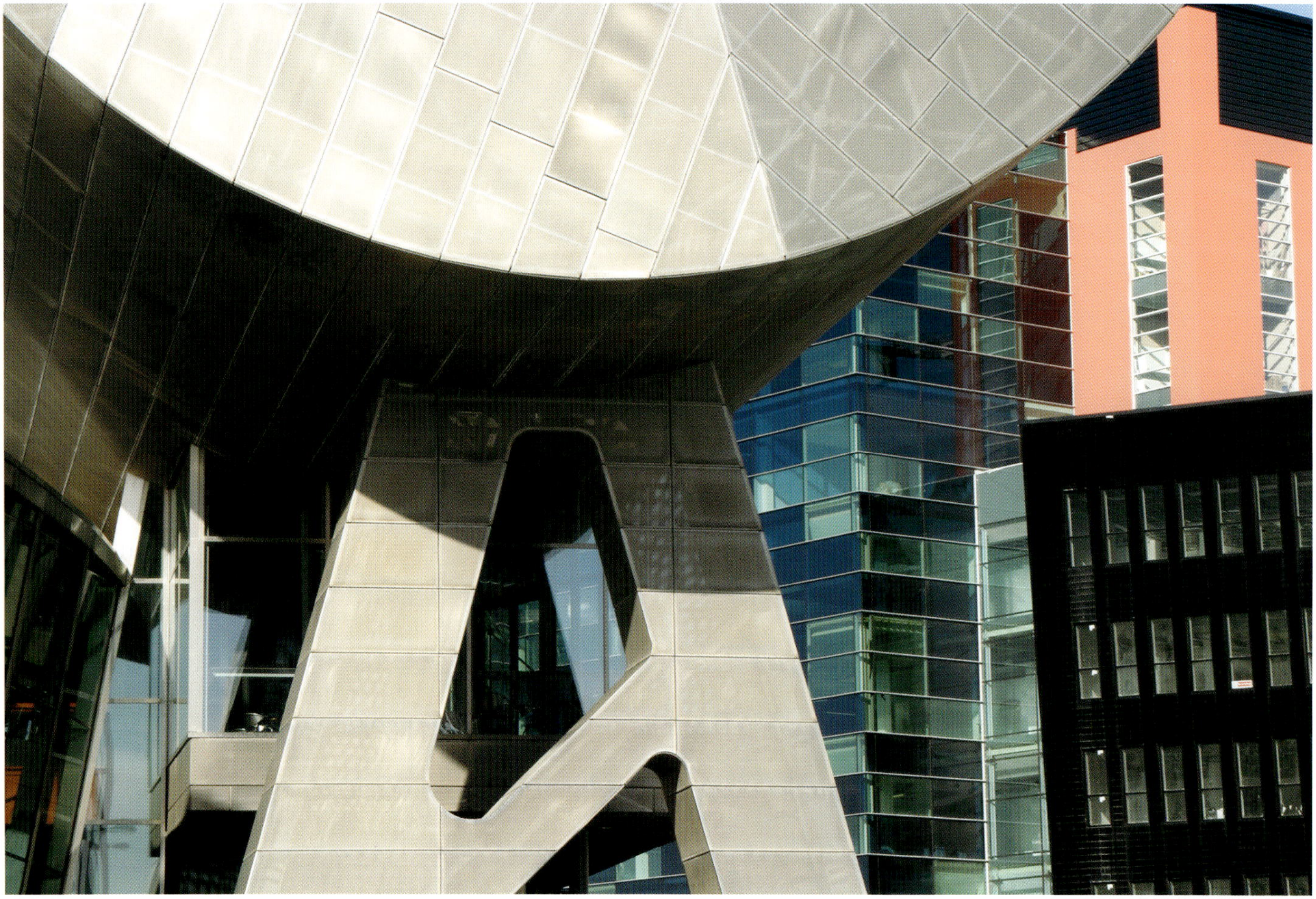

Designed by Michael Wilford and Partners, the contemporary style has not been to everyone's taste. This is the sweeping curve of the stainless steel-clad entrance canopy.

Adjacent to the internal promenade through the building, The Lowry restaurant caters for the arts centre's numerous visitors.

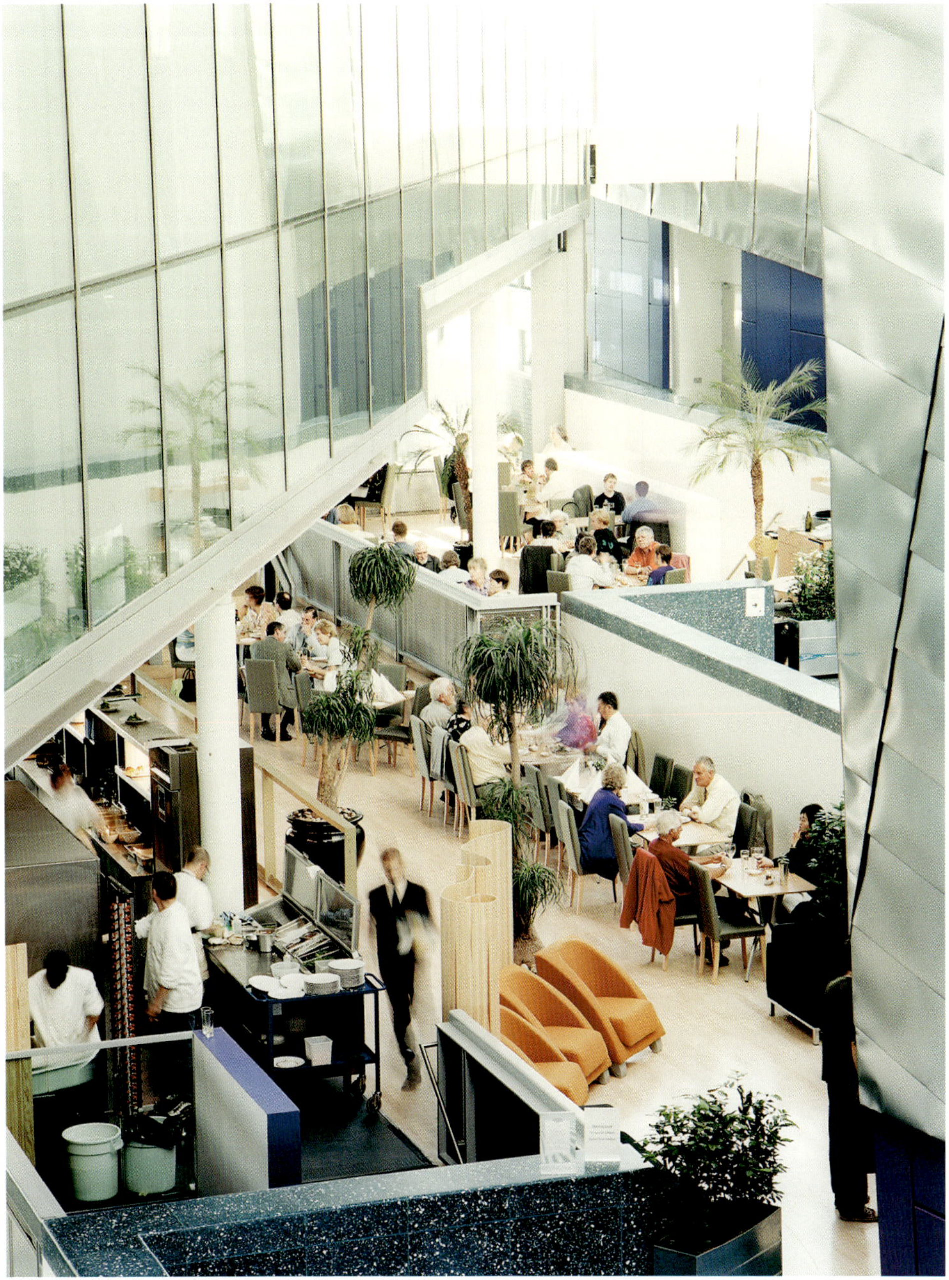

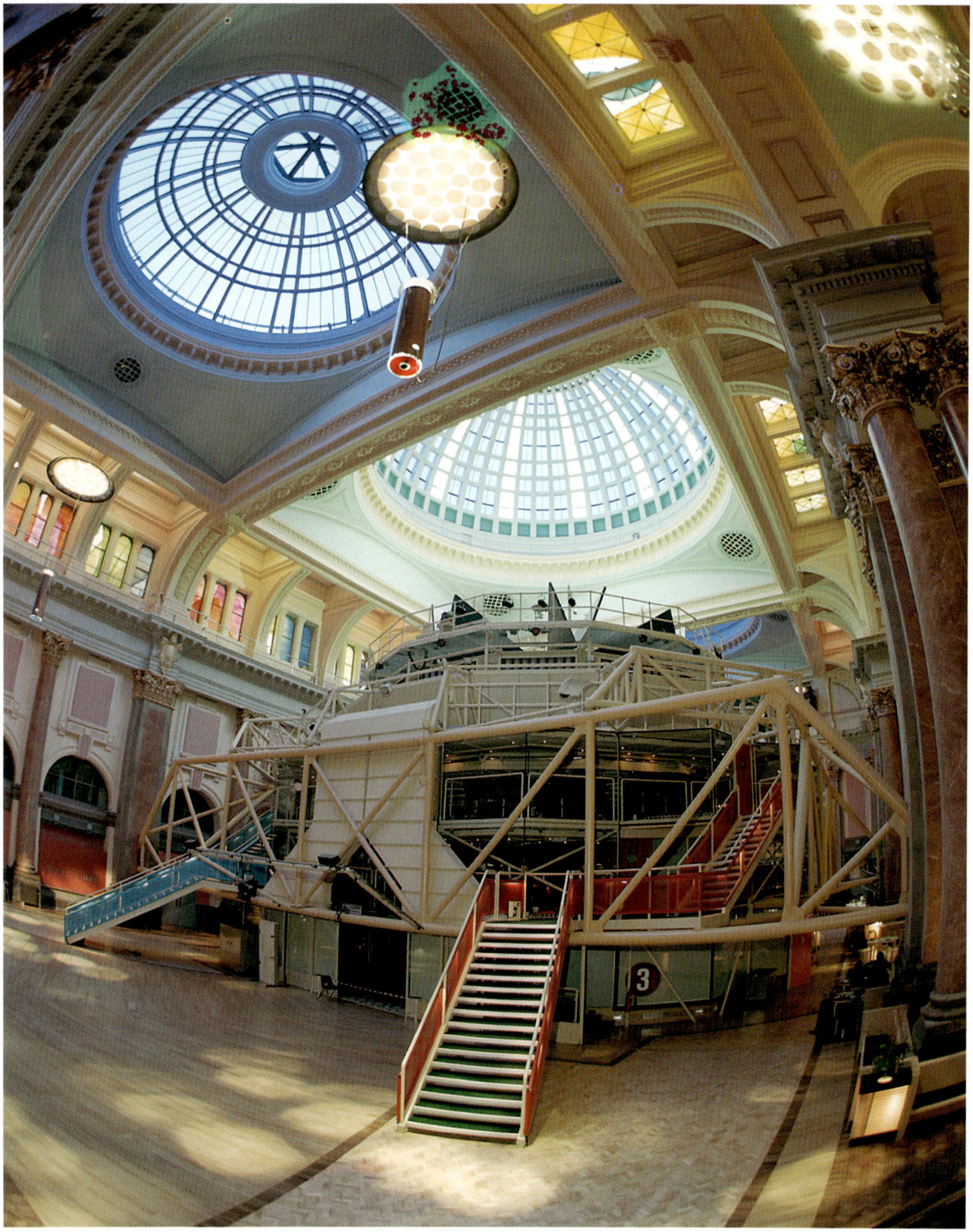

The Royal Exchange Theatre built as a free-standing theatre 'pod' in what was Manchester's Cotton Exchange.

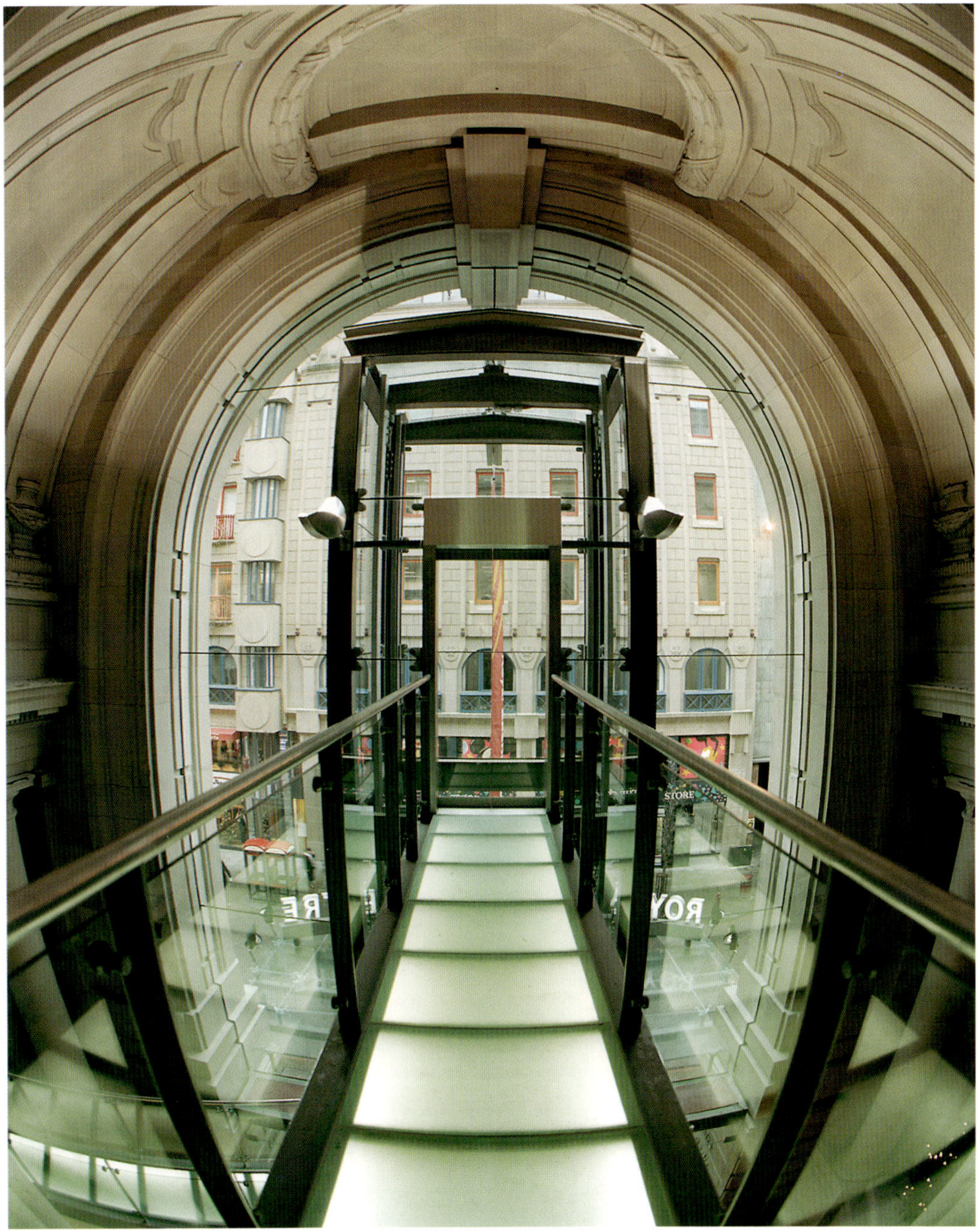

Refurbishment after the terrorist bomb of 1996 has included coloured glazing in the domes and improved access to St Ann's Square.

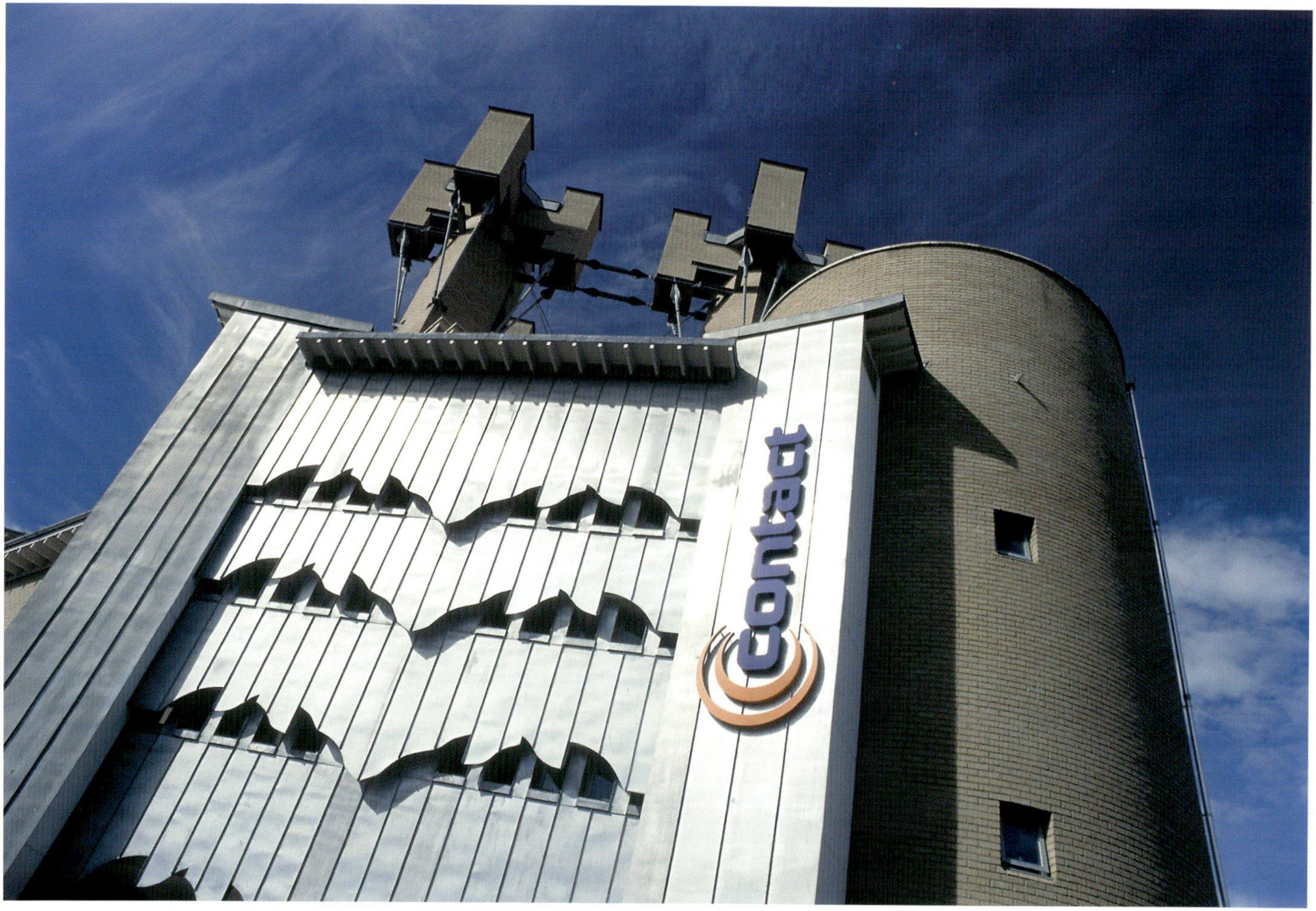

The Contact Theatre is acclaimed for its contemporary youth performances – and its policy of allowing drinks into the auditorium!

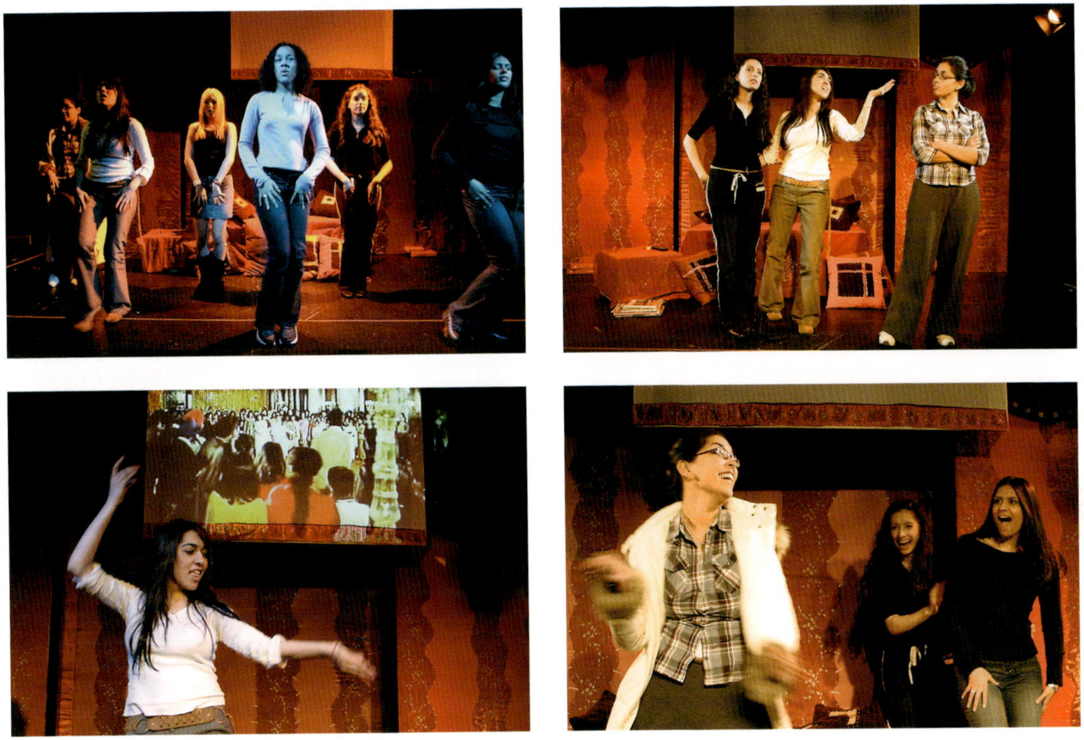

Oldham-based Peshkar productions rehearse for *Masala Girls: The Wedding*

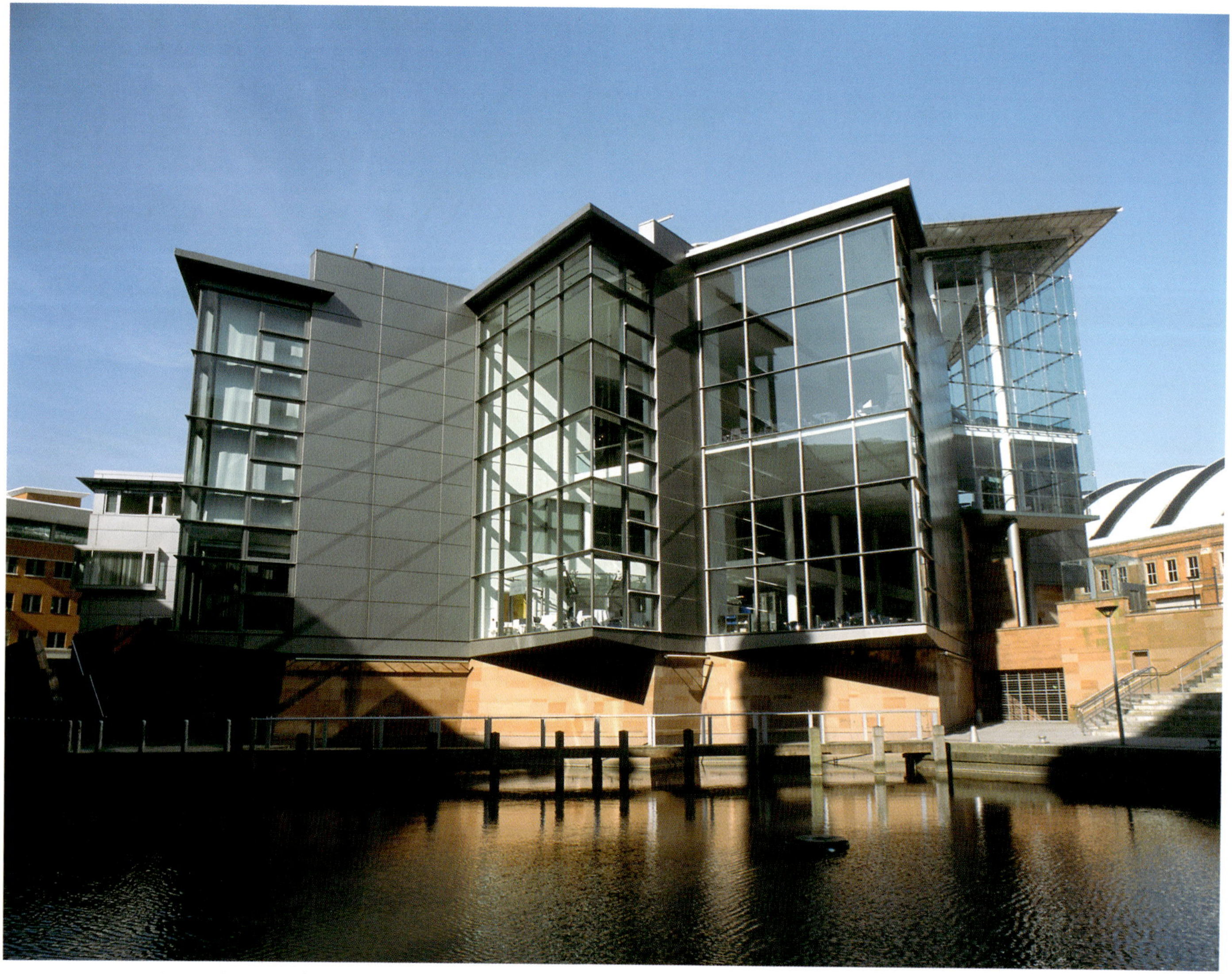

Opened in 1996, The Bridgewater Hall is Manchester's international concert venue and the home of the Hallé Orchestra. Its predecessor, the Free Trade Hall, is now a top-class hotel.

The hall's stunning design has won wide acclaim. A Civic Trust Award praised the hall for doing most to enhance the appearance of a city centre.

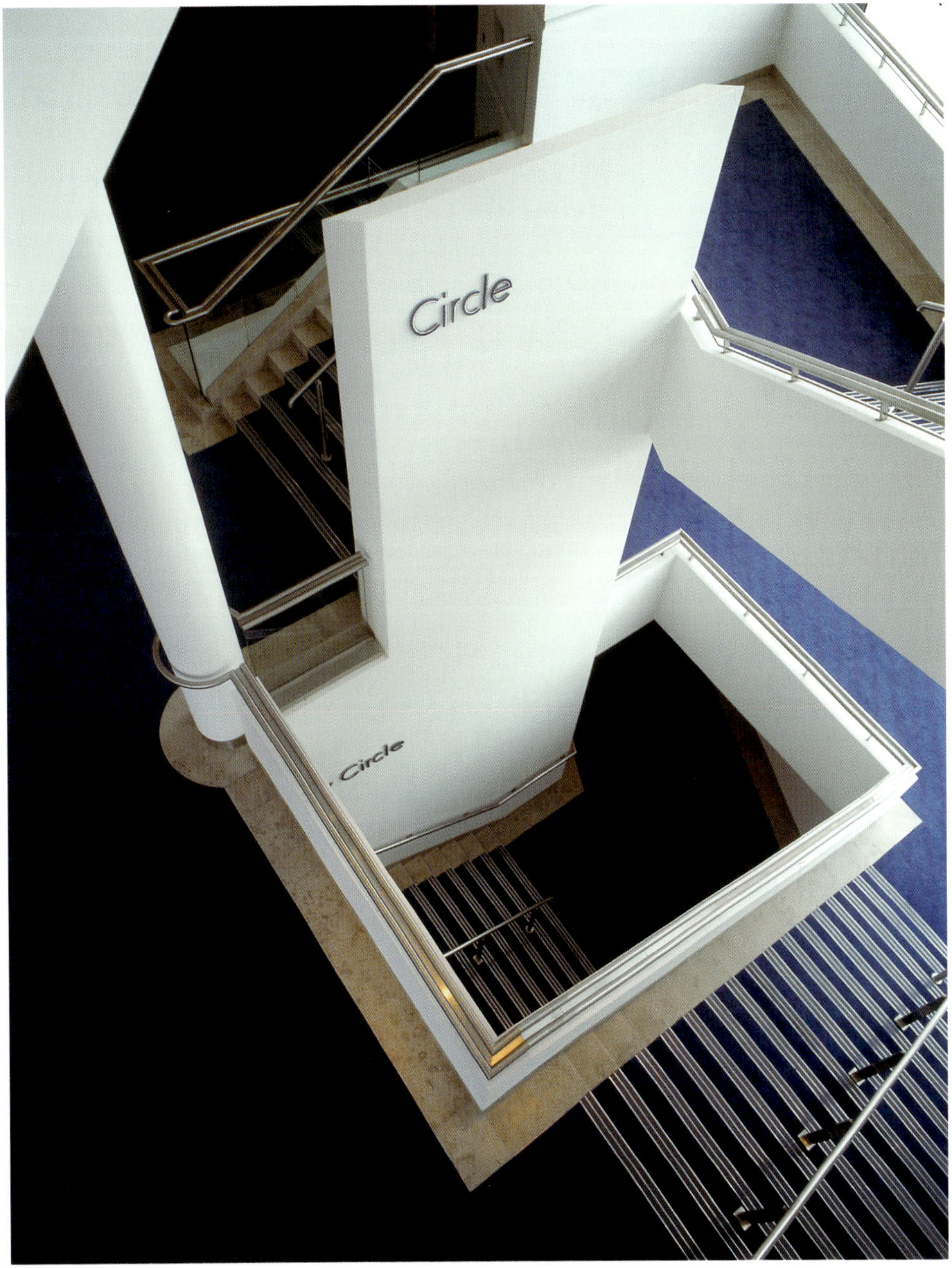

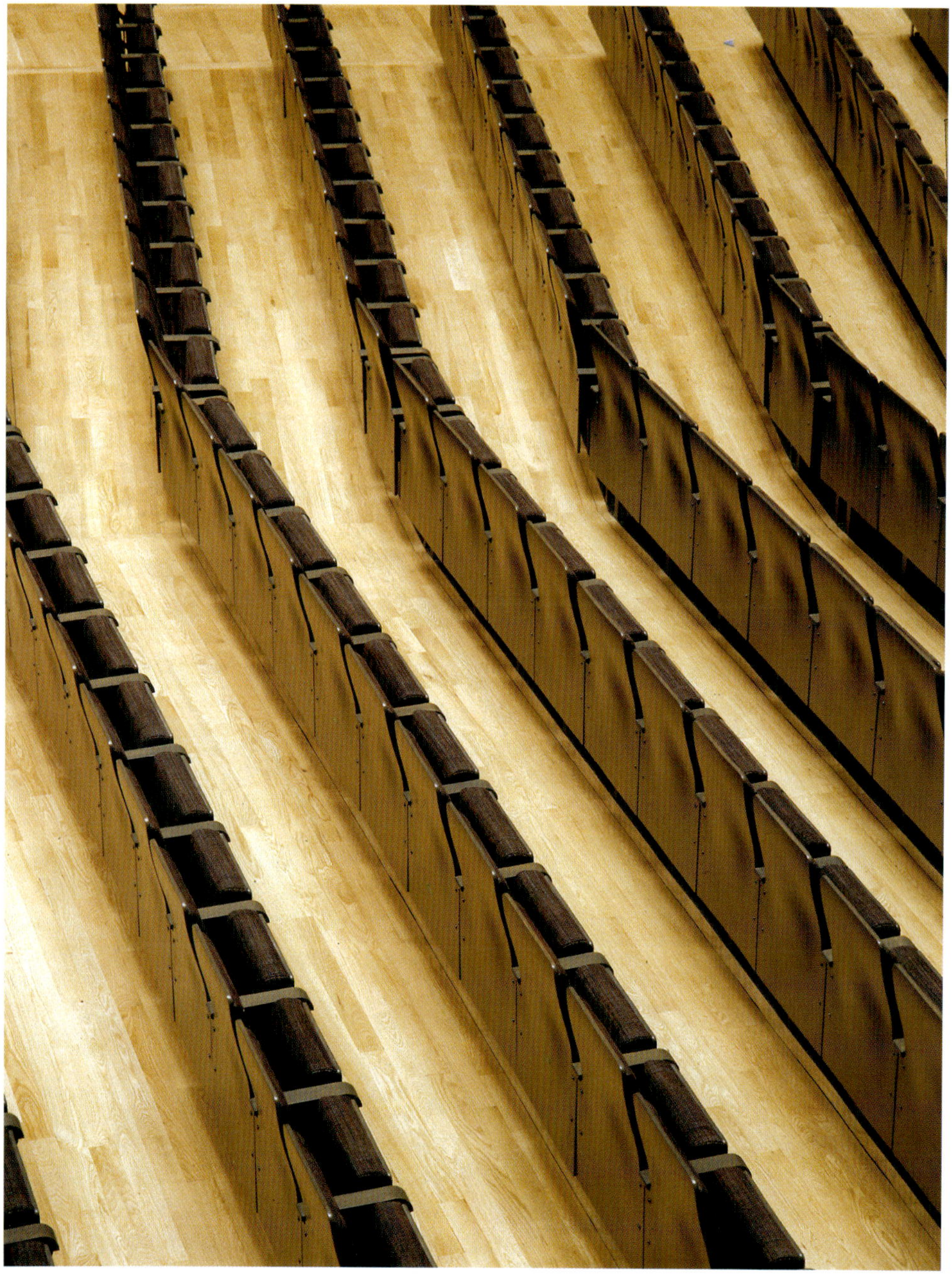

In this state-of-the-art venue, even the seats are acoustically designed.

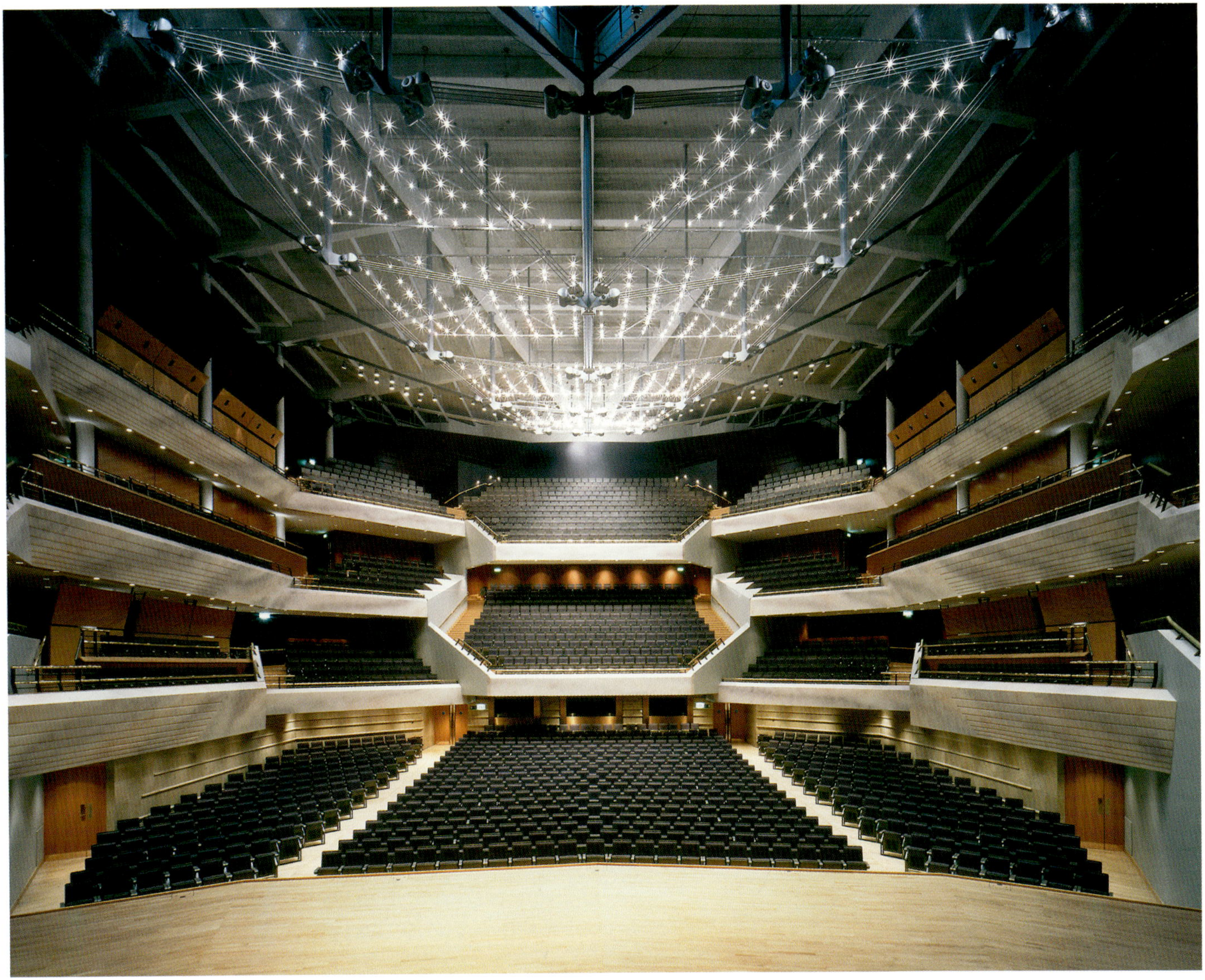

The Bridgewater Hall can seat over 2300 and stages 250 performances each year.

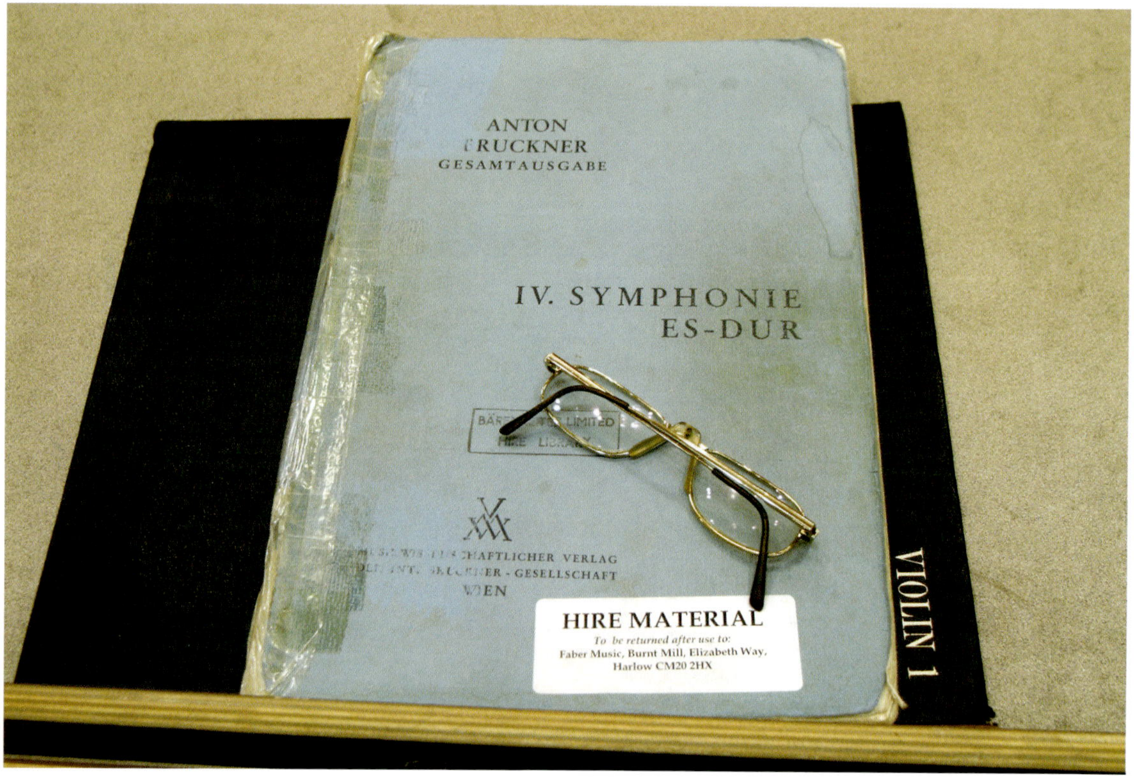

The BBC Philharmonic, a regular at the Bridgewater Hall, rehearsing a Bruckner symphony *(above)* under conductor Vassily Sinaisky in Studio 7 Concert Hall at the BBC studios on Oxford Road*(opposite)*.

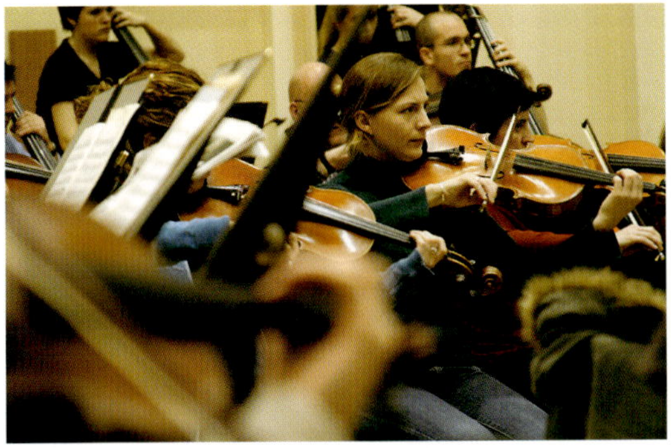

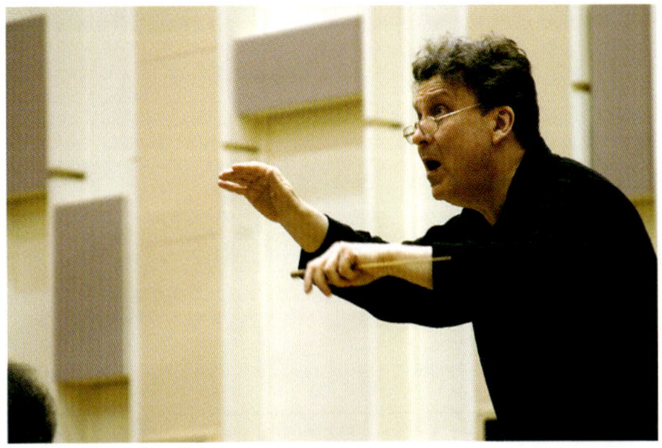

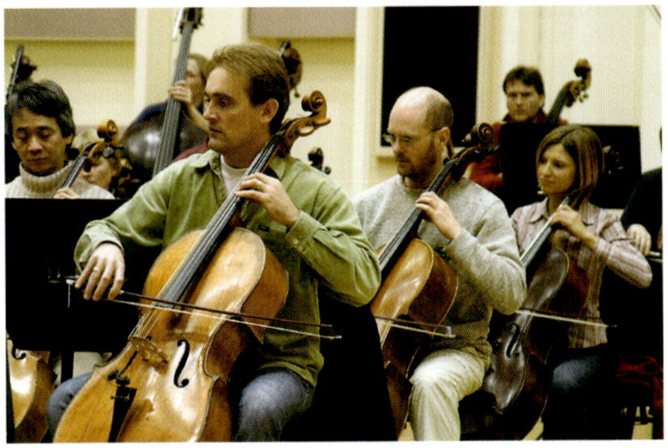

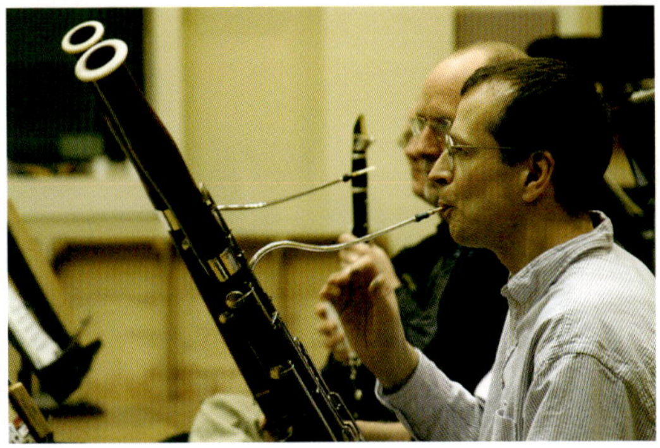

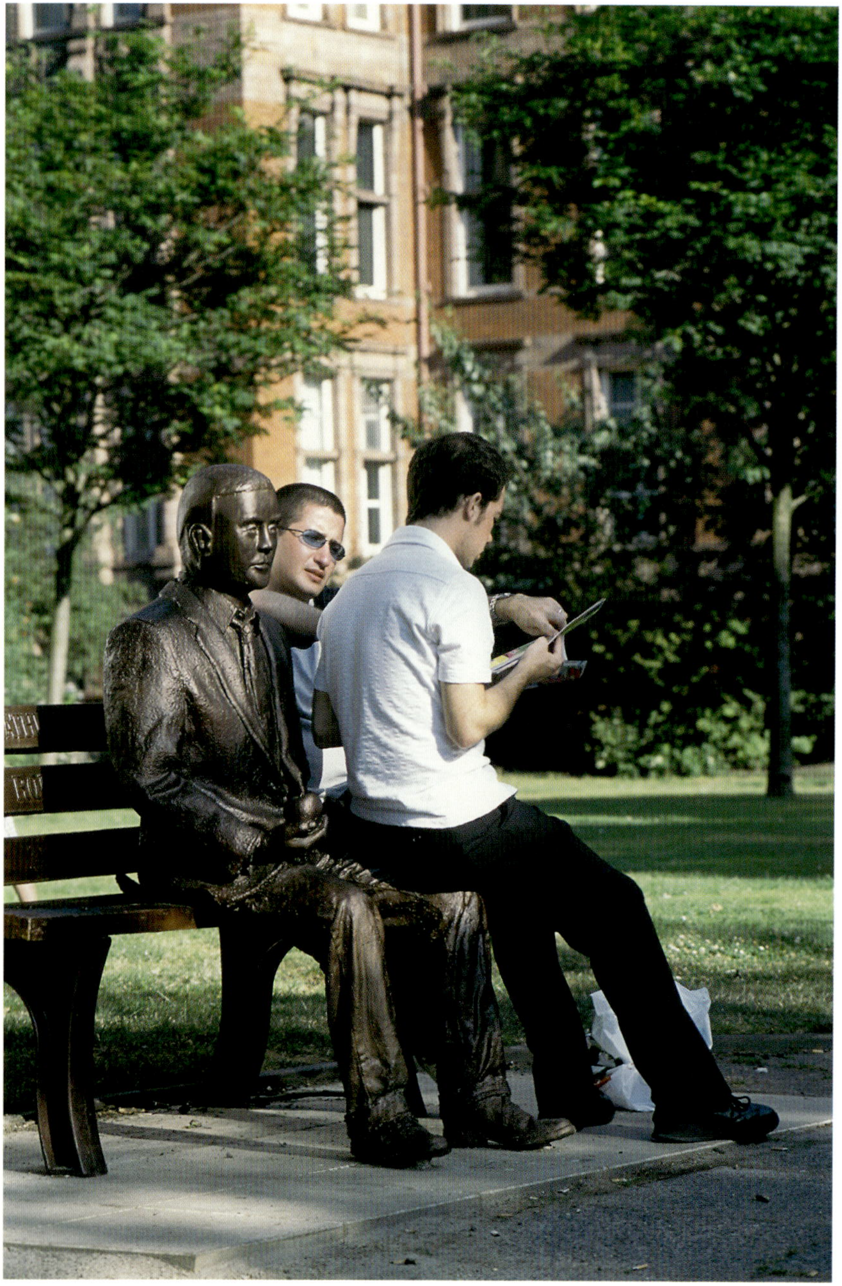

Sited in the Gay Village, this sculpture by Glyn Hughes is a tribute to Alan Turing, the computer scientist and code-breaker, persecuted for his homosexuality.

In St Peter's Square, the bronze figures in Phillip Jackson's Struggle for Peace and Freedom confront passers-by.

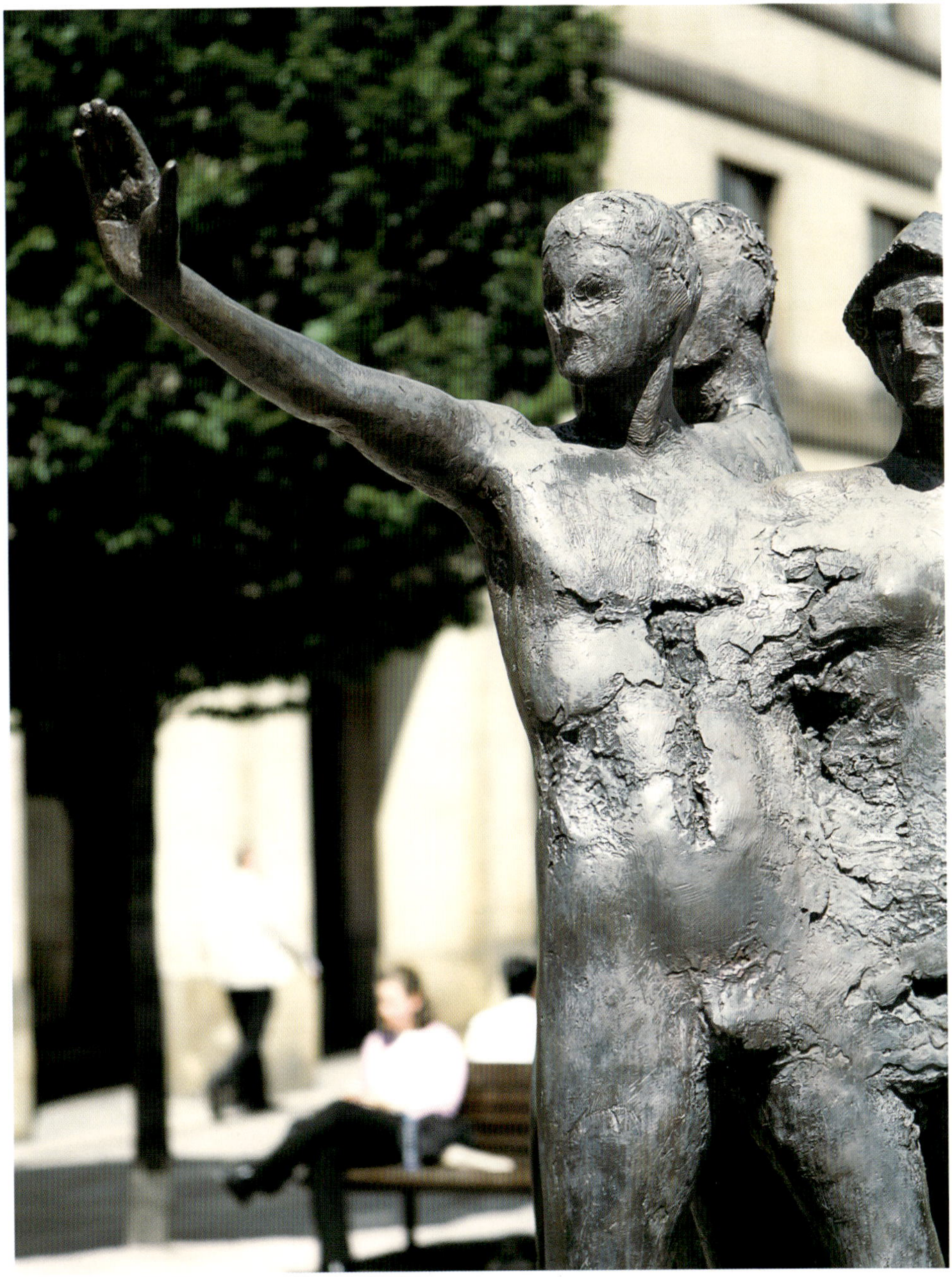

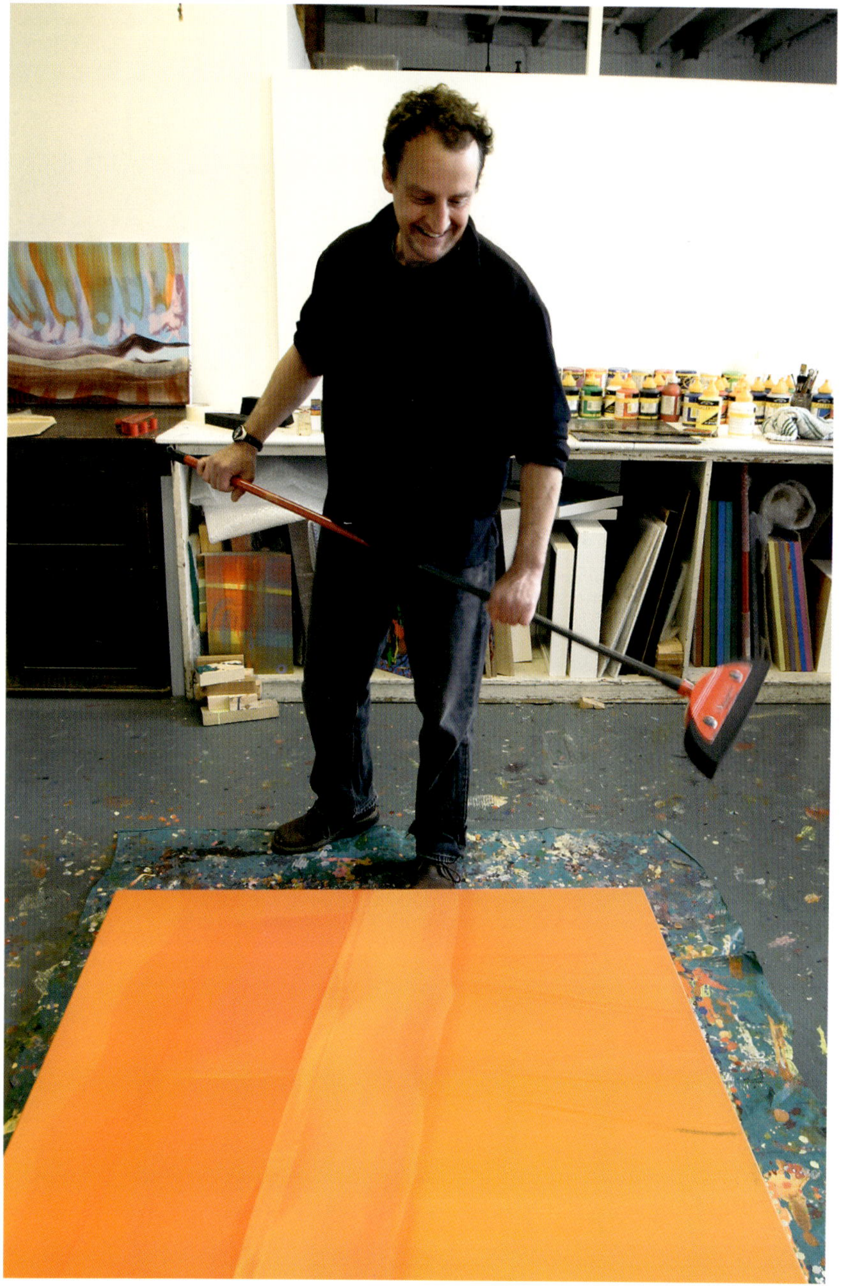

Painter Martin Nash based at Rogue Studios, is part of a thriving artistic community typically housed in redundant mills on the edge of the city centre.

Japenese-born metal artist Junko Mori was attracted to the city by its diverse cultural scene. In her Salford workshop, she makes everything from solid silver jewellery to large site-specific sculptures.

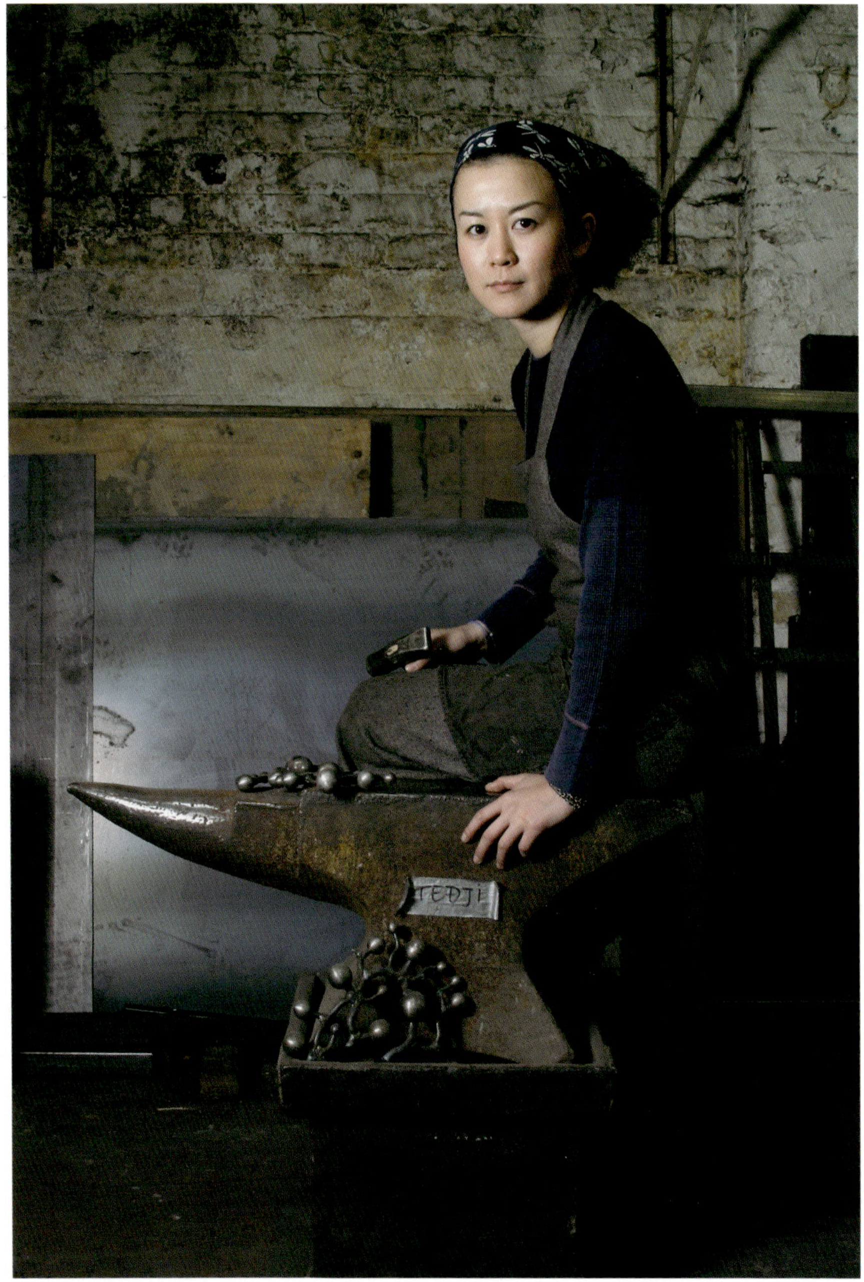

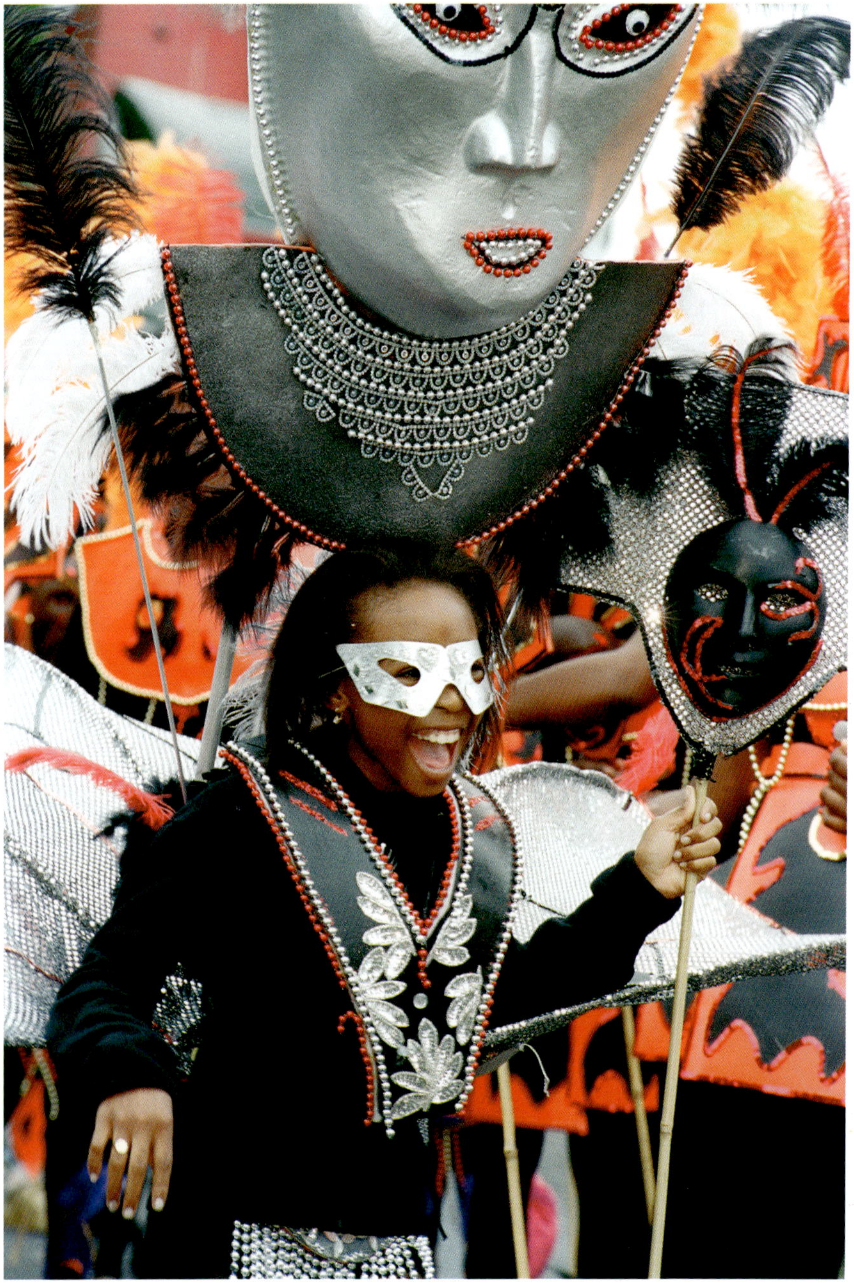

The annual Moss Side Carnival gives participants the chance to show off their stunning costumes.

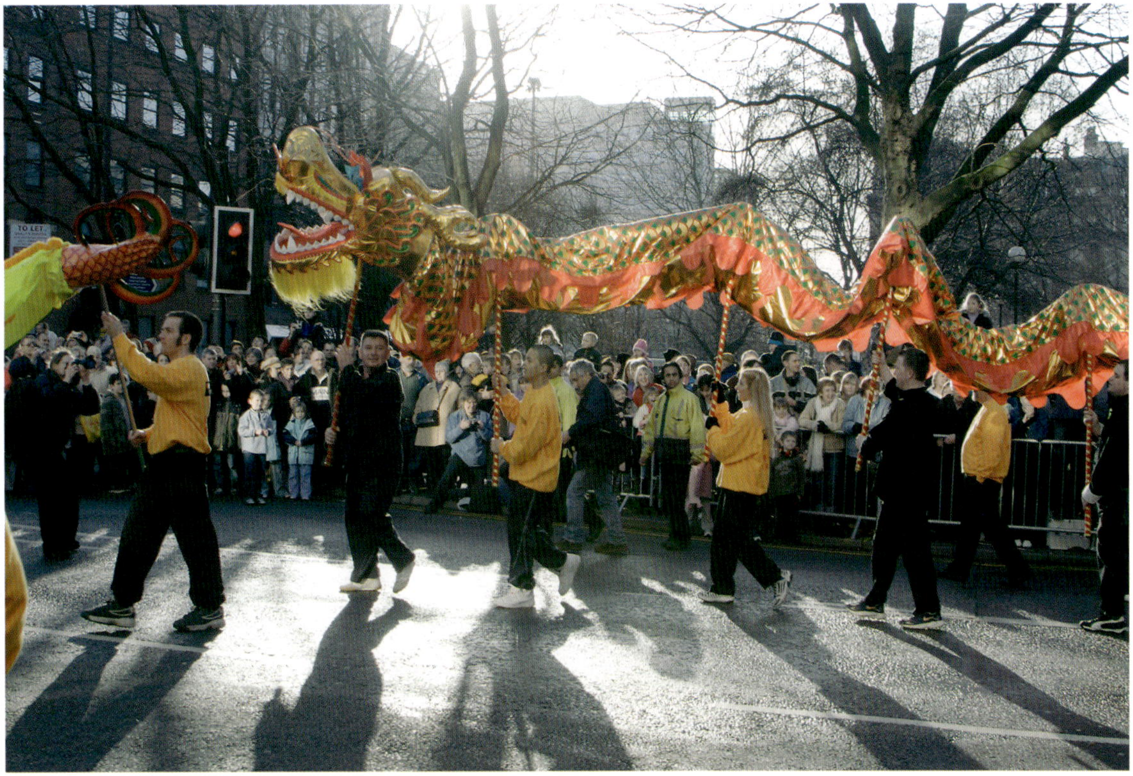

The Dragon Dance making its way at the Chinese New Year along Princess Street towards Chinatown.

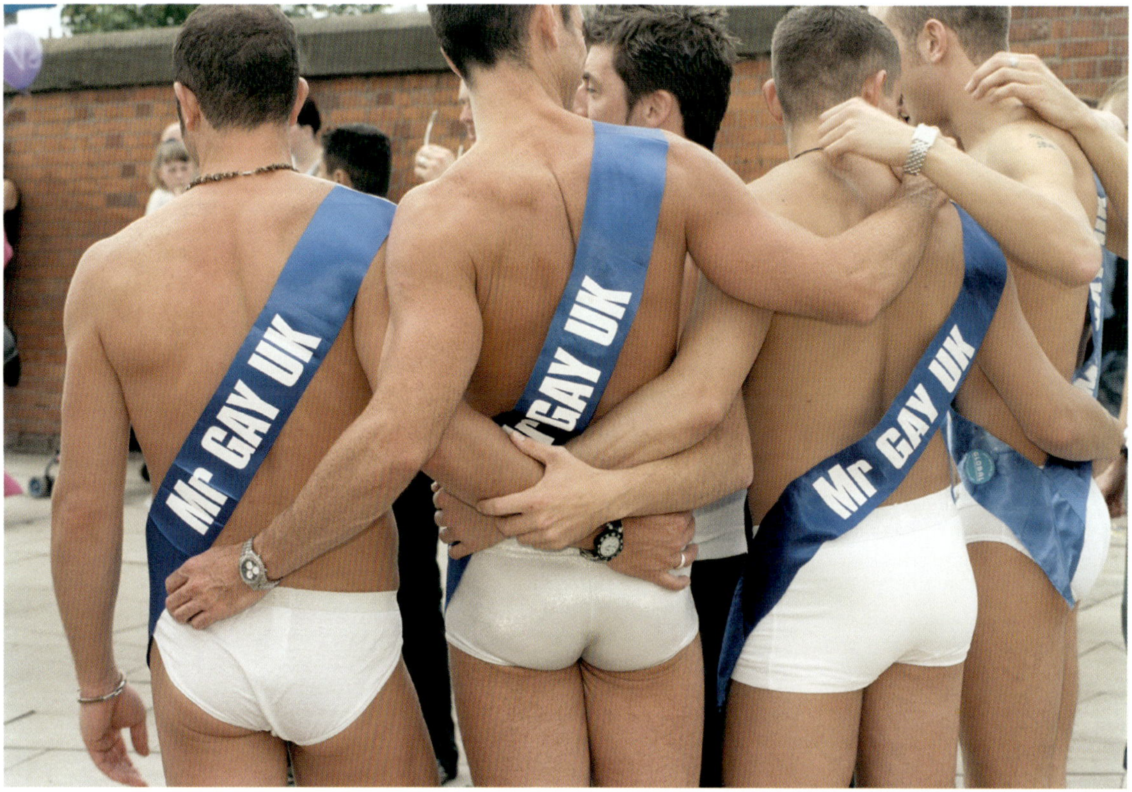

Manchester has one of the largest gay communities outside London, so the annual Mardi Gras in August is always very popular.

The festival centres on Canal Street, where crowds converge throughout the day and into the night.

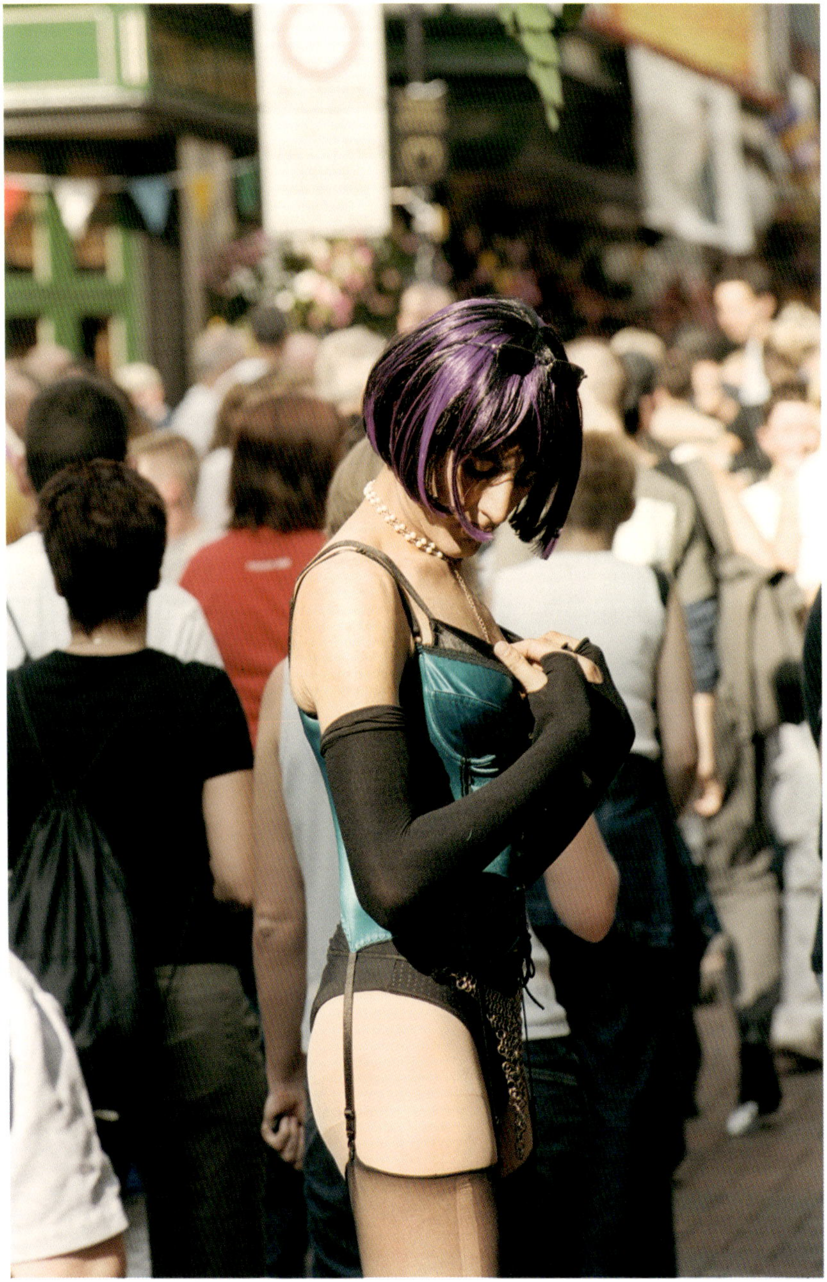

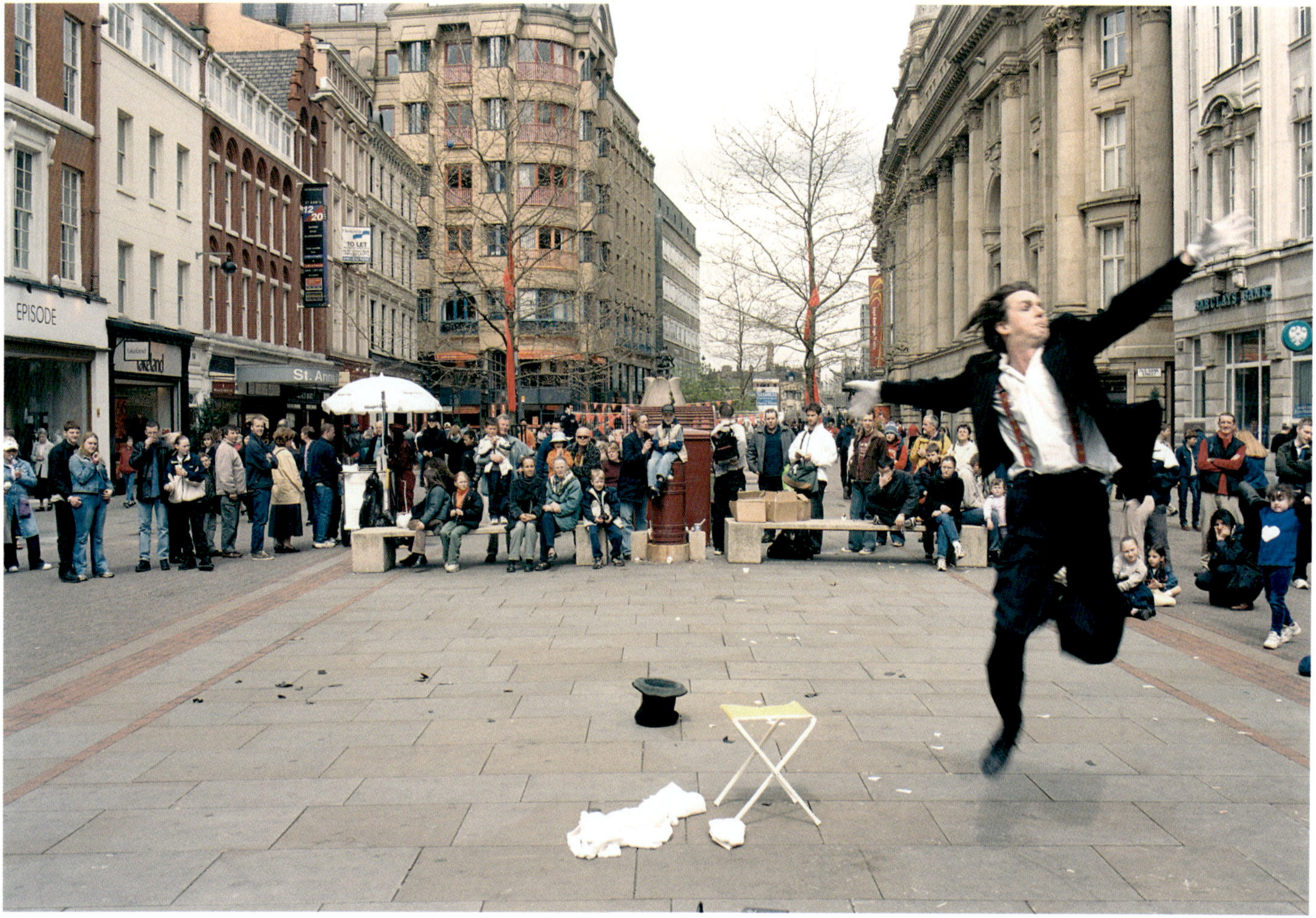

In recent years, Mancunians and visitors have been entertained by a succession of hugely popular street festivals.

A Catalan 'gegant' mingles with the crowds in Exchange Square.

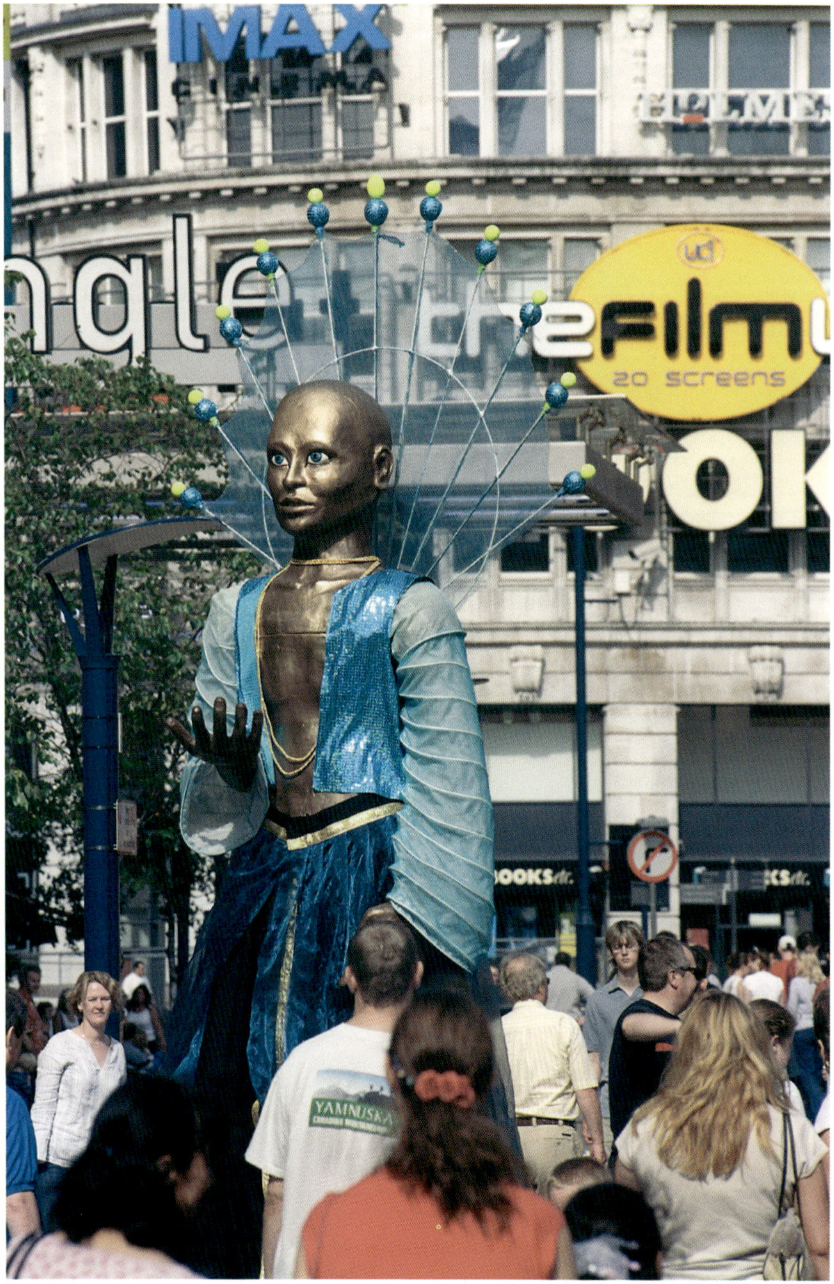

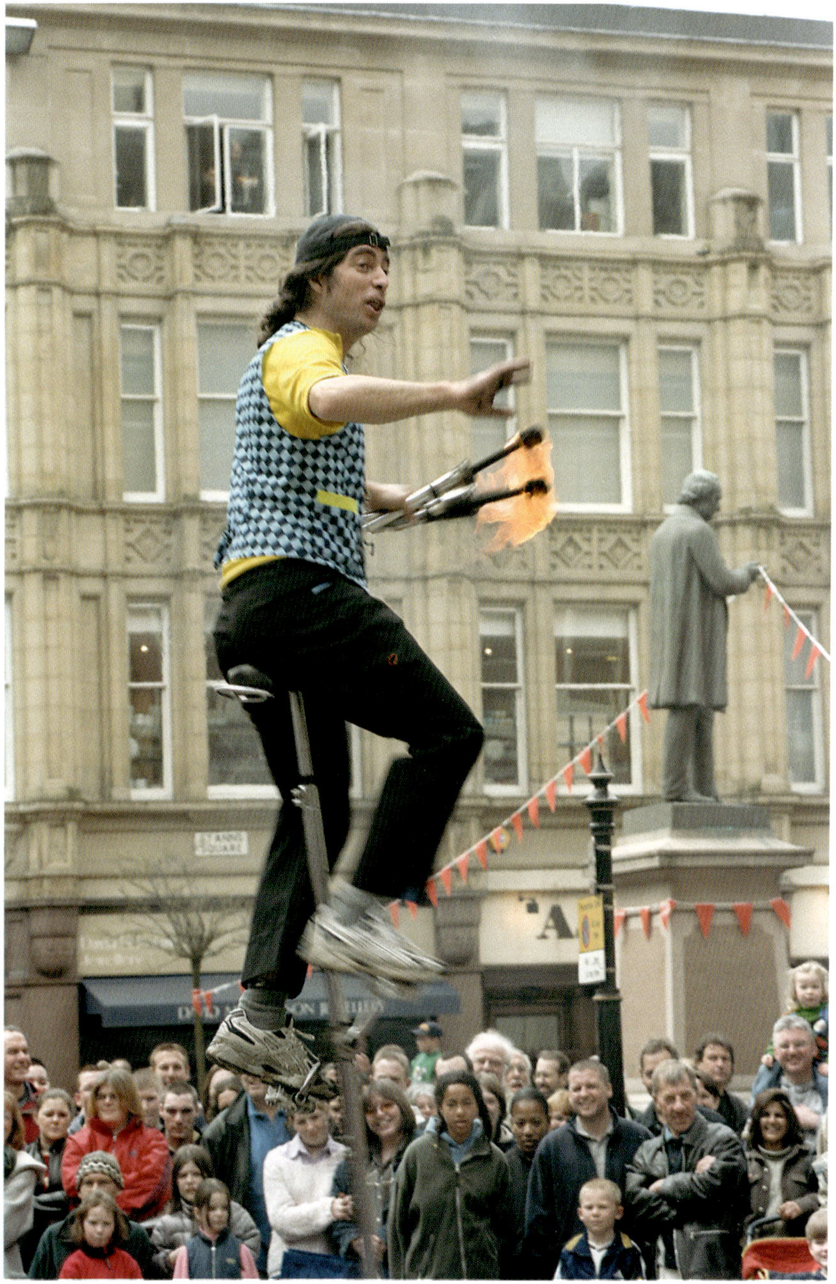

A fire-juggling unicyclist performs in St Ann's Square.

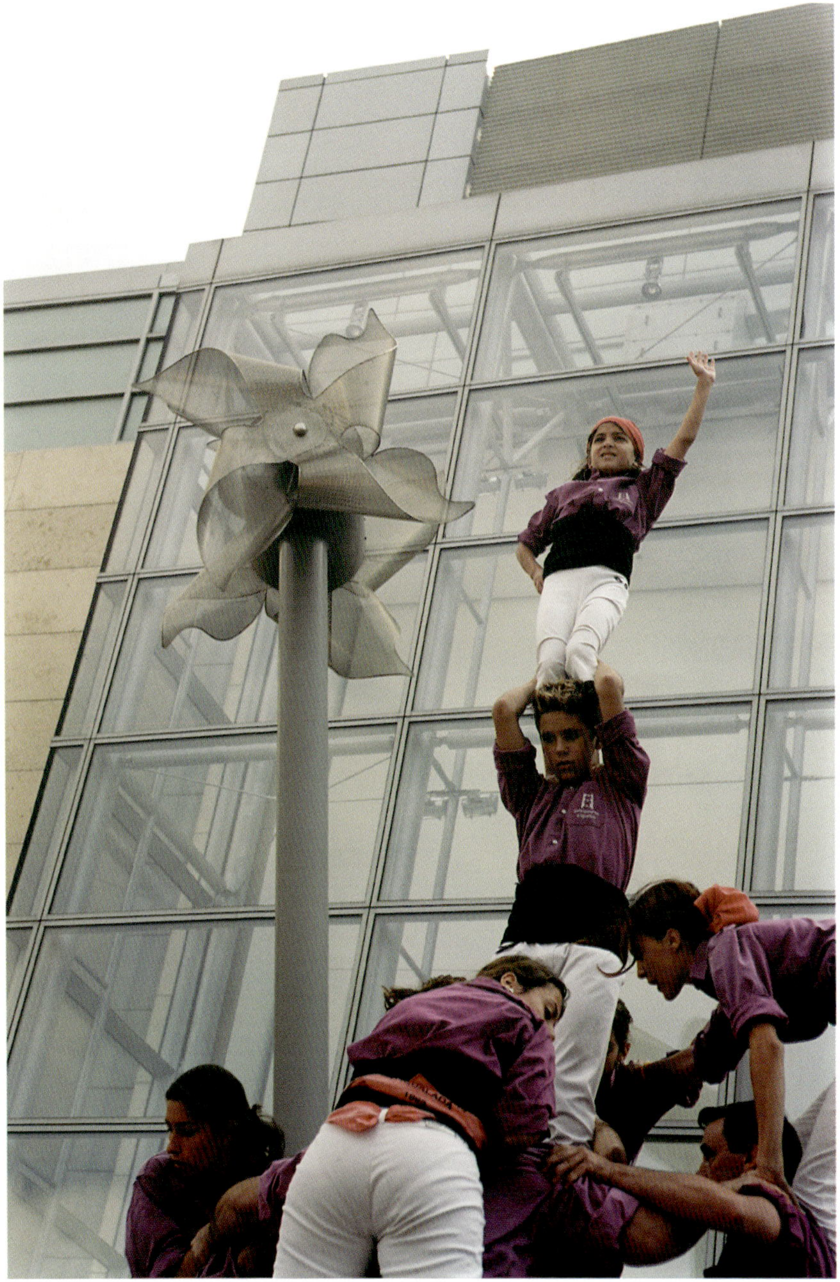

Catalan performers build a human castle outside Selfridges.

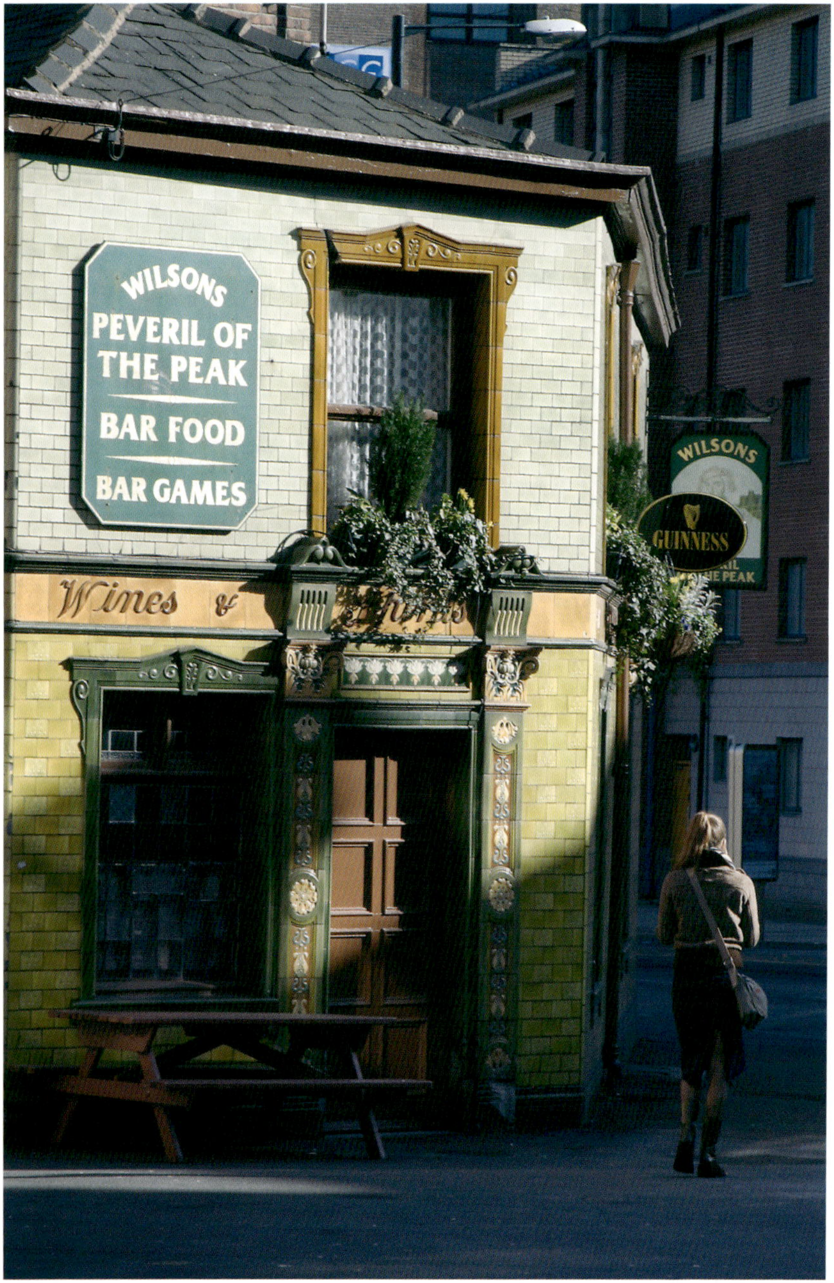

Many a happy hour... The Peveril of the Peak remains a favourite among pub-goers content with a good pint and a table football machine. The pub is nearly 200 years old and deserves its Grade II listed status.

A couple of hundred metres away, new trendy bars and restaurants make use of refurbished railway arches alongside the Rochdale Canal.

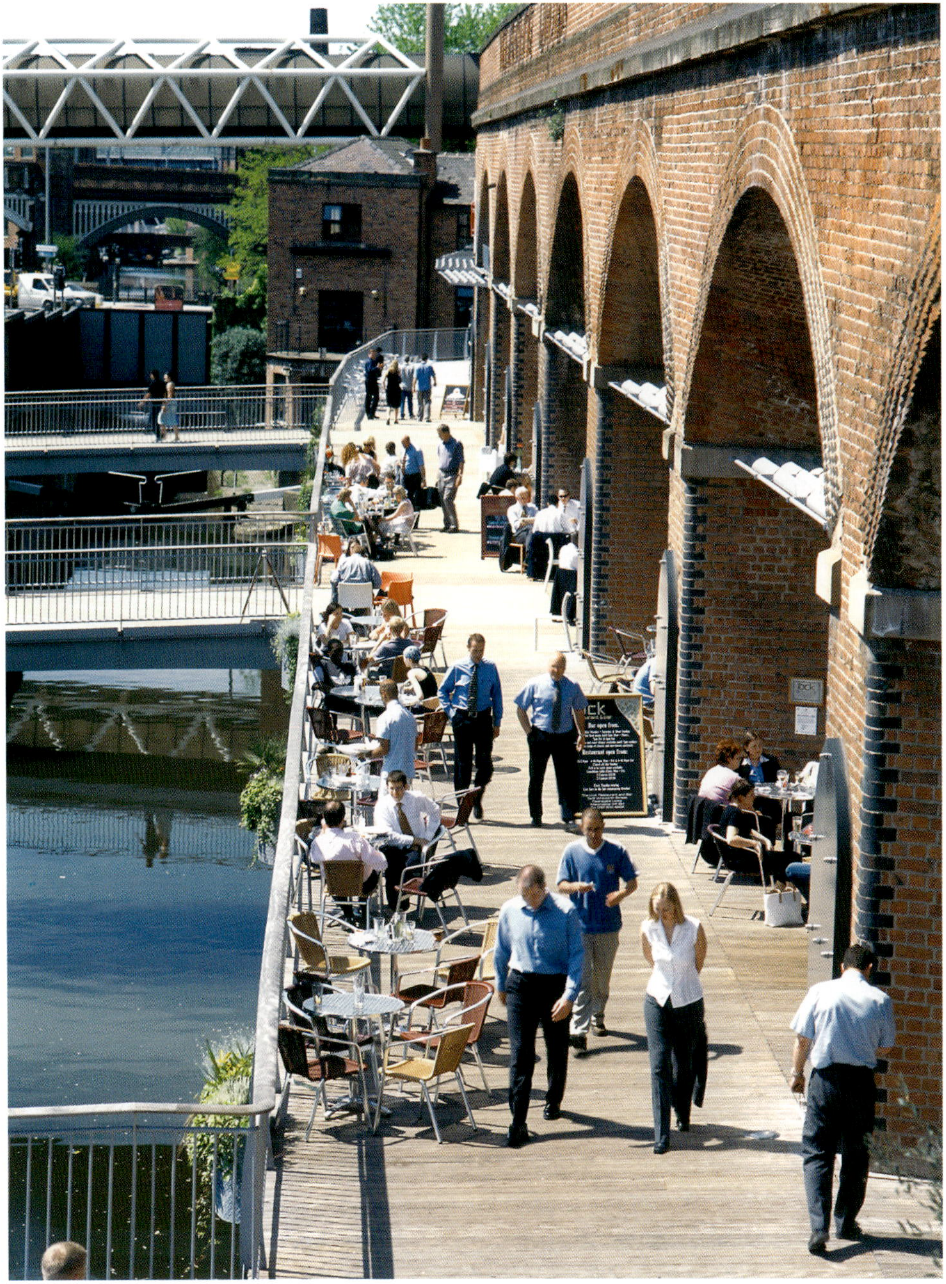

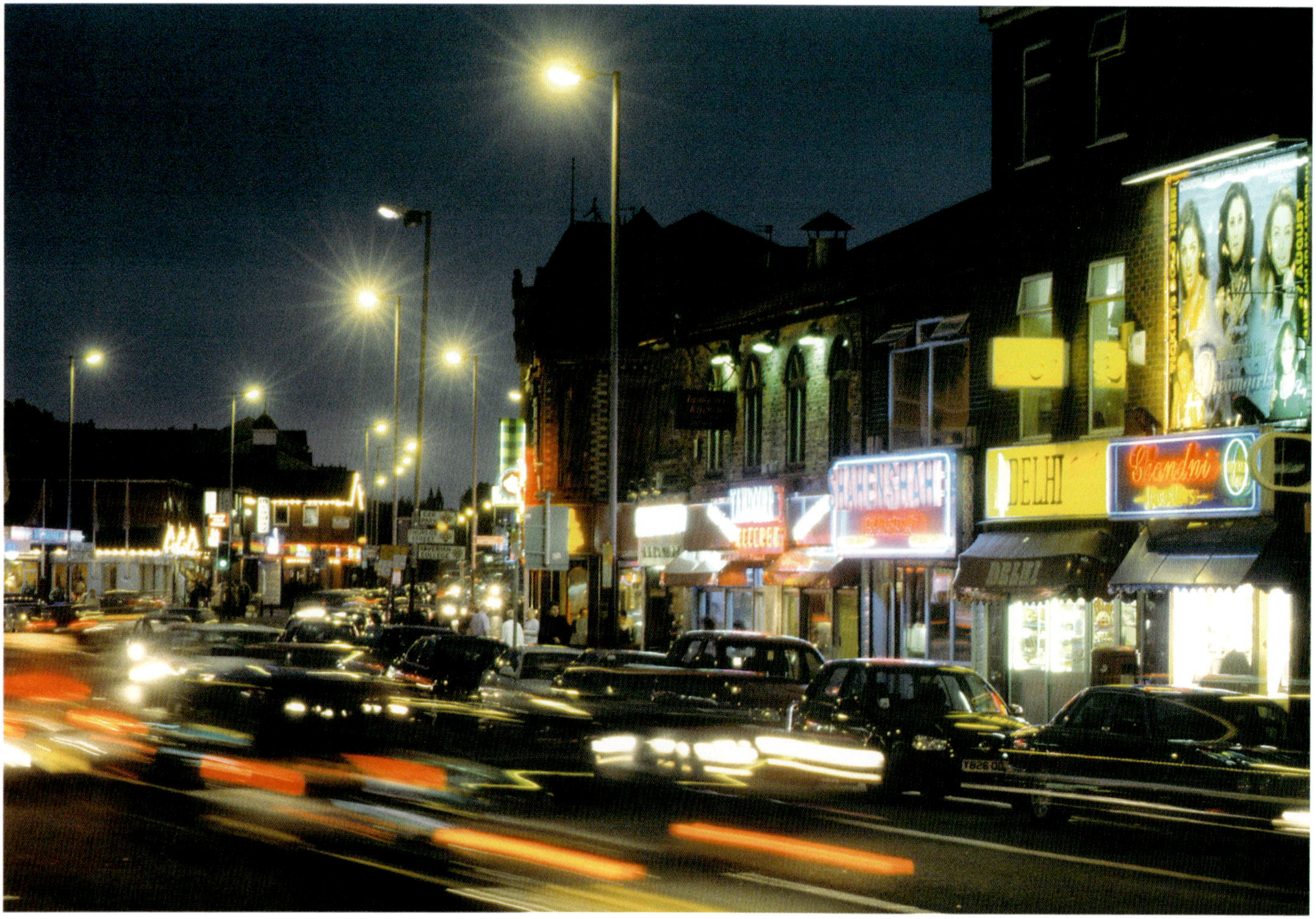

Rusholme's 'Curry Mile' is a stretch of Oxford Road with more than 50 restaurants and cafés displaying varying amounts of neon to attract the thousands who dine there each week.

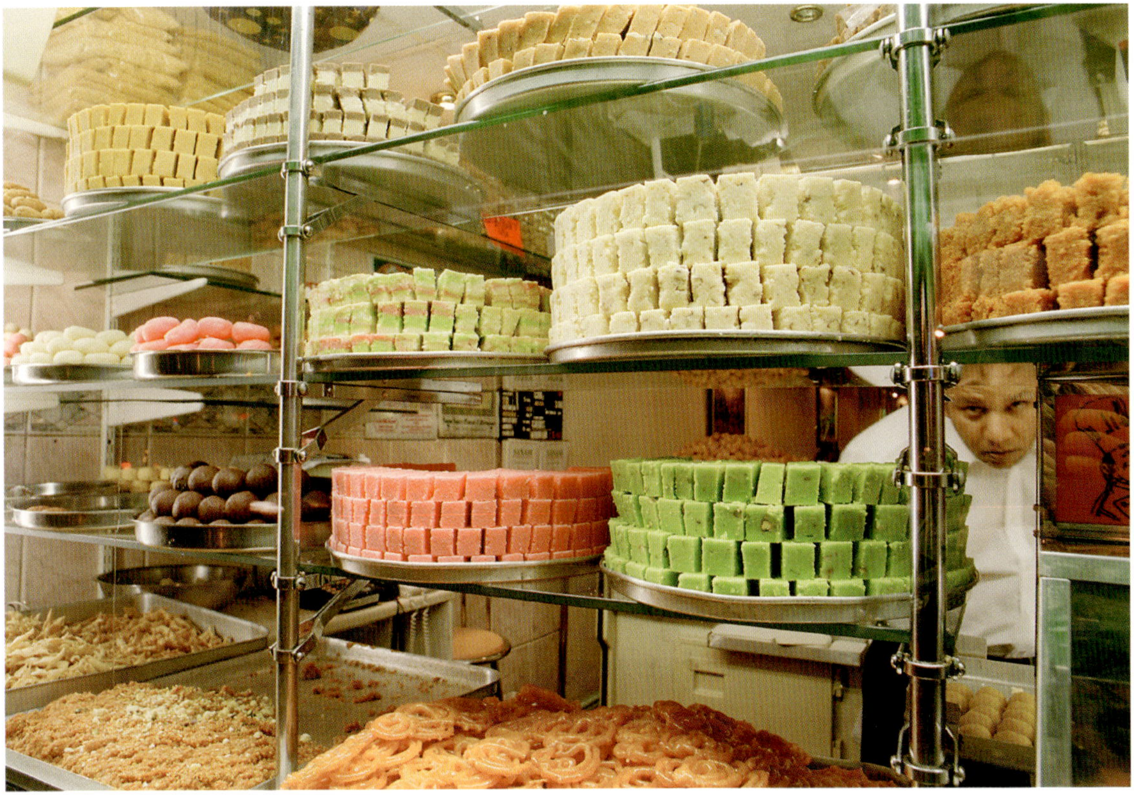

With ingredients like cardamom, pistachio, almond and cashew, the multicoloured sweets are stacked high in numerous sweet centres along the 'mile'.

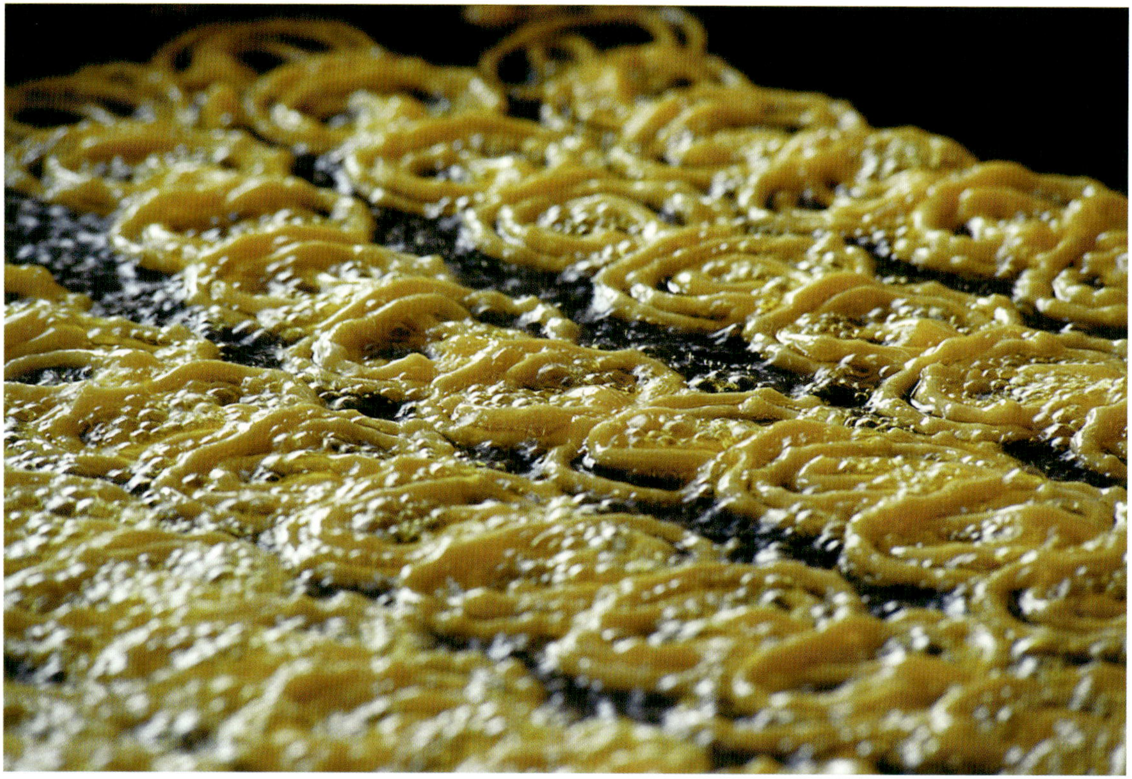

Frying swirls of golden brown jalebi batter are dipped in a sugary syrup to make a mouth-watering sweet. Best when it's still hot!

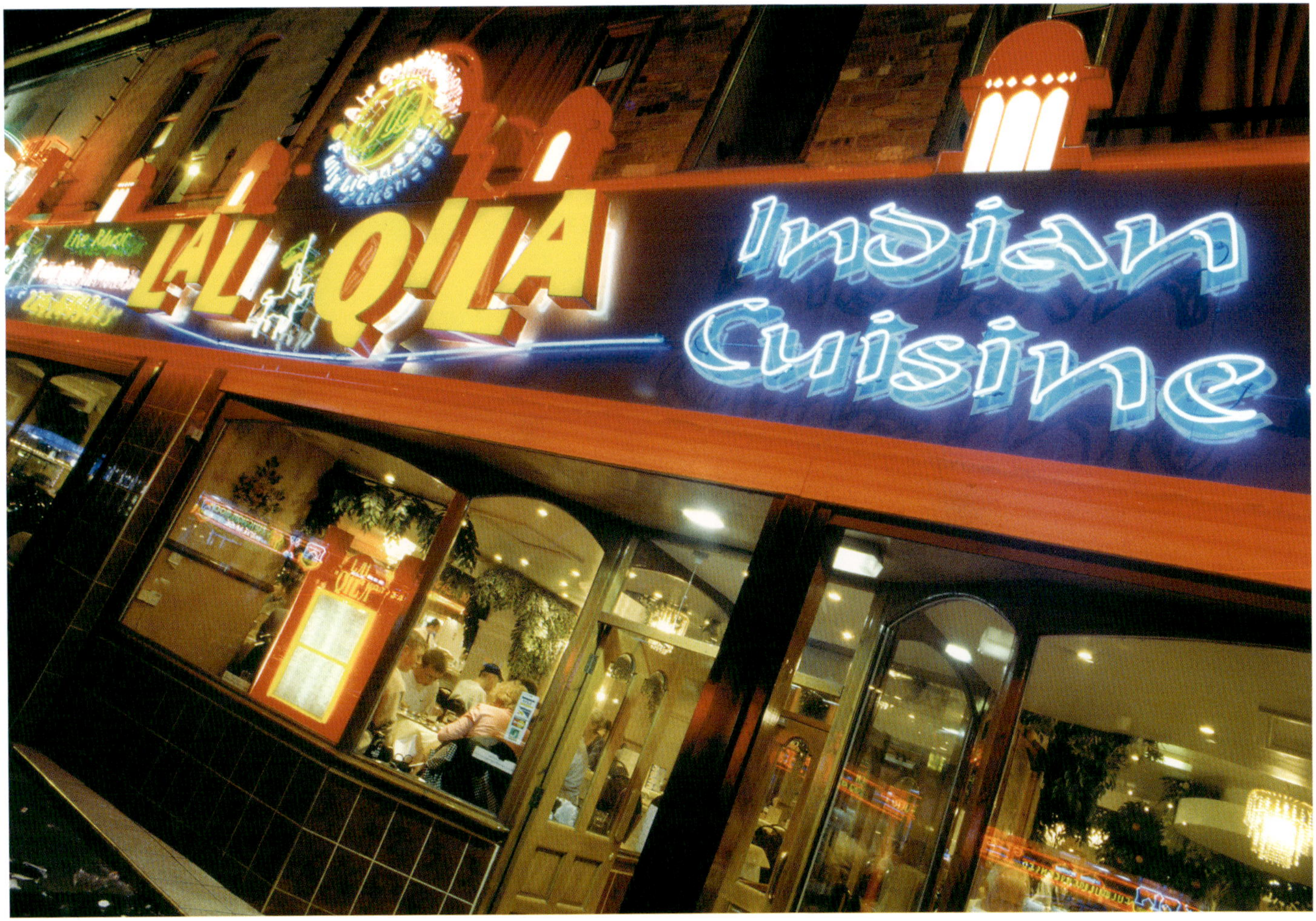

The cafés first appeared thirty years ago to serve an increasing Asian immigrant population. The appeal has since broadened with baltis, kaharis, kormas and vindaloos now on the menu.

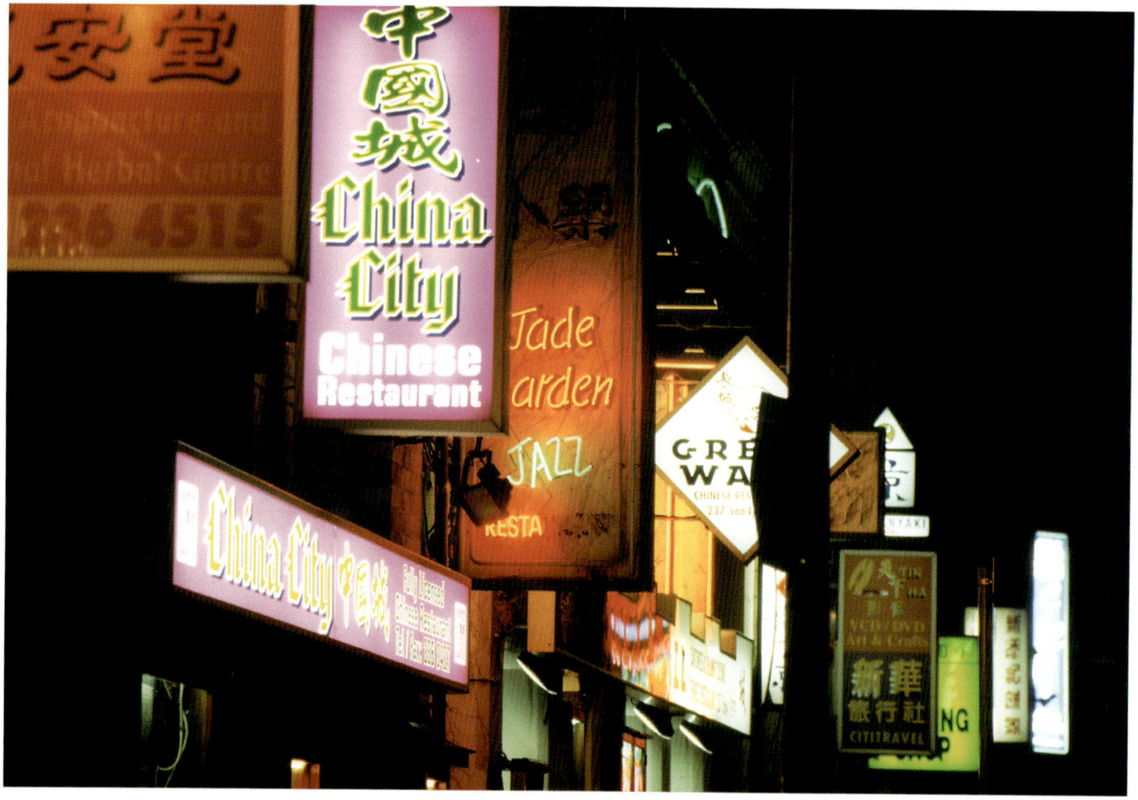

Manchester's Chinatown grew up among the redundant cotton warehouses around Nicholas Street. The earliest restaurants date back to the early 1970s, and now provide culinary diversity for the city.

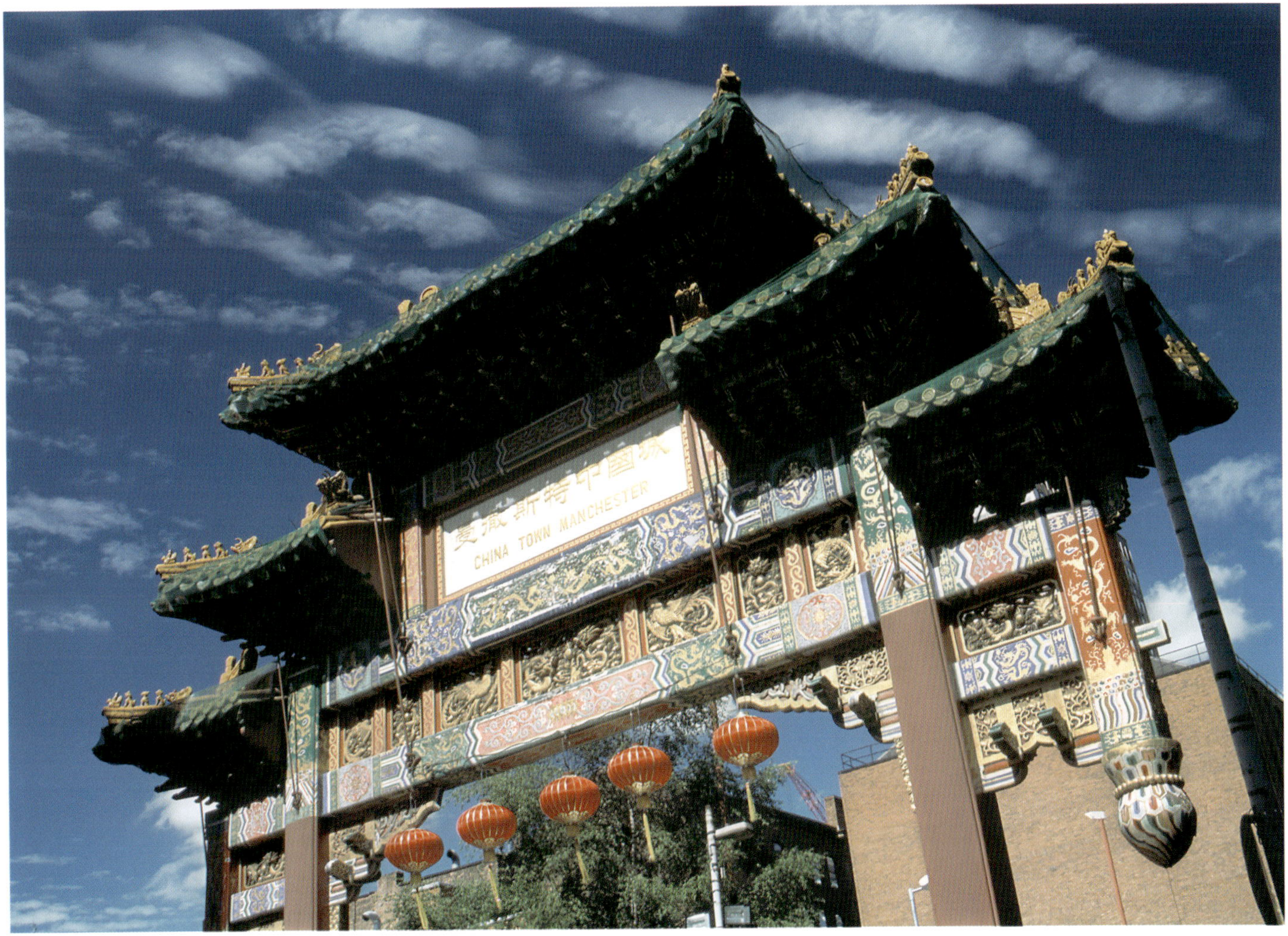

The Chinese arch on Faulkner Street in Chinatown. On the same junction is Ho's Bakery, whose pork buns and chicken curry pasties make a welcome change to the usual city centre lunchtime fare.

Overleaf Empty for many years, the Joshua Hoyle building at the bottom of Piccadilly Approach has since been refurbished as part of the Malmaison Hotel.

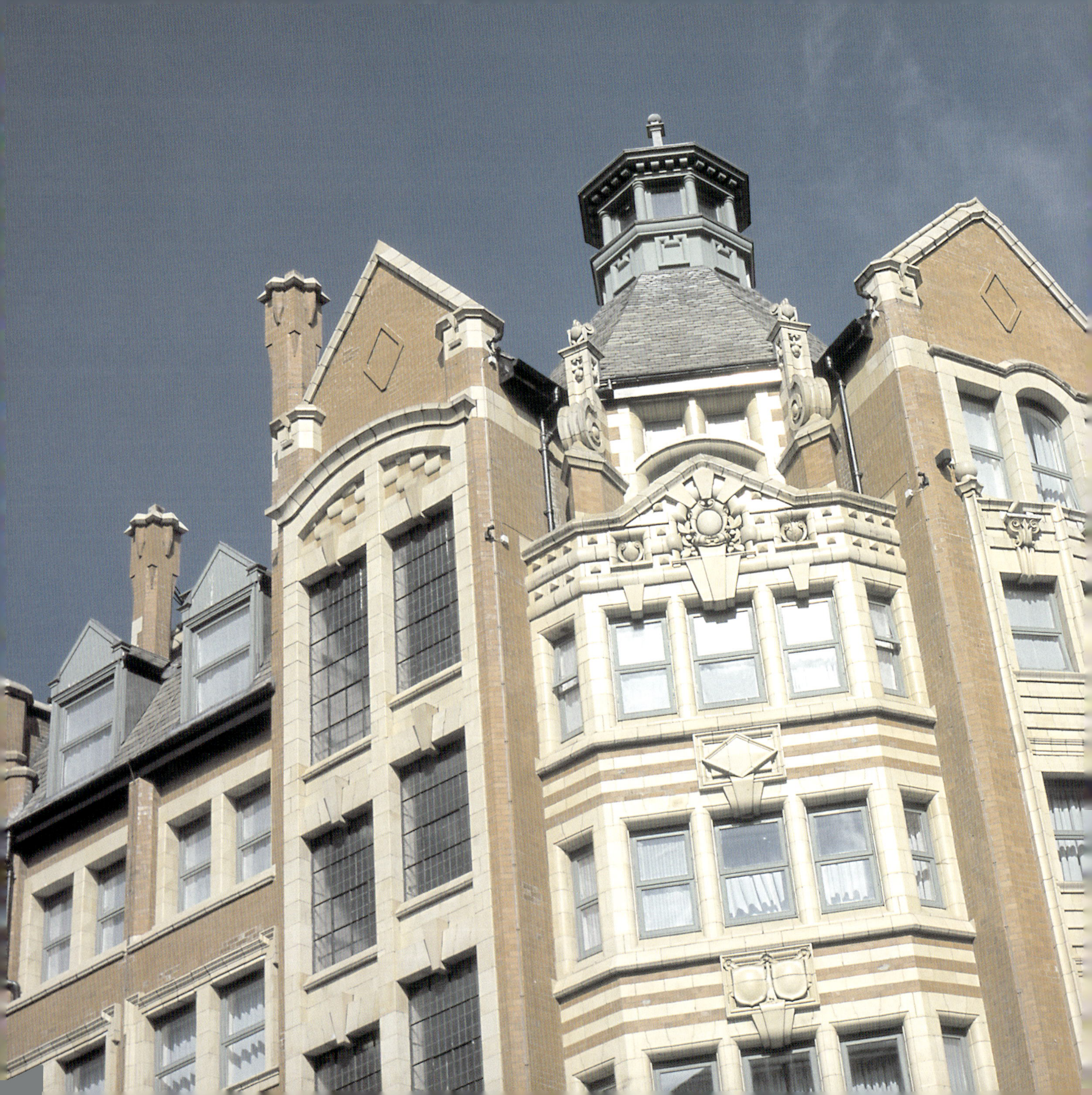

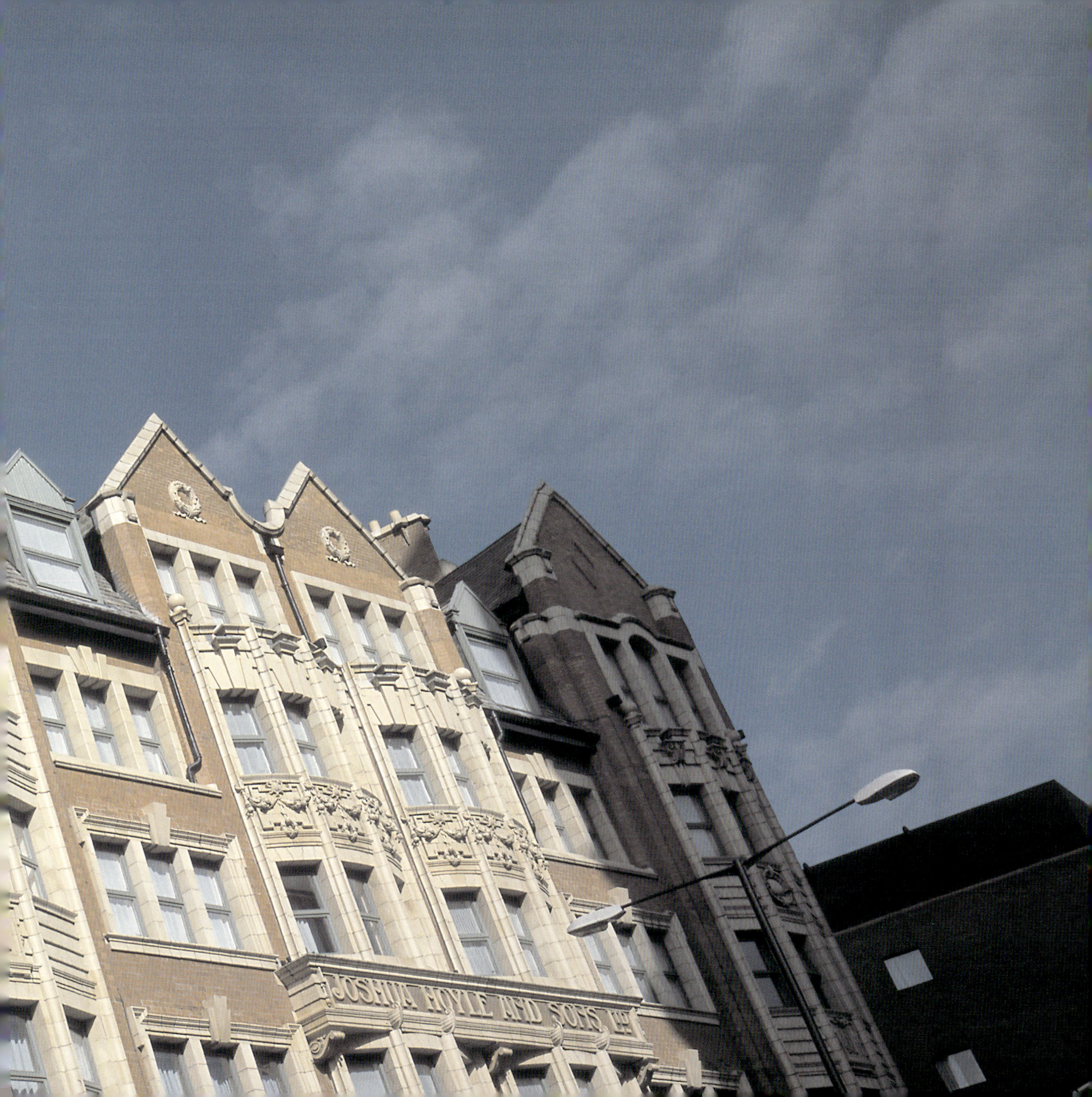
JOSHUA HOYLE AND SONS LTD

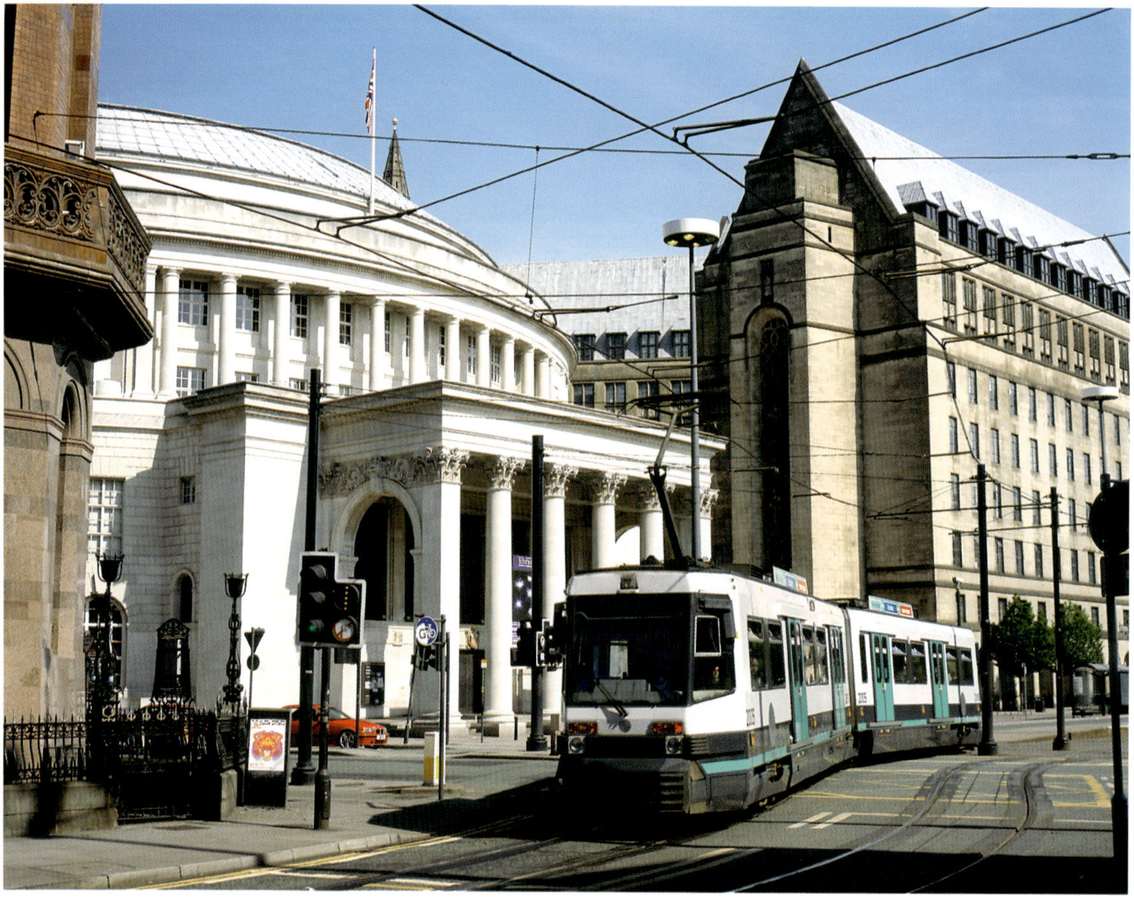

A regular sight on the city streets since 1992, the Metrolink light rapid transport system *(above and right)* continues to be extended. It will soon serve east Manchester and Manchester Airport.

Overleaf Known locally as the 'Lazy S' building, Gateway House leads passengers up Station Approach to the newly-refurbished Piccadilly Station.

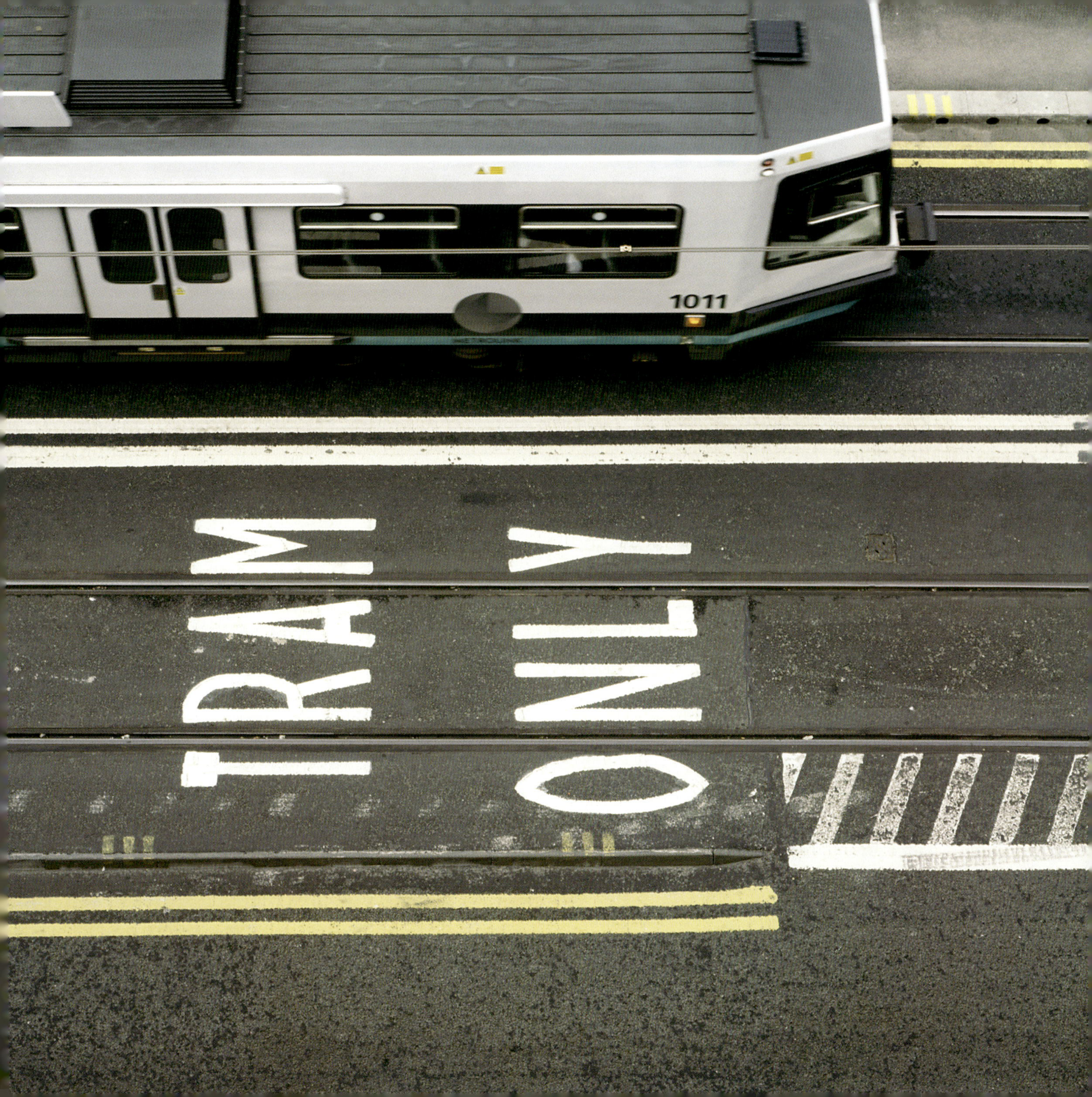
1011
TRAM
ONLY

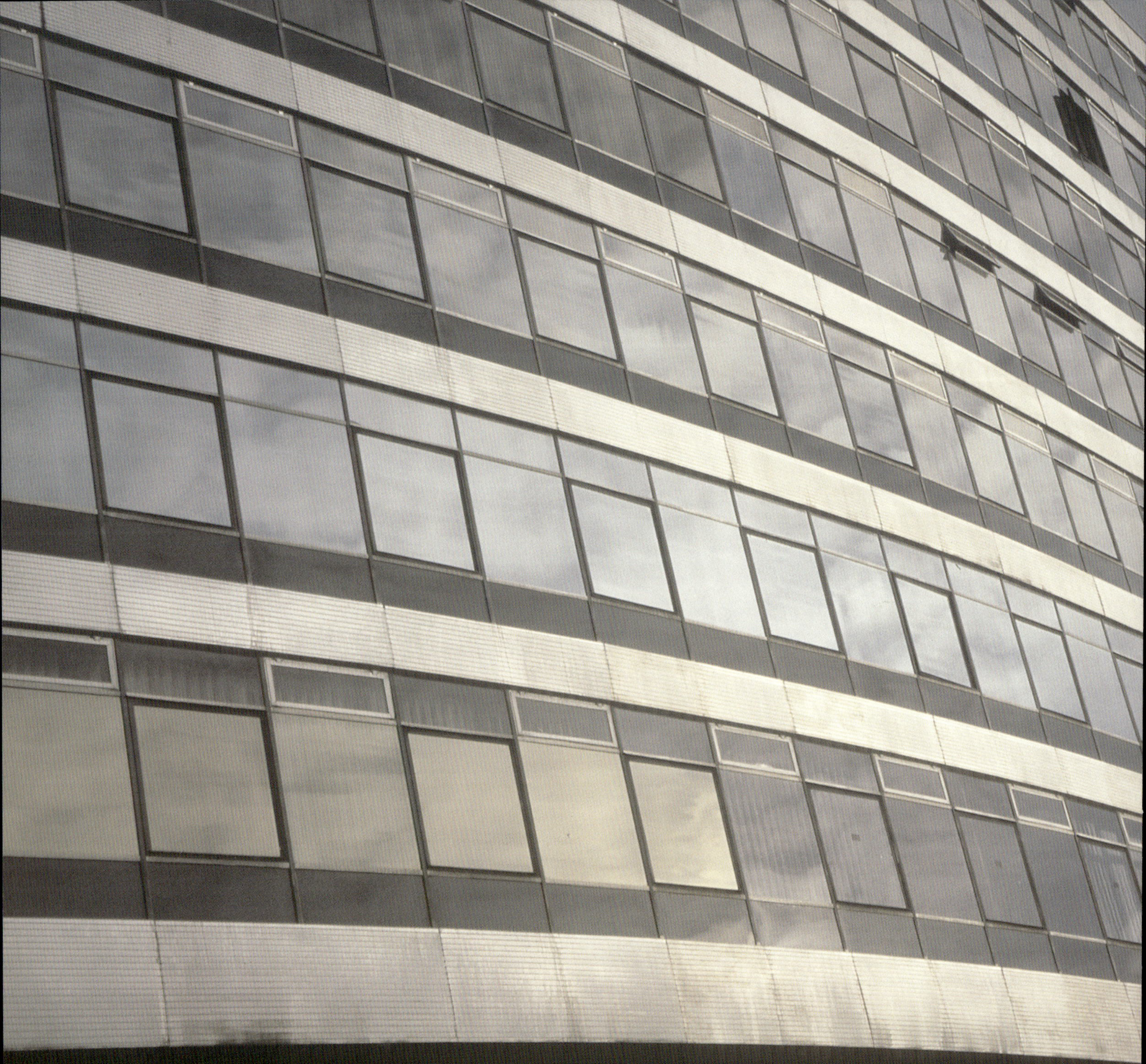

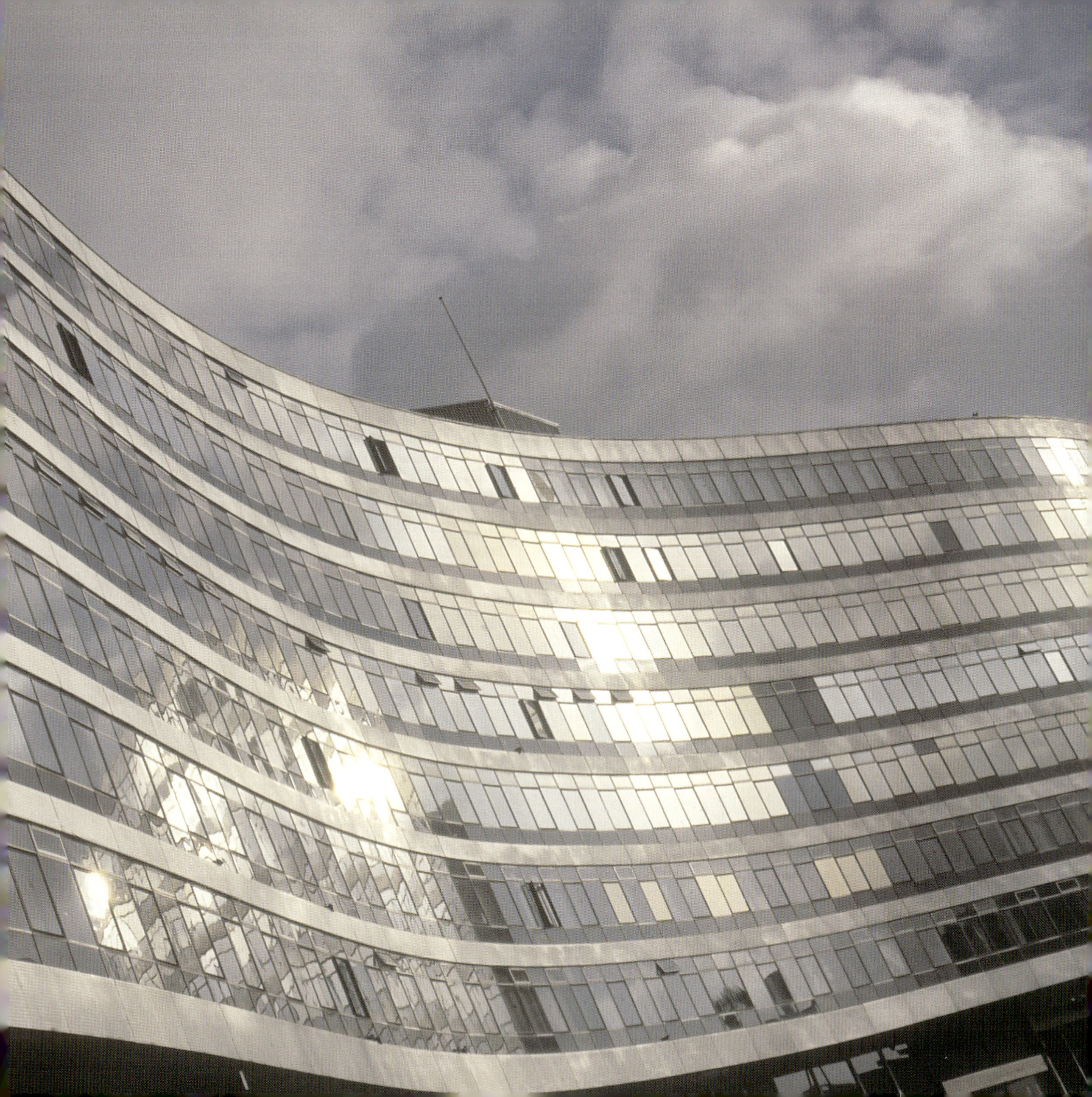

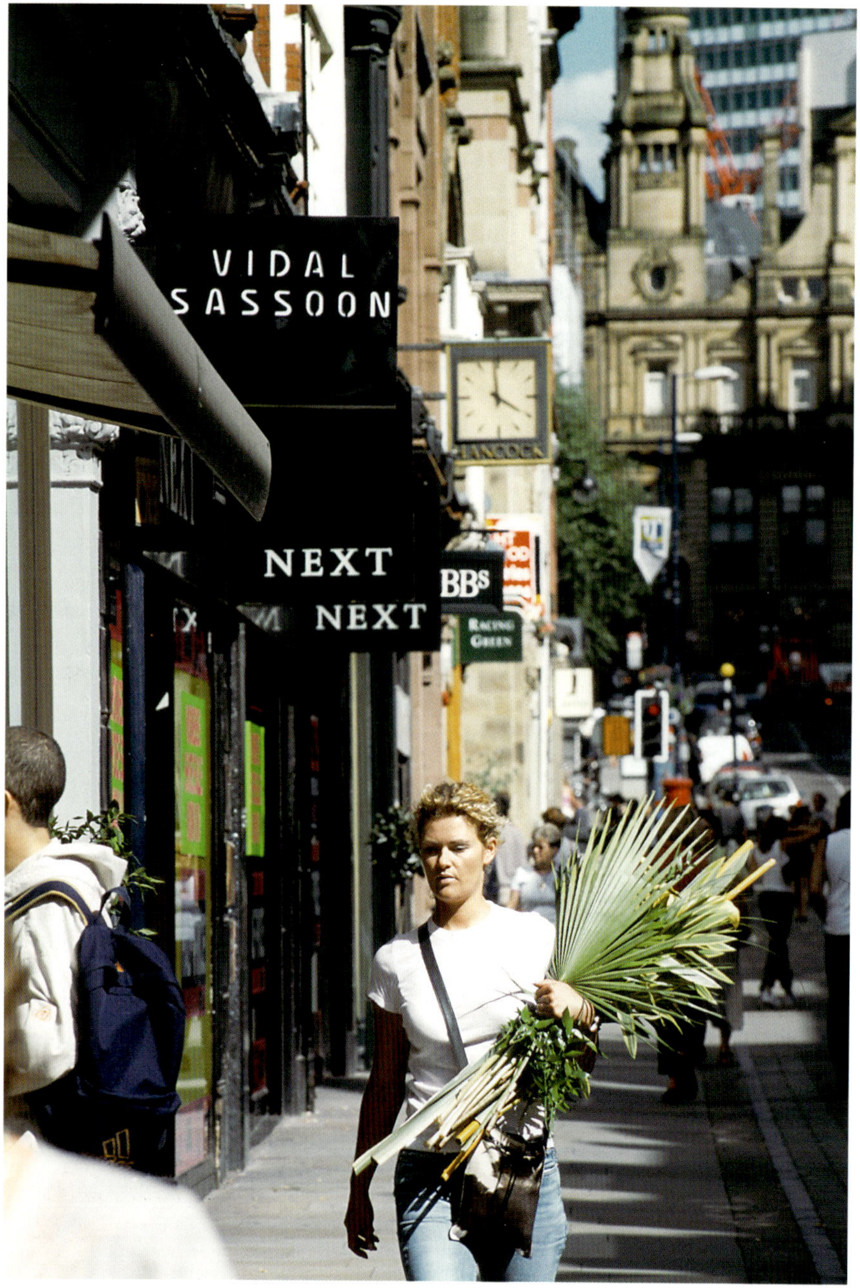

Once the heart of the city's financial district, King Street *(left and opposite)* is fast becoming home to the trendiest shops in town with Vivienne Westwood, Whistles and Armani now in residence.

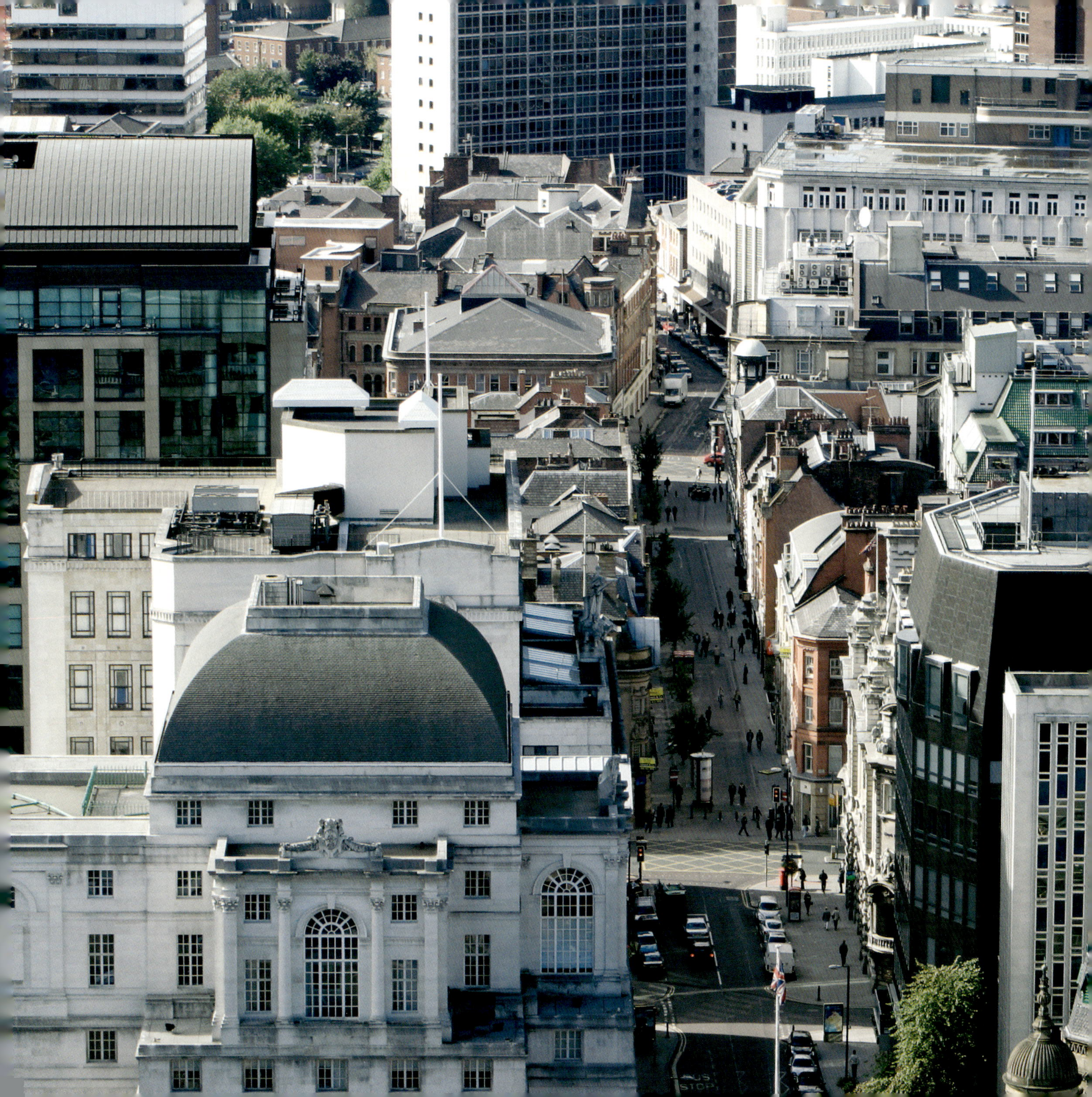

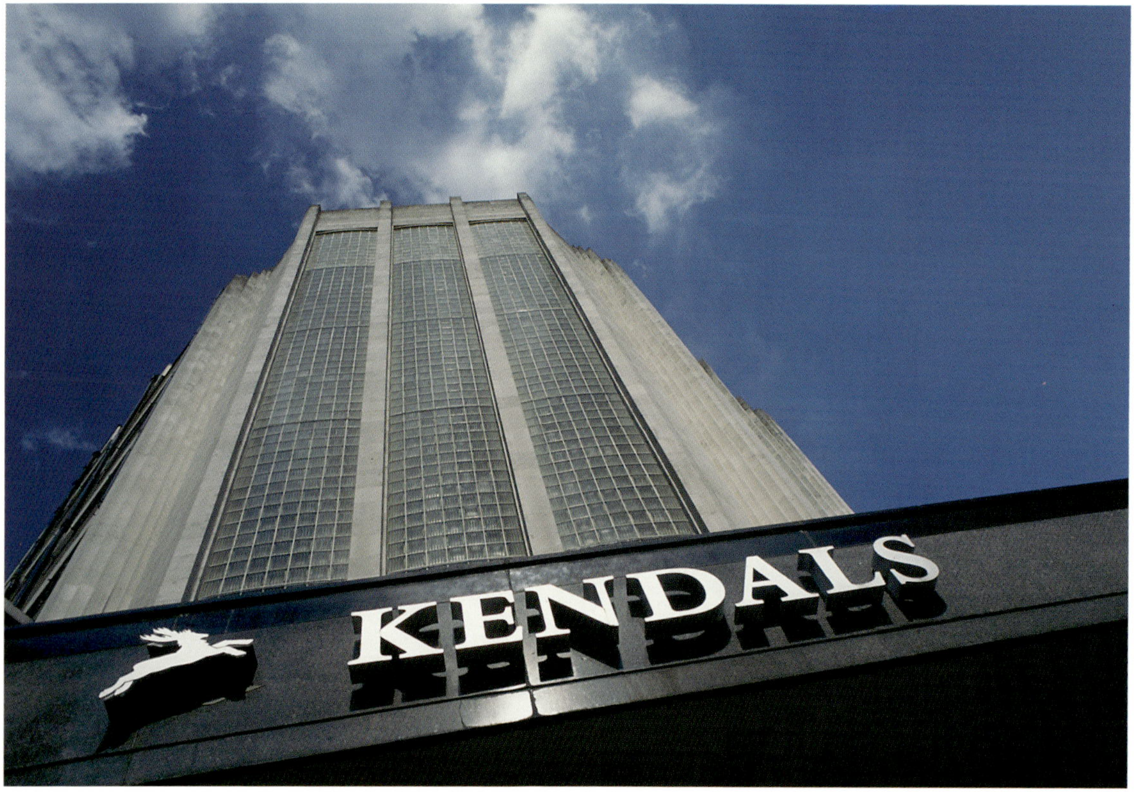

Much-loved Kendals, one of the city's oldest department stores, is often referred to as the 'Harrods of the North'.

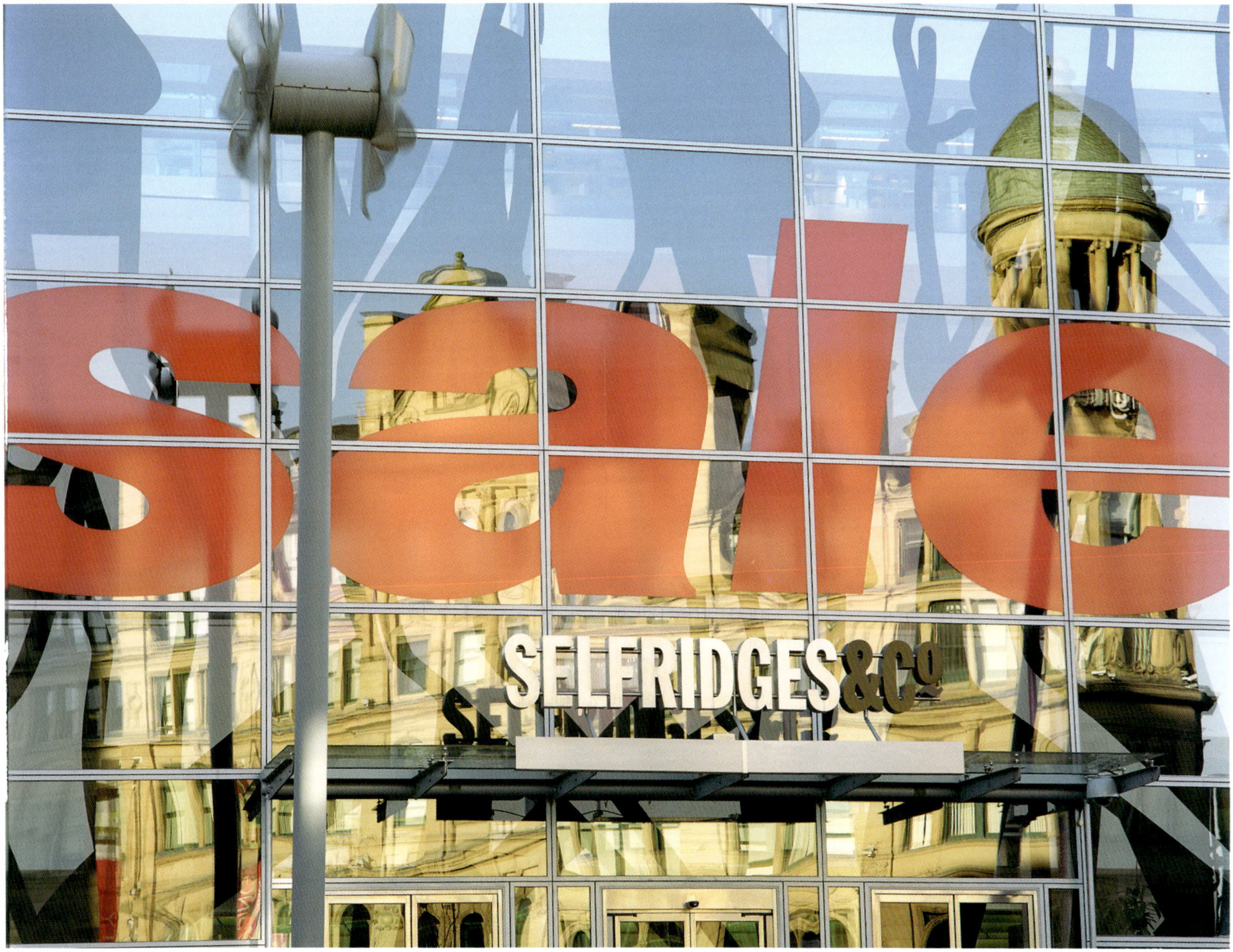

Selfridges, a relative newcomer to the retail scene, reflects
The Triangle shopping complex in its huge glass façade.

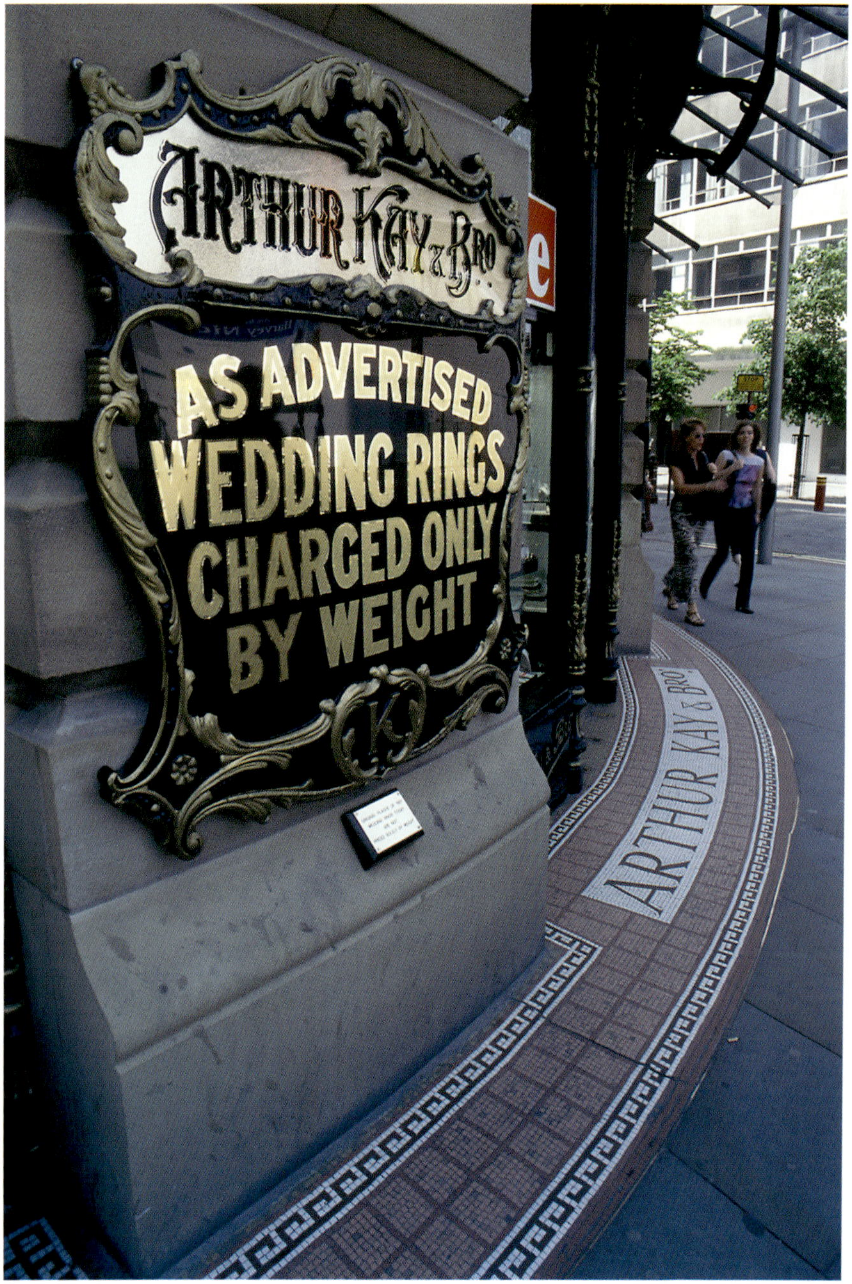

From wedding rings in St Ann's Square...

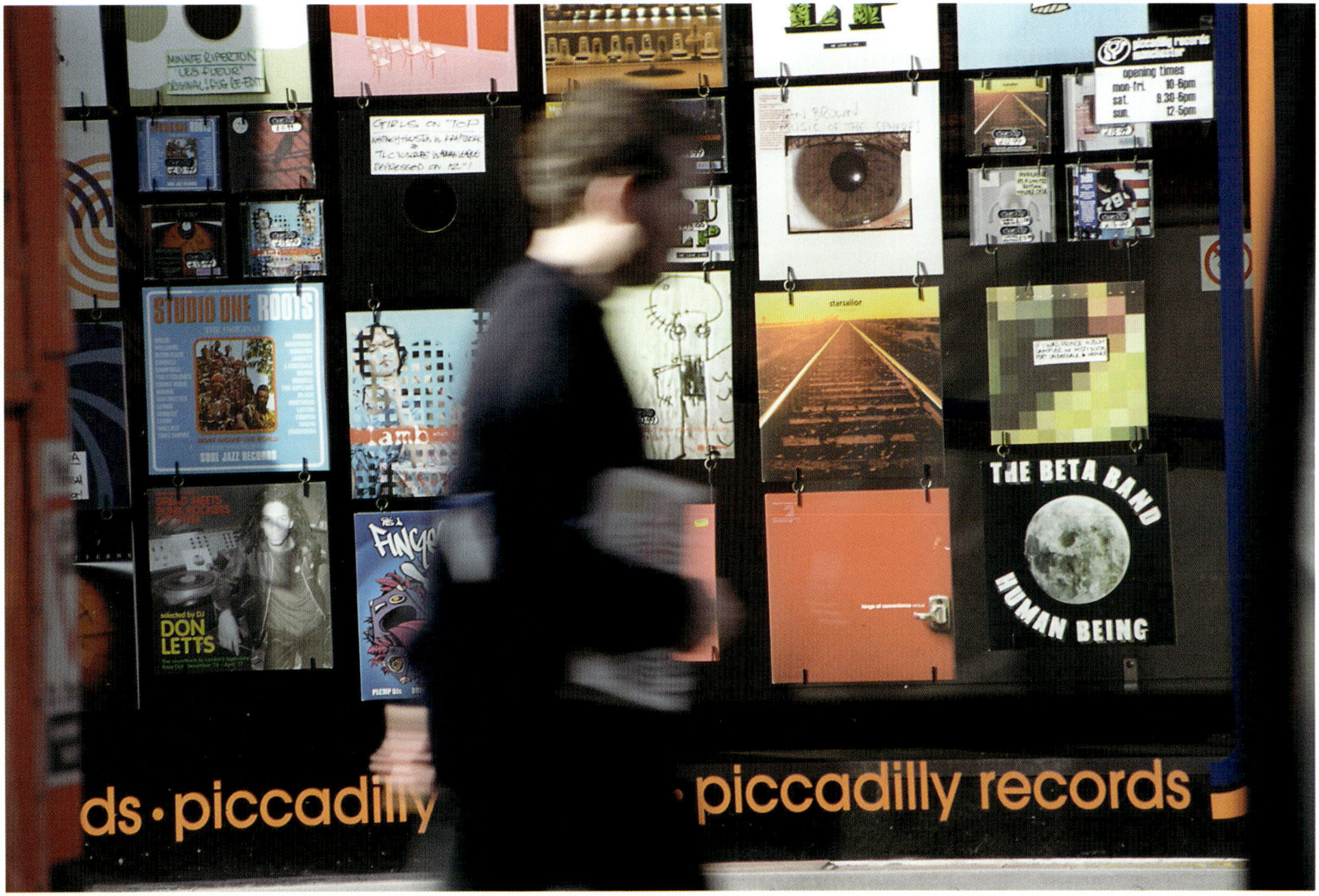

... to old-fashioned vinyl at Piccadilly Records in the avant-garde
Northern Quarter, Manchester has it all.

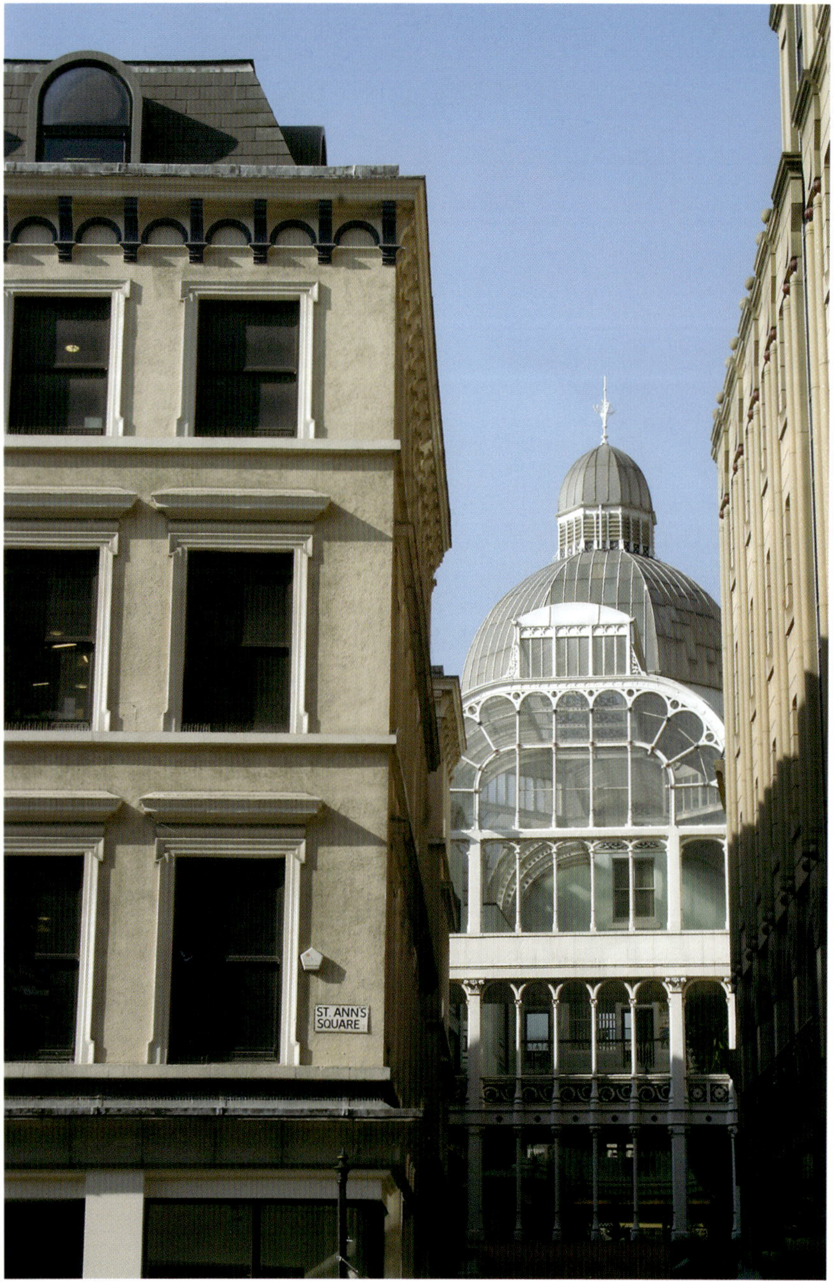

You step out of St Ann's Square into Barton Arcade, three storeys of iron and glass topped by twin glass domes *(left and opposite)*.

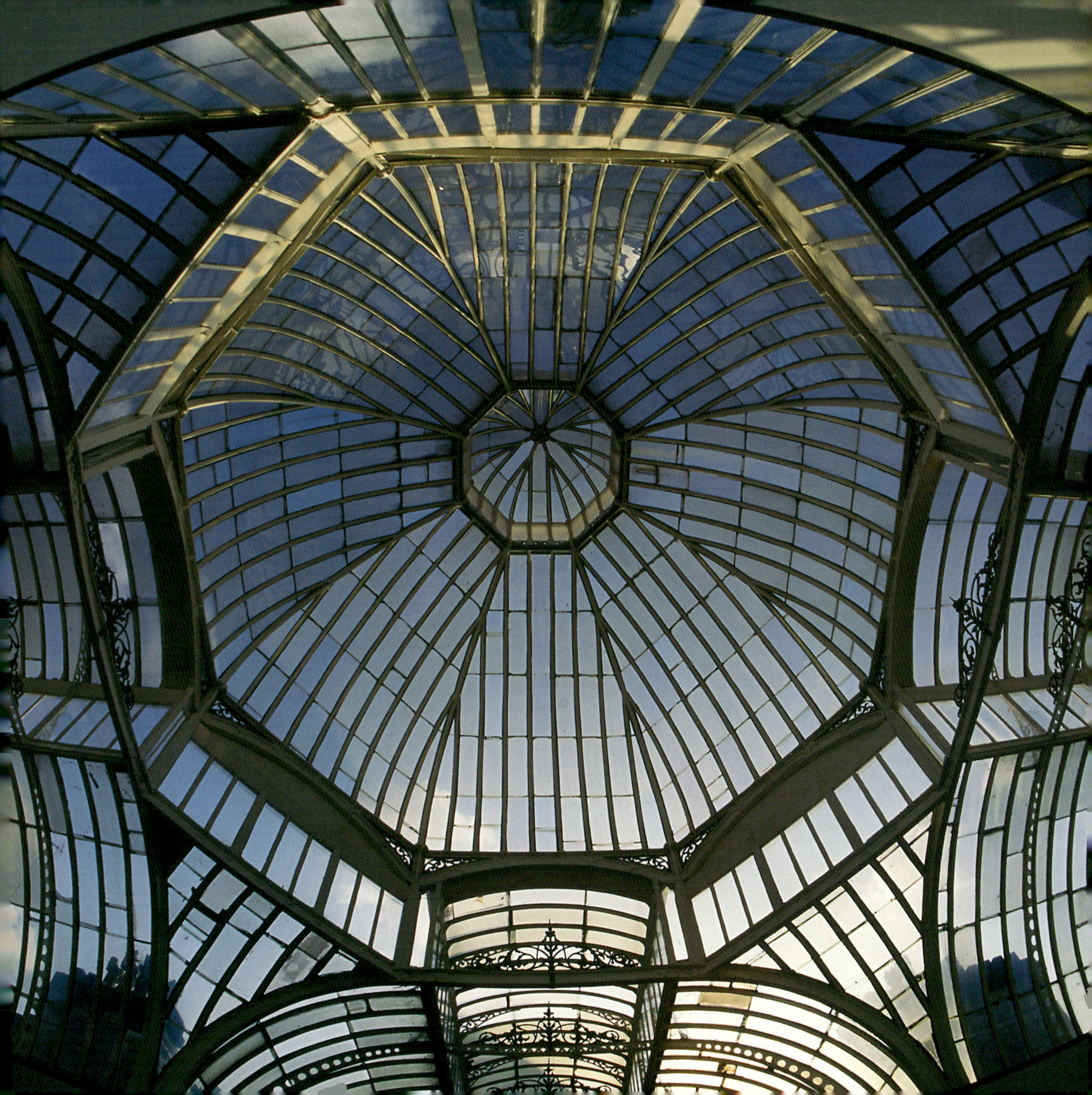

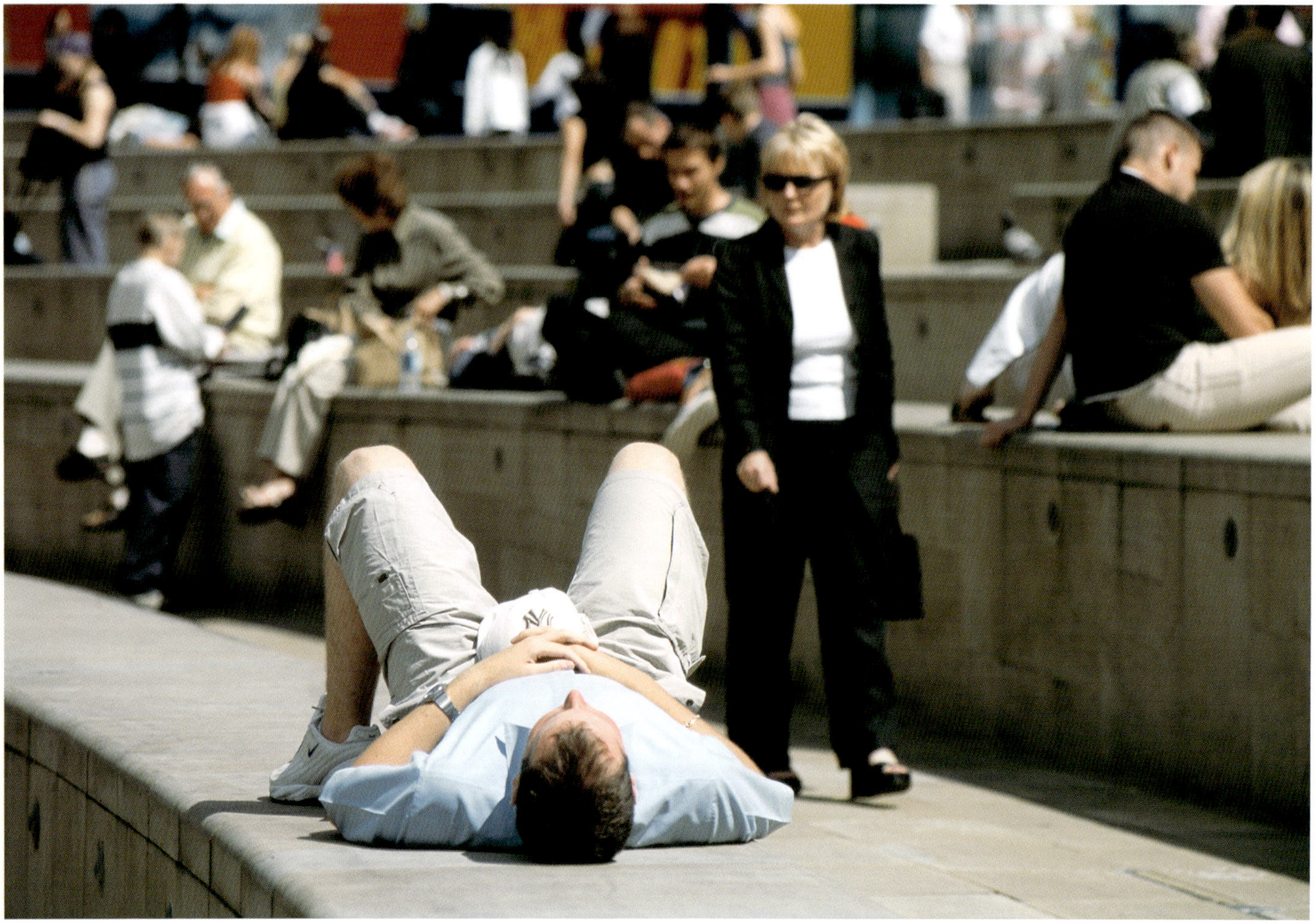

Lunchtime in the city: chilling out in Exchange Square...

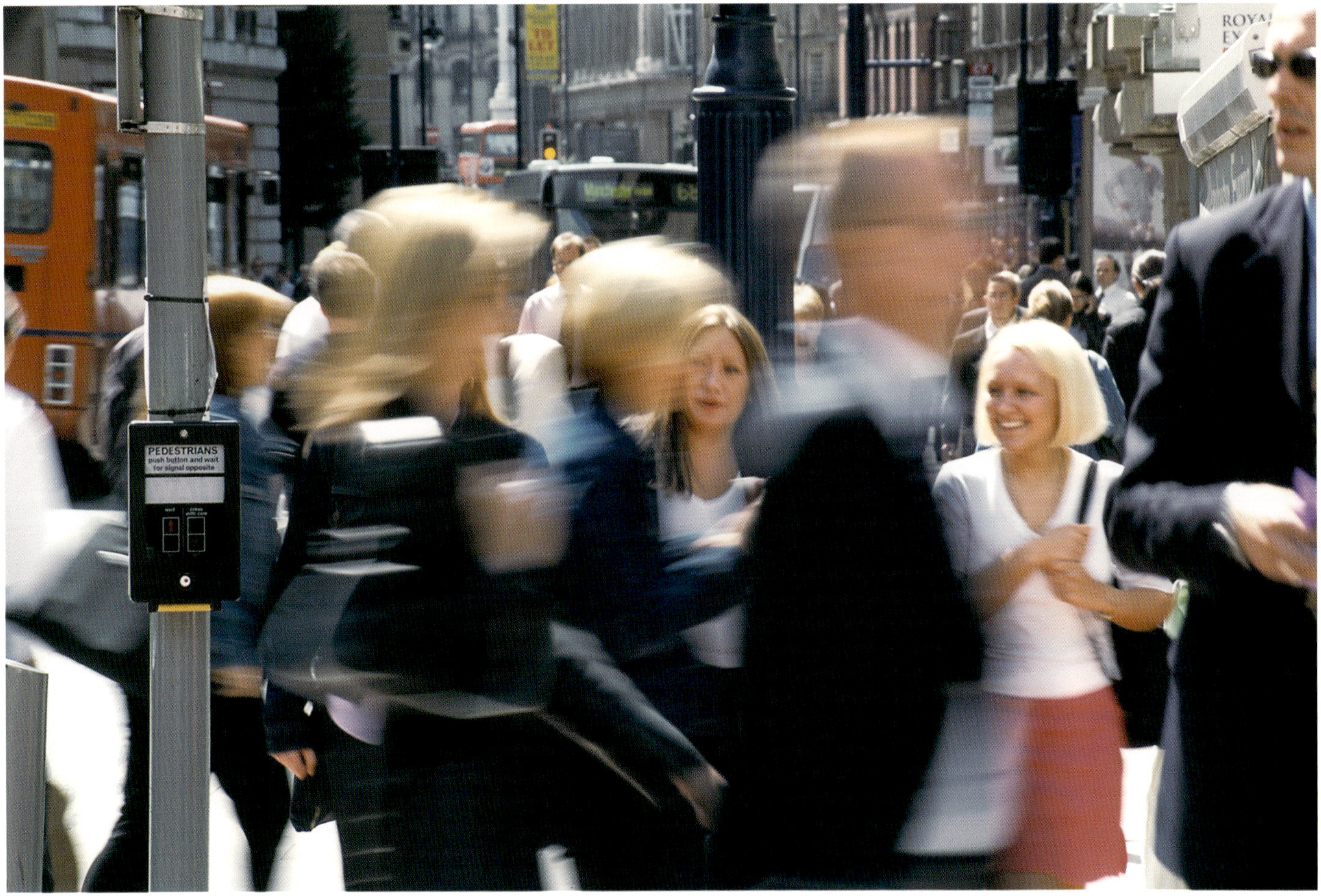

... or enjoying a stroll down Cross Street.

The redesign of Piccadilly Gardens by Japanese architect Ando Tadao includes a sweeping concrete wall and glass-fronted pavilion.

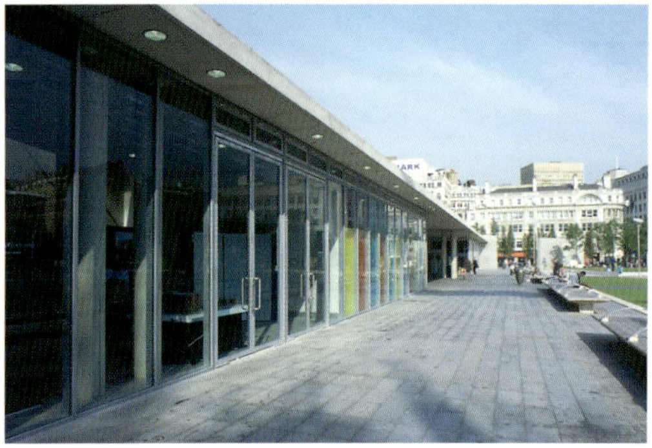

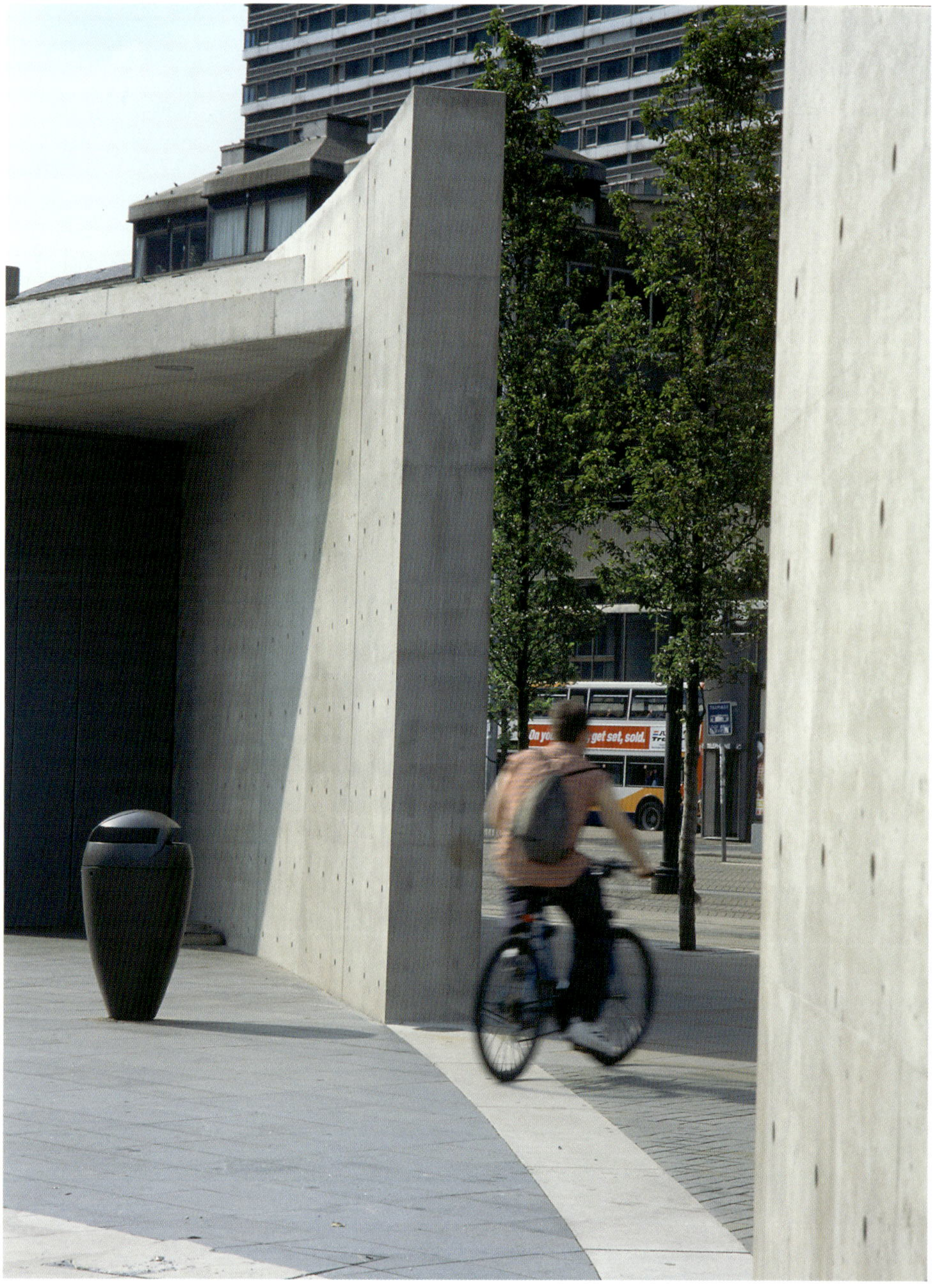

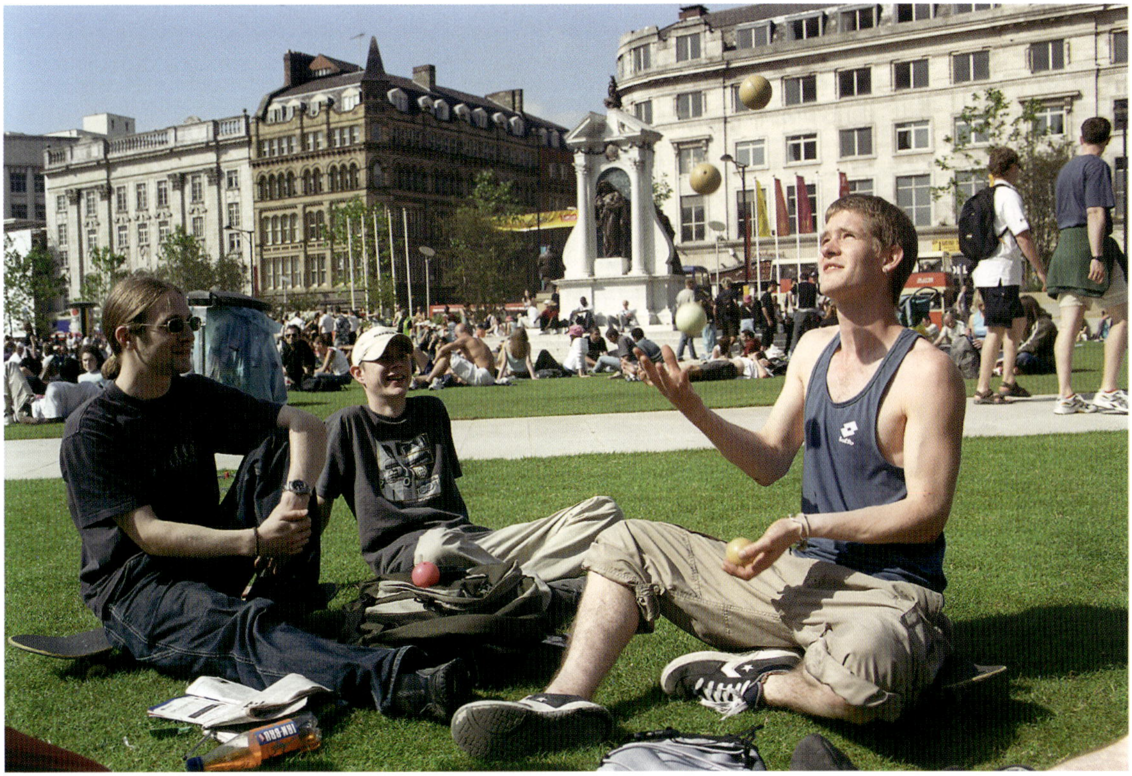

Piccadilly Gardens is a great place to sit out and enjoy the sunshine.

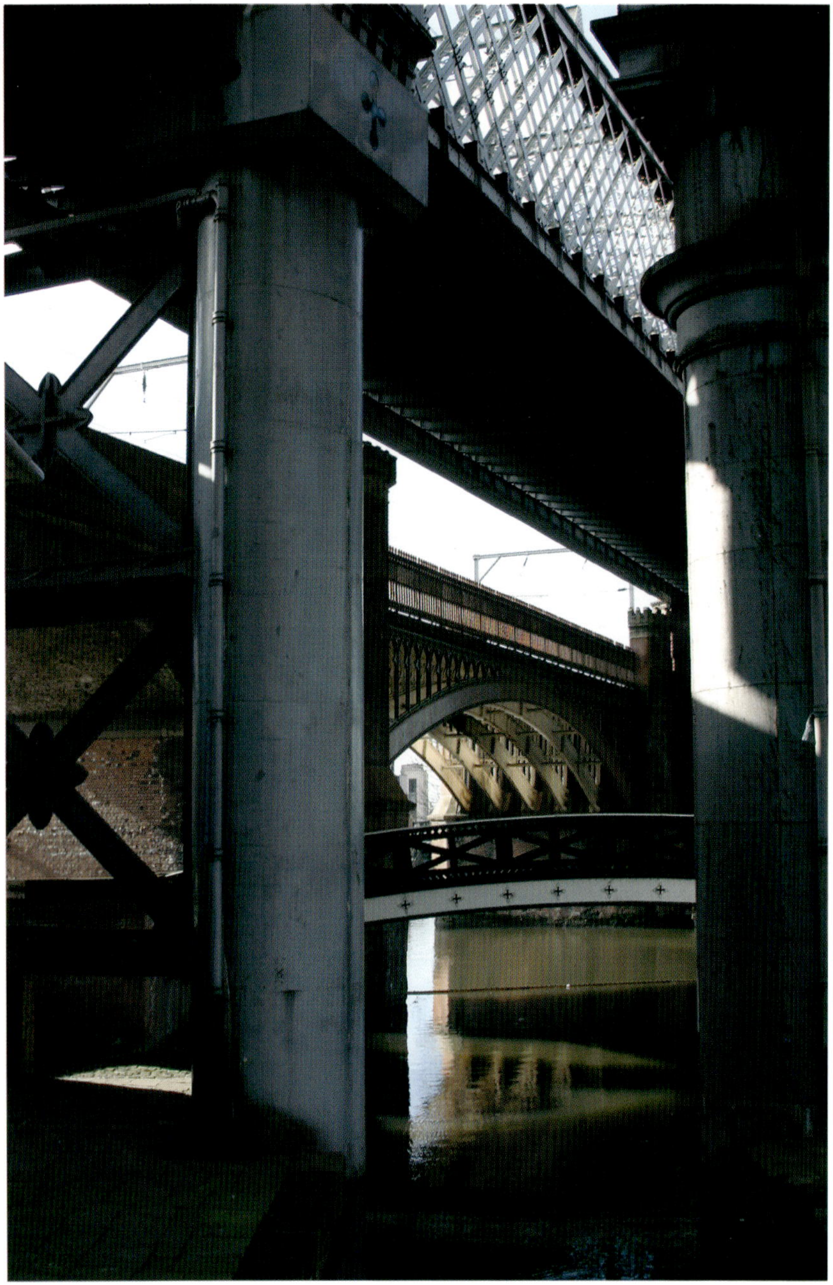

Characterised by its imposing railway viaduct and canal system, Castlefield originally developed as a 'goods inward' location for 'Cottonopolis'.

Eastgate, formerly known as Gail House, was a rundown Victorian canalside warehouse. Now it's home to media and creative companies.

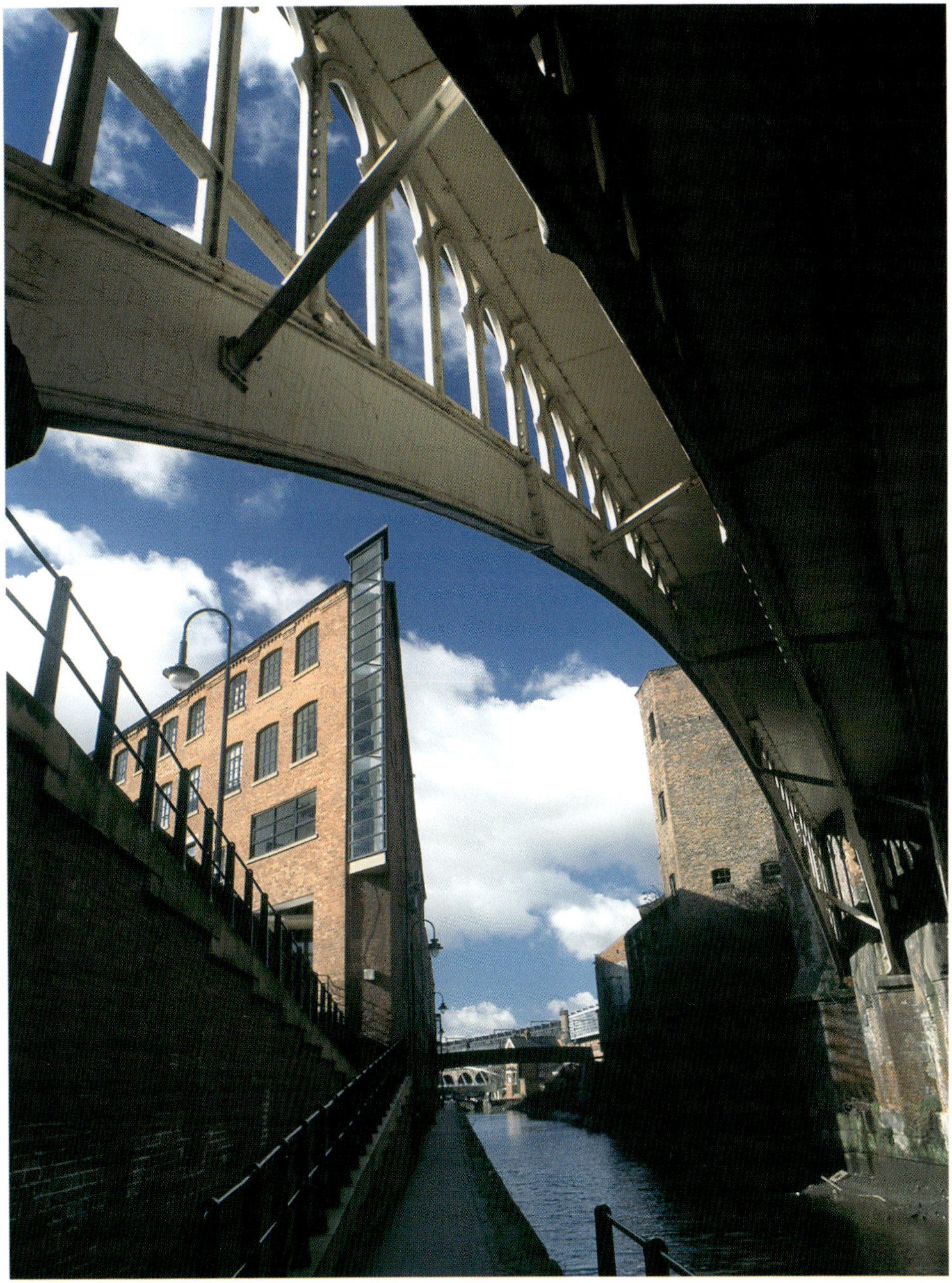

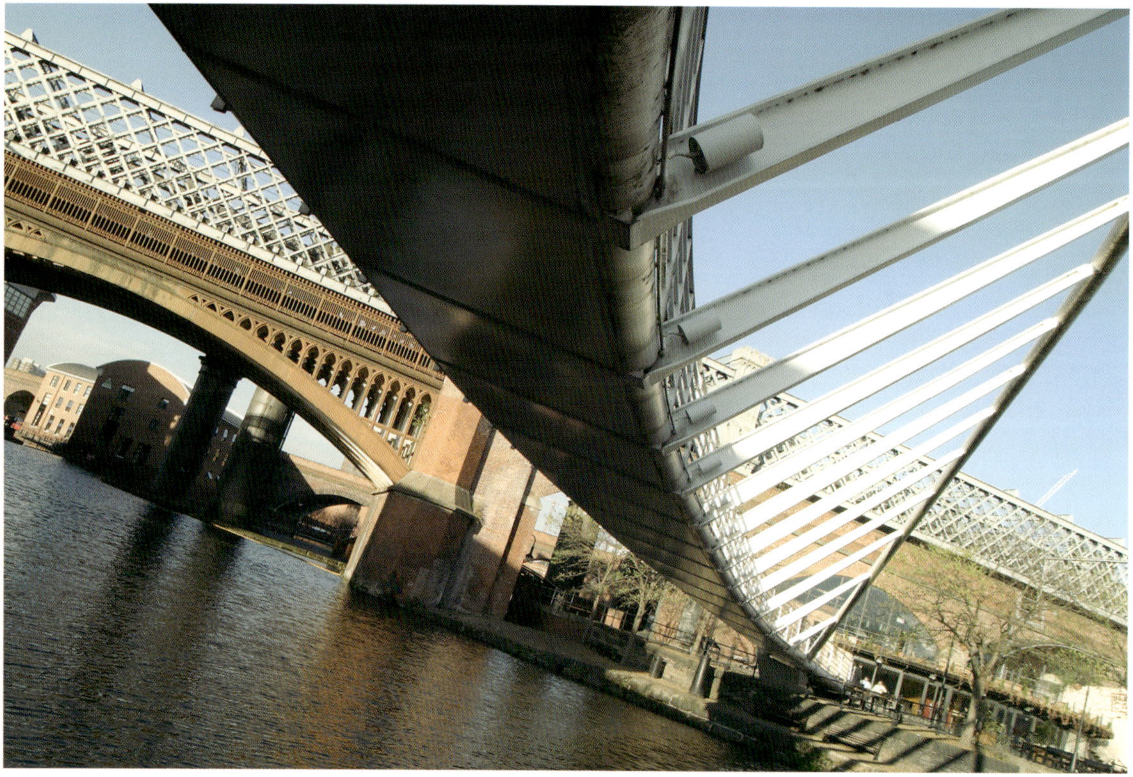

Over recent years several new footbridges *(above)* have been built to span the Bridgewater and Rochdale Canals which meet here *(opposite)*.

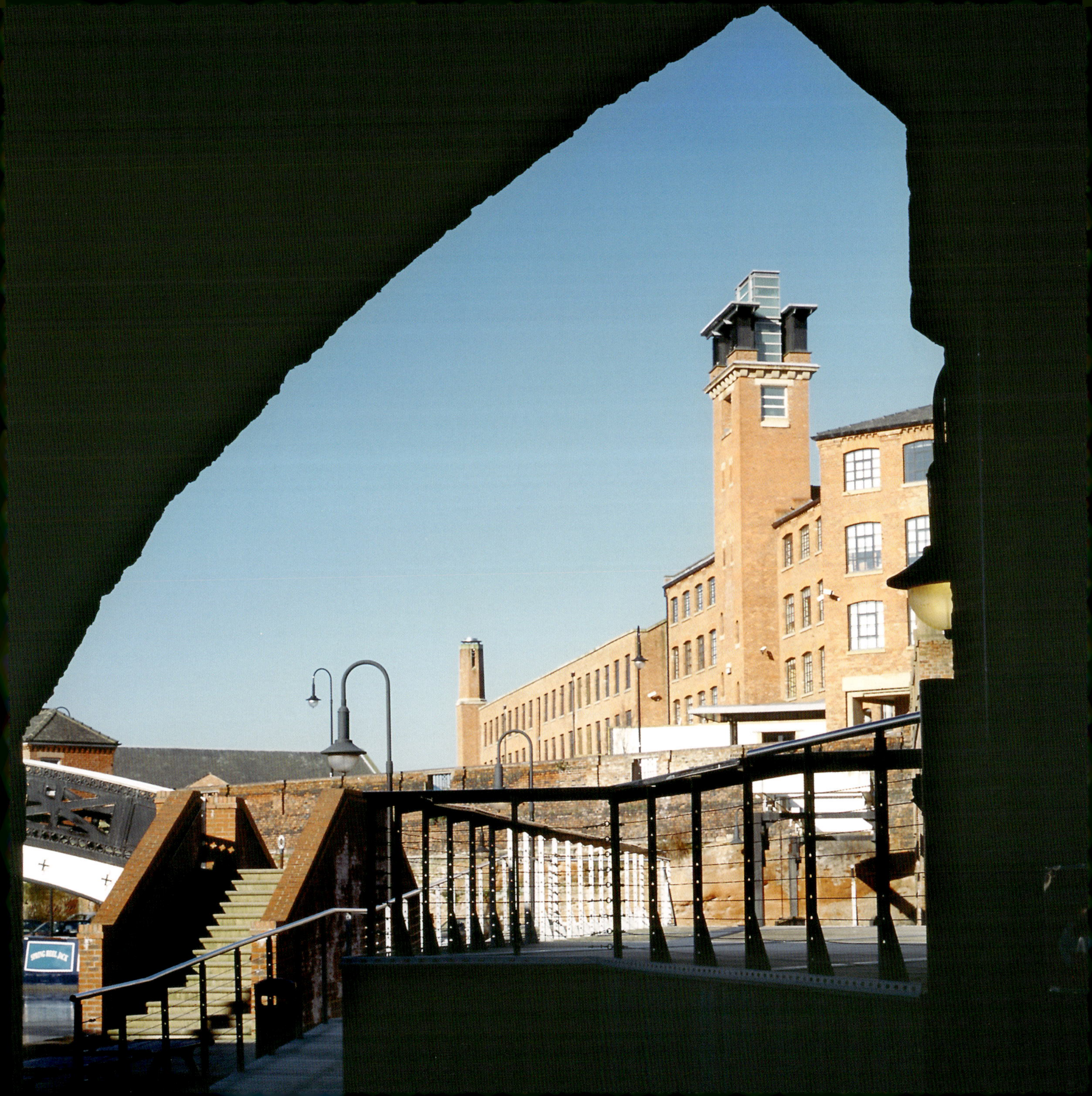

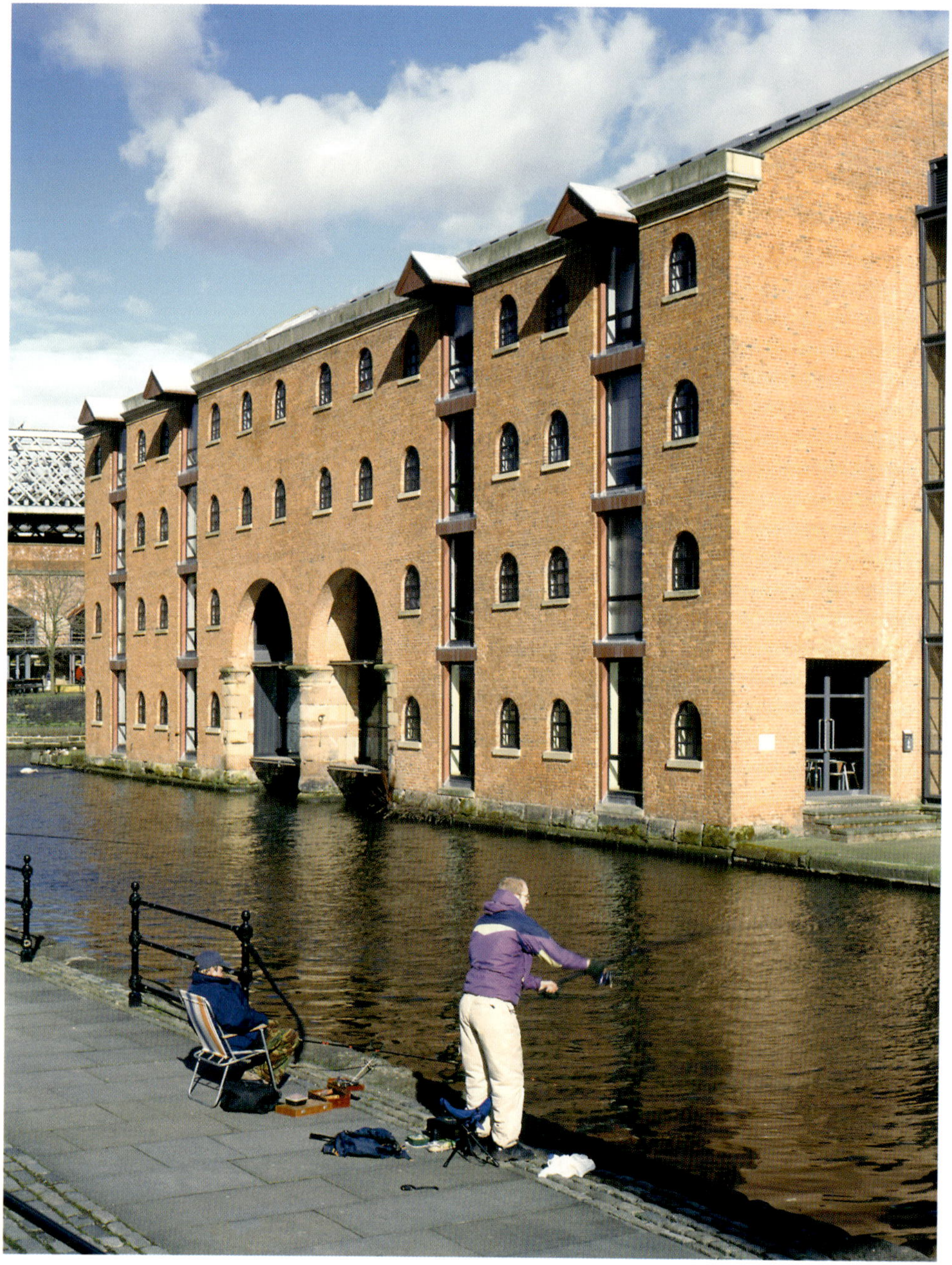

Built in 1827, Merchants' Warehouse is the oldest surviving canalside warehouse.

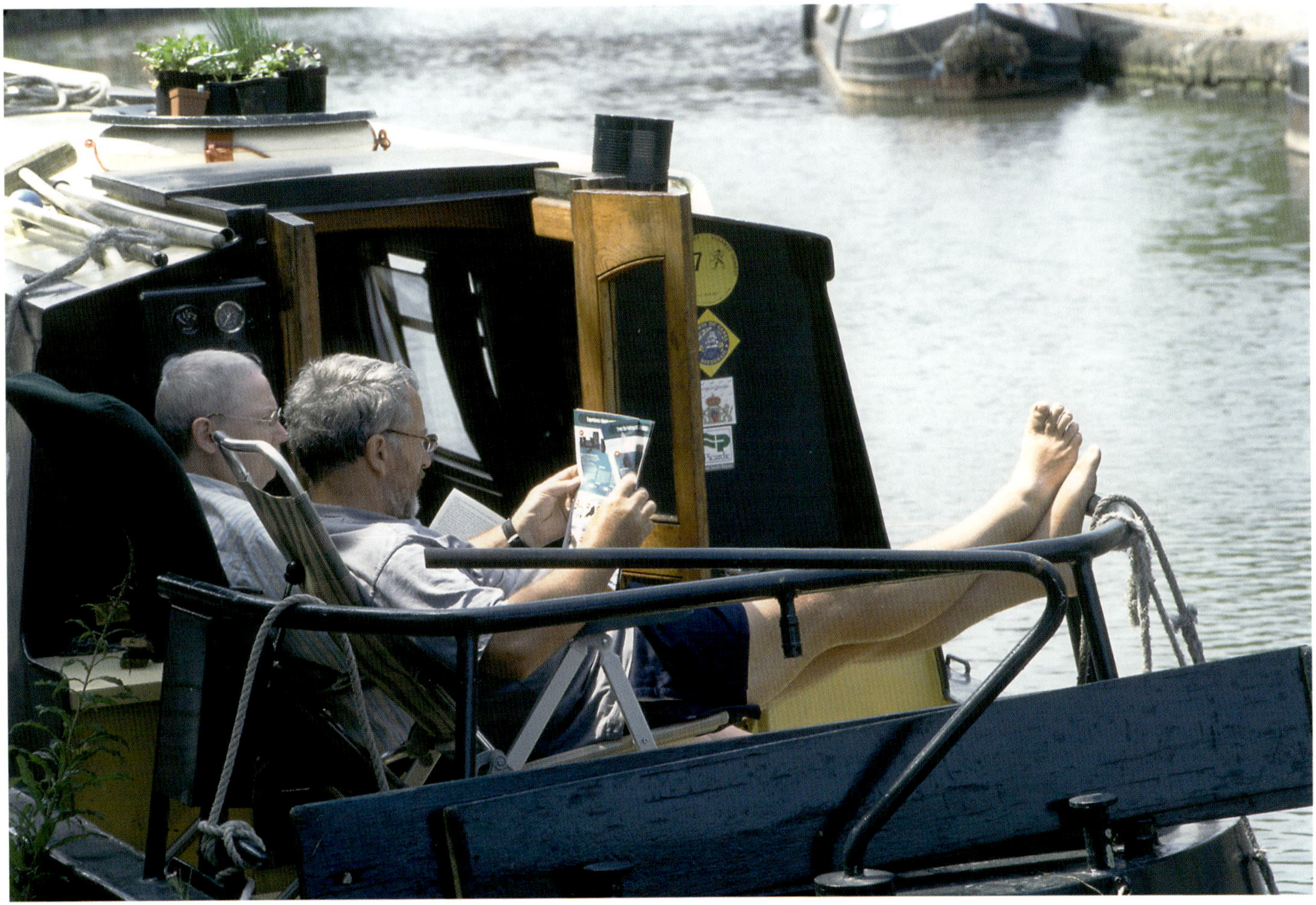

Castlefield was designated the first ever Urban Heritage Park.

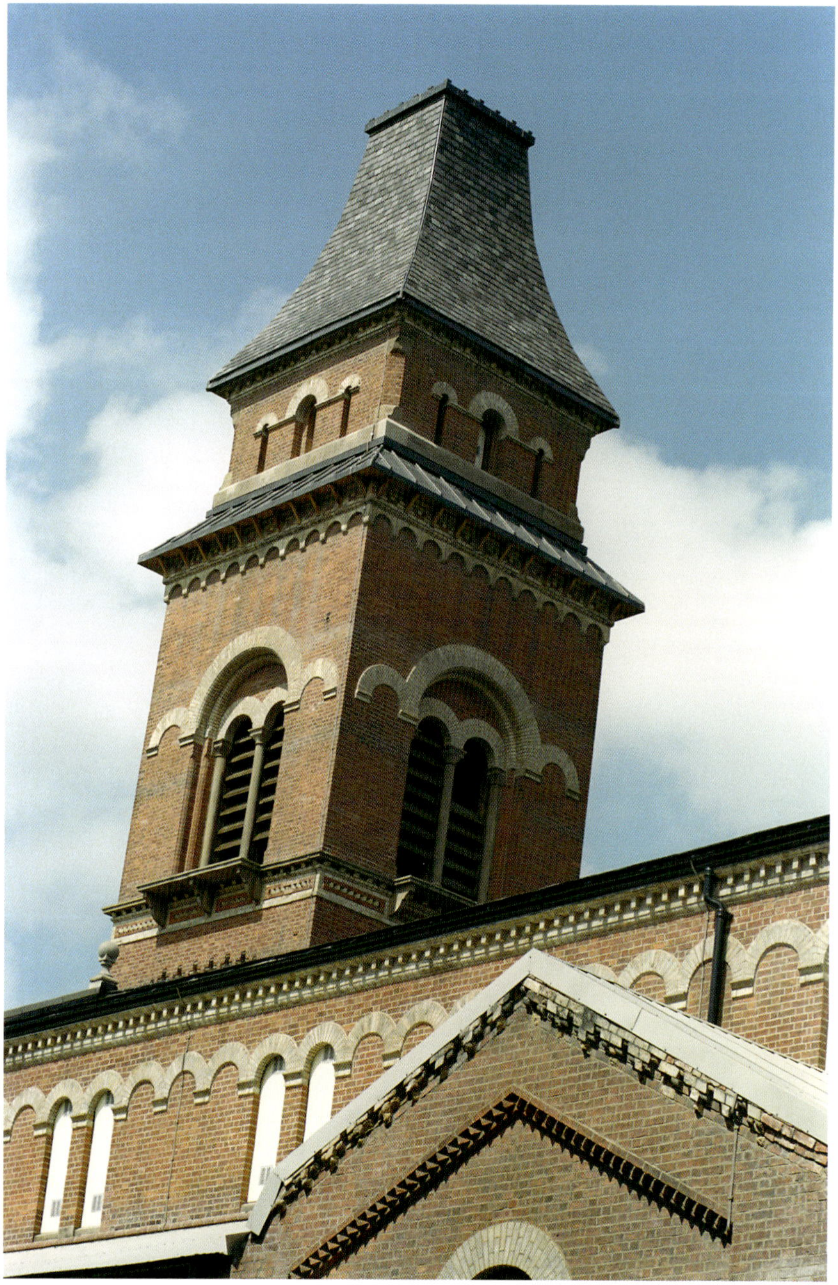

Manchester's industrial past is nowhere more evident than in Ancoats, the world's first industrial suburb. This is St Peter's Church, the centrepiece of what is now Ancoats Urban Village.

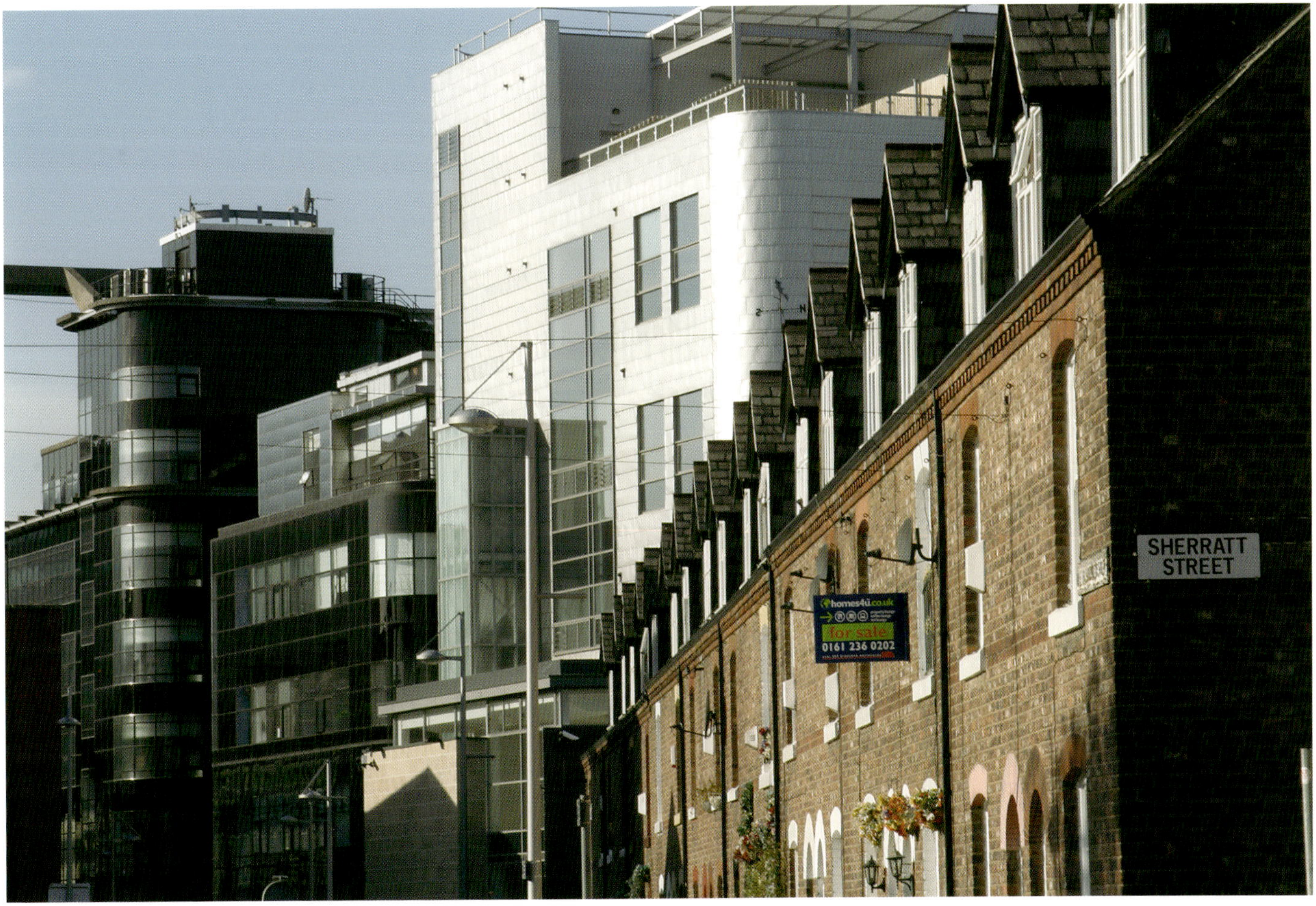

The Victorian terraces of George Leigh Street contrast sharply with the black and green Daily Express Building of the 1930s, and the ultra modern metallic cladding of Express Networks.

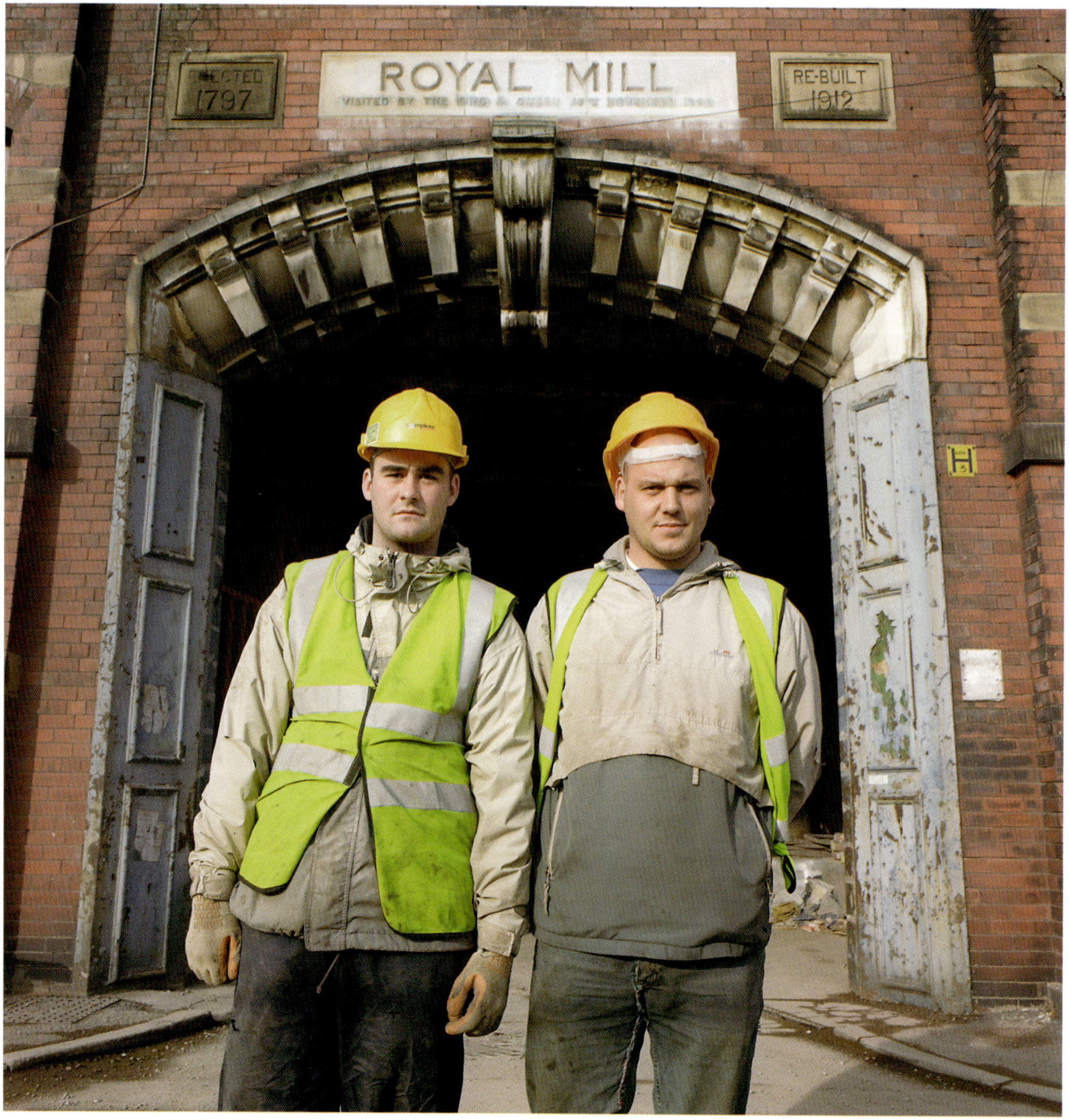

The Royal Mill complex in Ancoats *(opposite)*, formerly known as McConnel's and Kennedy's Mills, was the largest in the region, employing 1500 workers in the 1830s. The eight-storey structures were marvelled at by all who visited them. The mills are now being restored *(above)* after many years of dereliction and neglect.

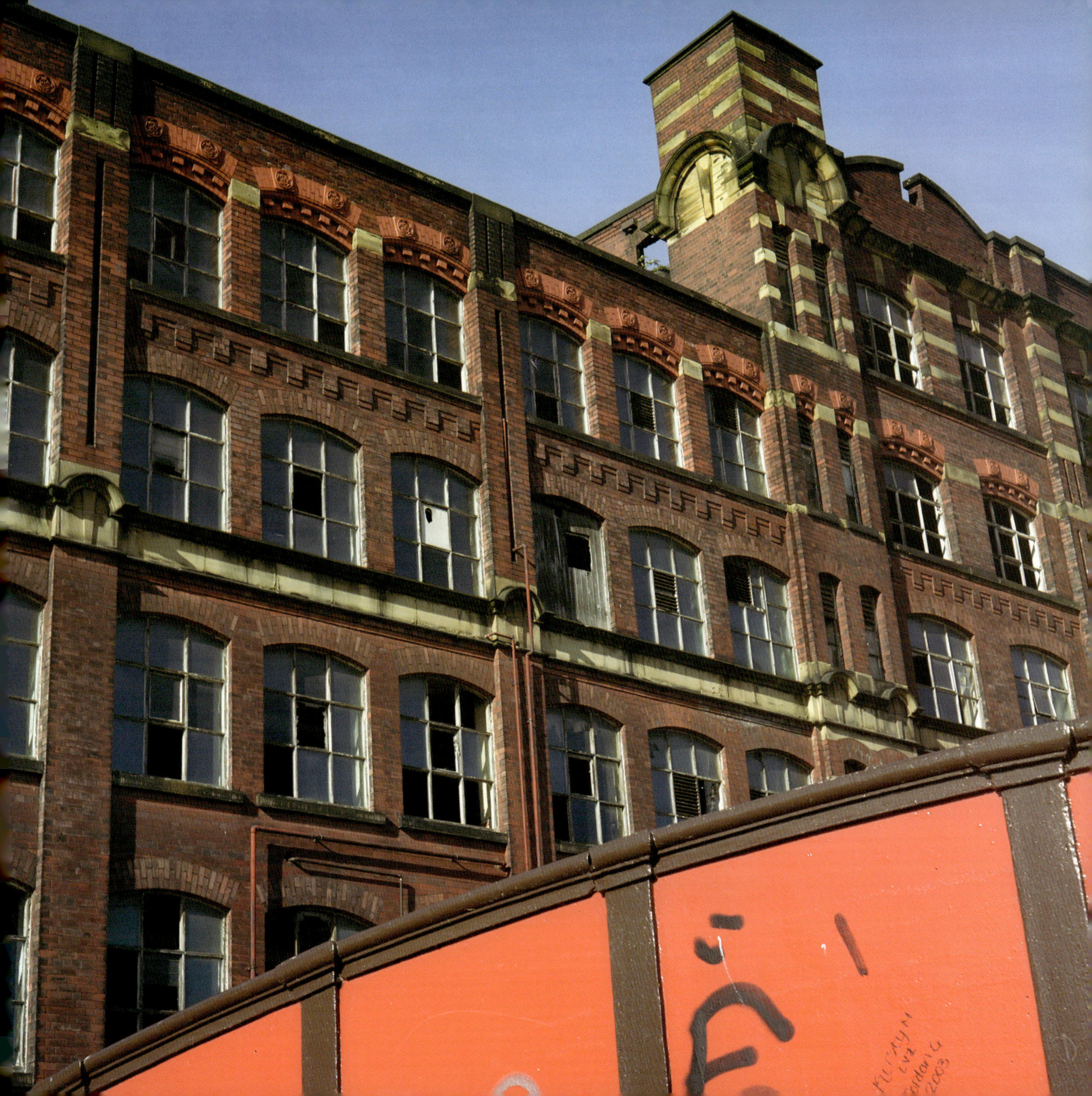

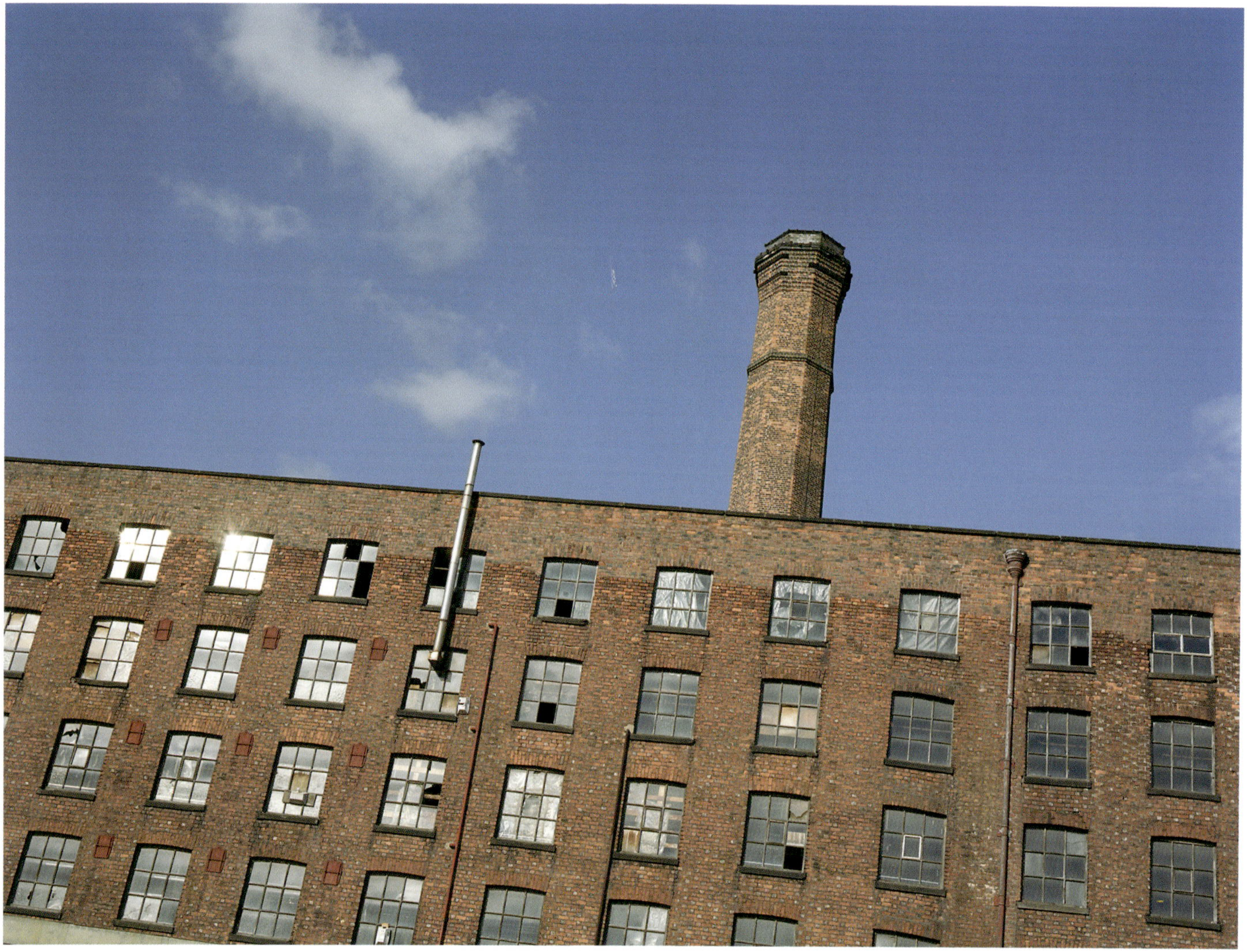

Scotsmen Adam and George Murray built their mills in Ancoats 200 years ago.
The fine yarns spun here in Manchester were originally sent back to hand-loom weavers in Scotland.

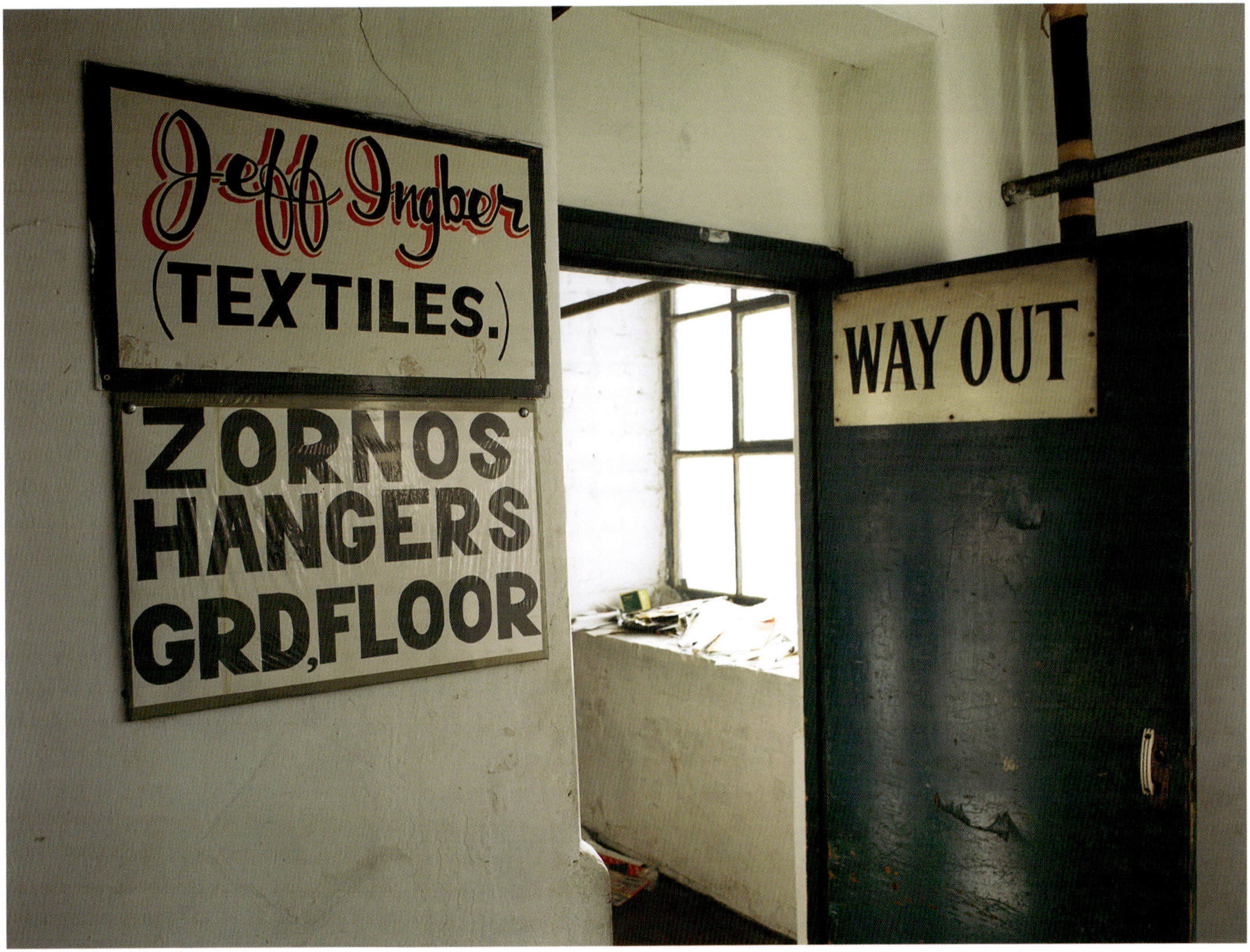

Even after cotton spinning came to an end, the Ancoats mills continued to be used by textile trades before the buildings were acquired for redevelopment.

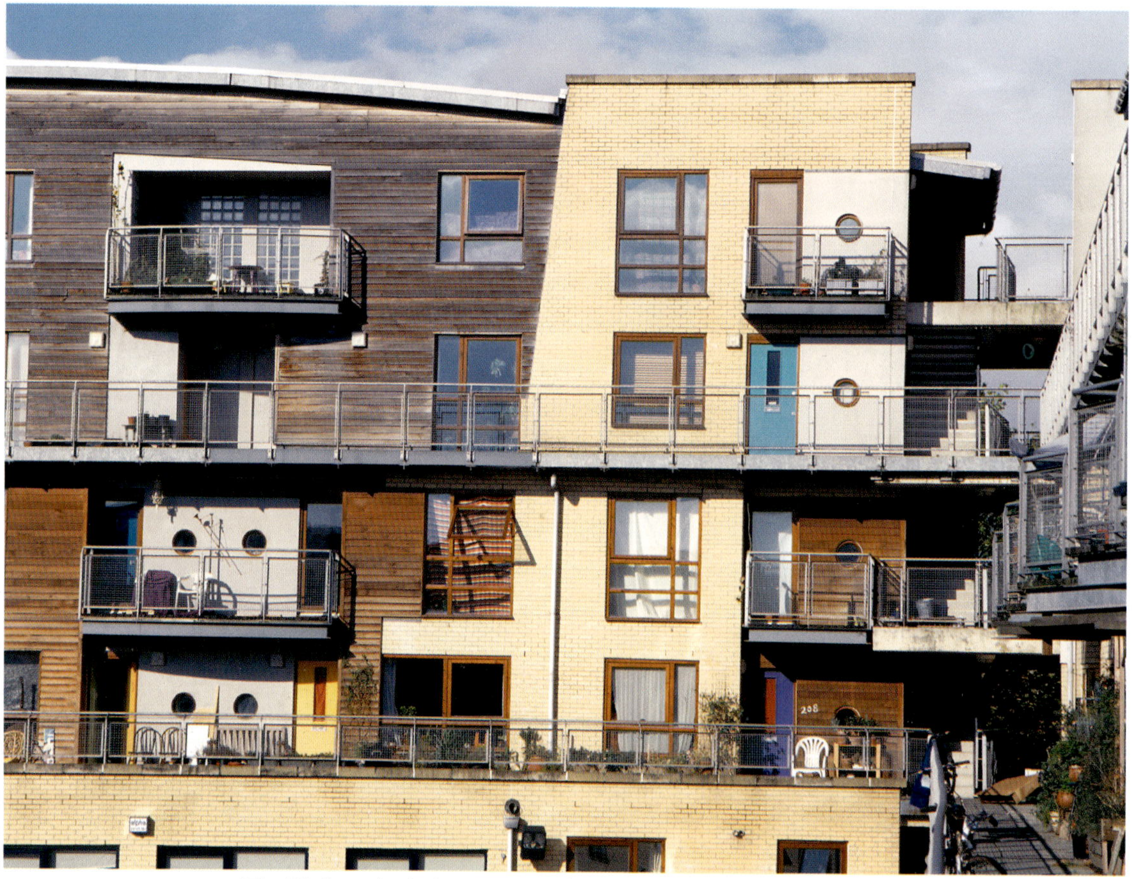

The Hulme Arch *(opposite)* symbolises the major rejuvenation for this part of the city. Numerous award-winning housing schemes have developed in the past decade. *(Above)* This is Homes for Change by MBLC architects.

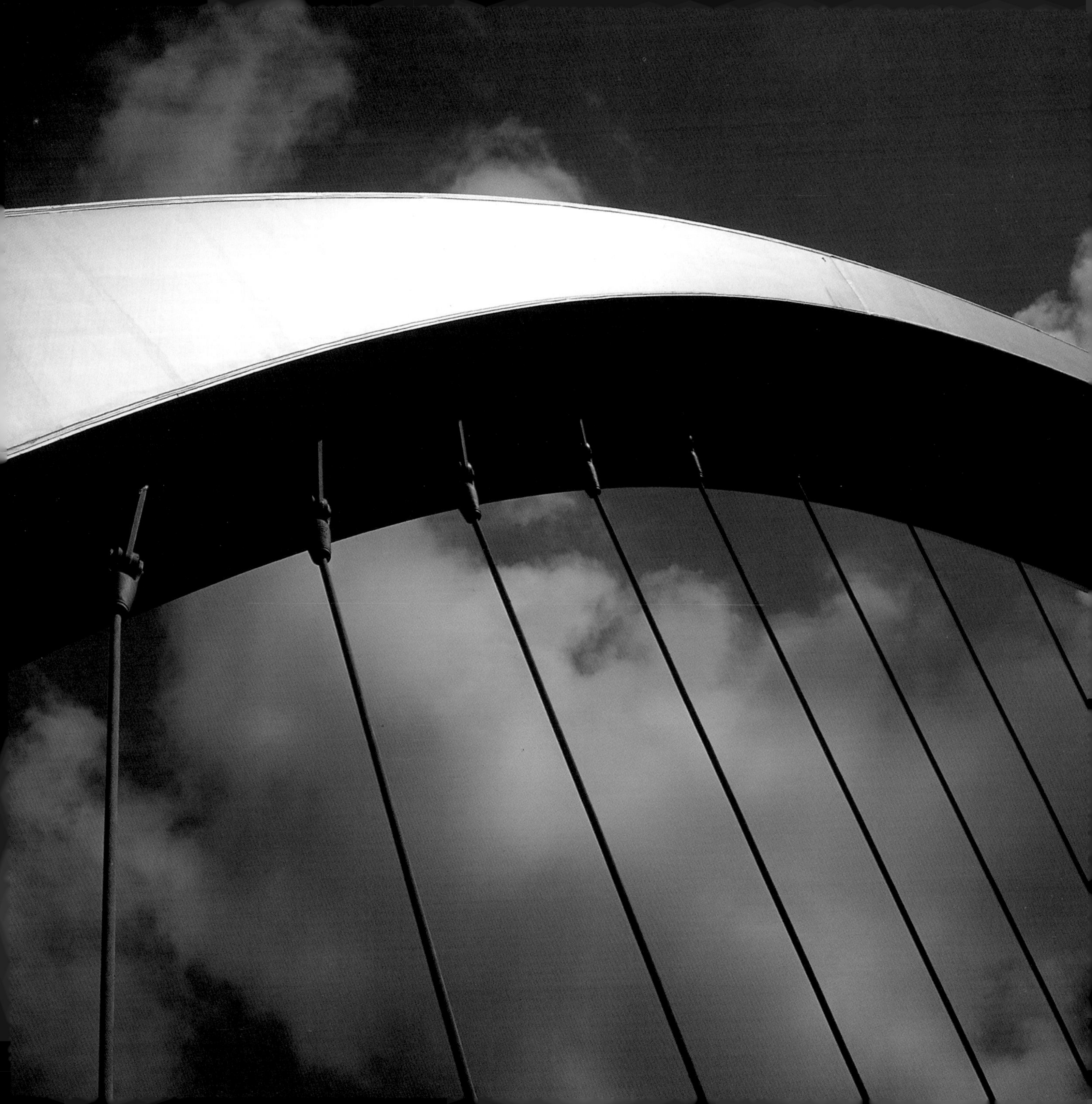

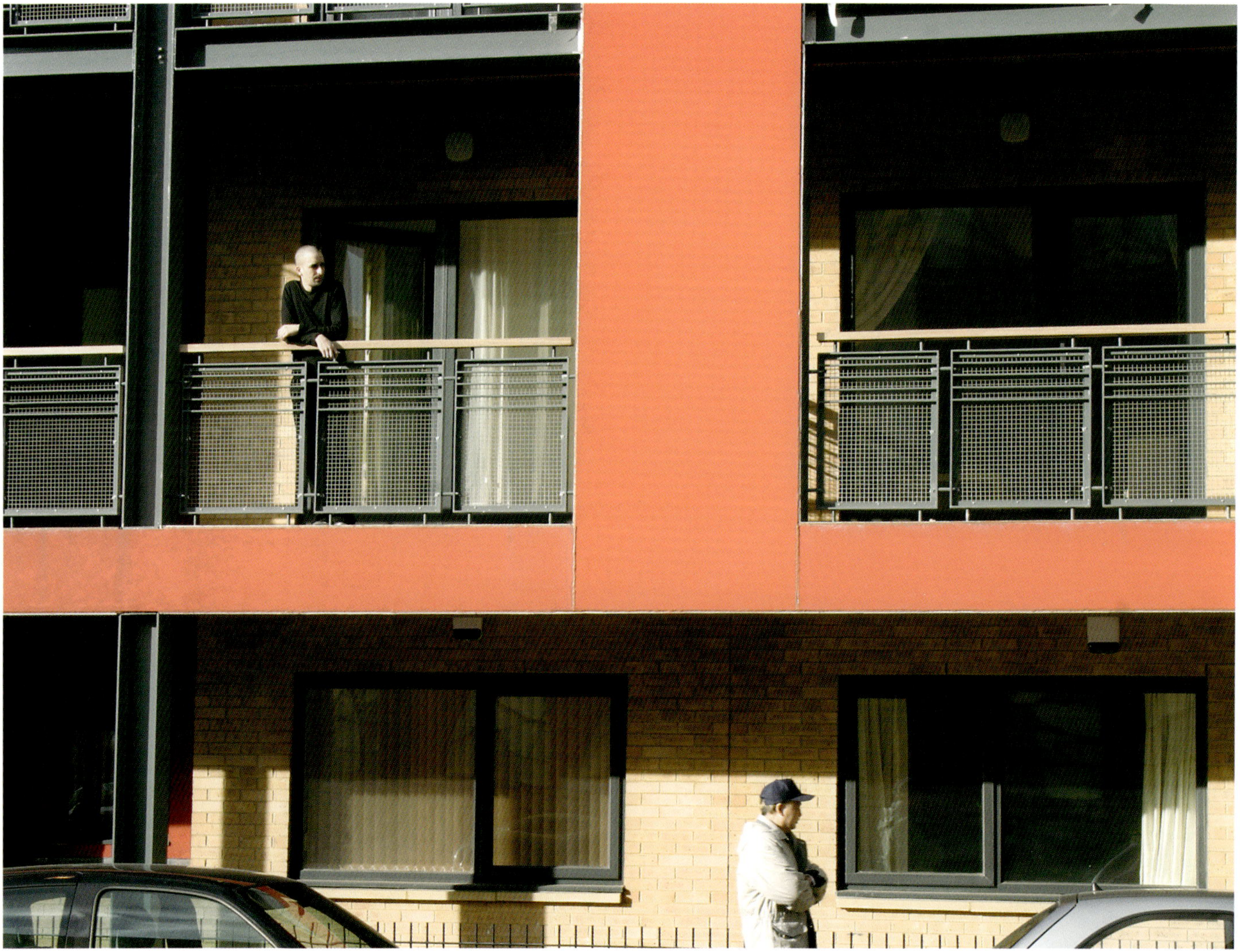

In Hulme, attractive houses and apartments have replaced badly-constructed, concrete housing blocks.

The first new park in the city for fifty years, Hulme Park provides a place to play and relax with friends.

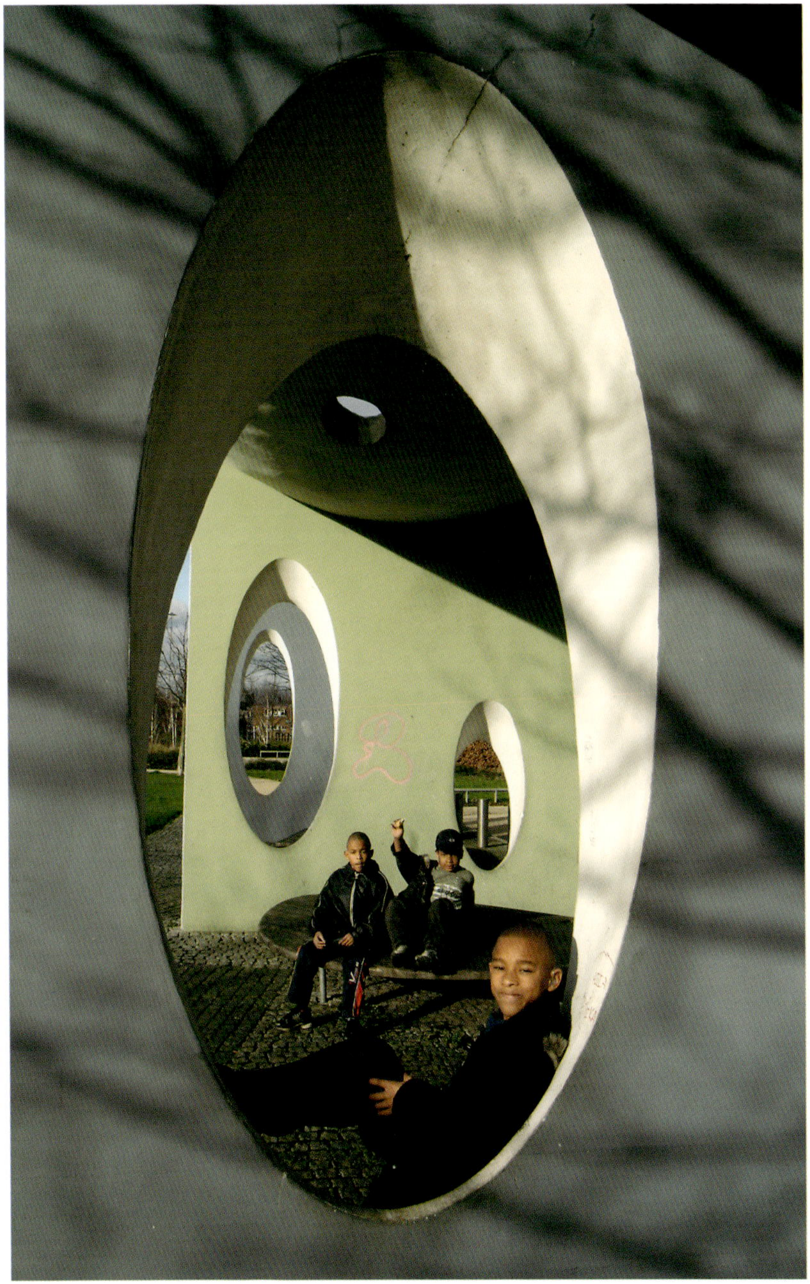

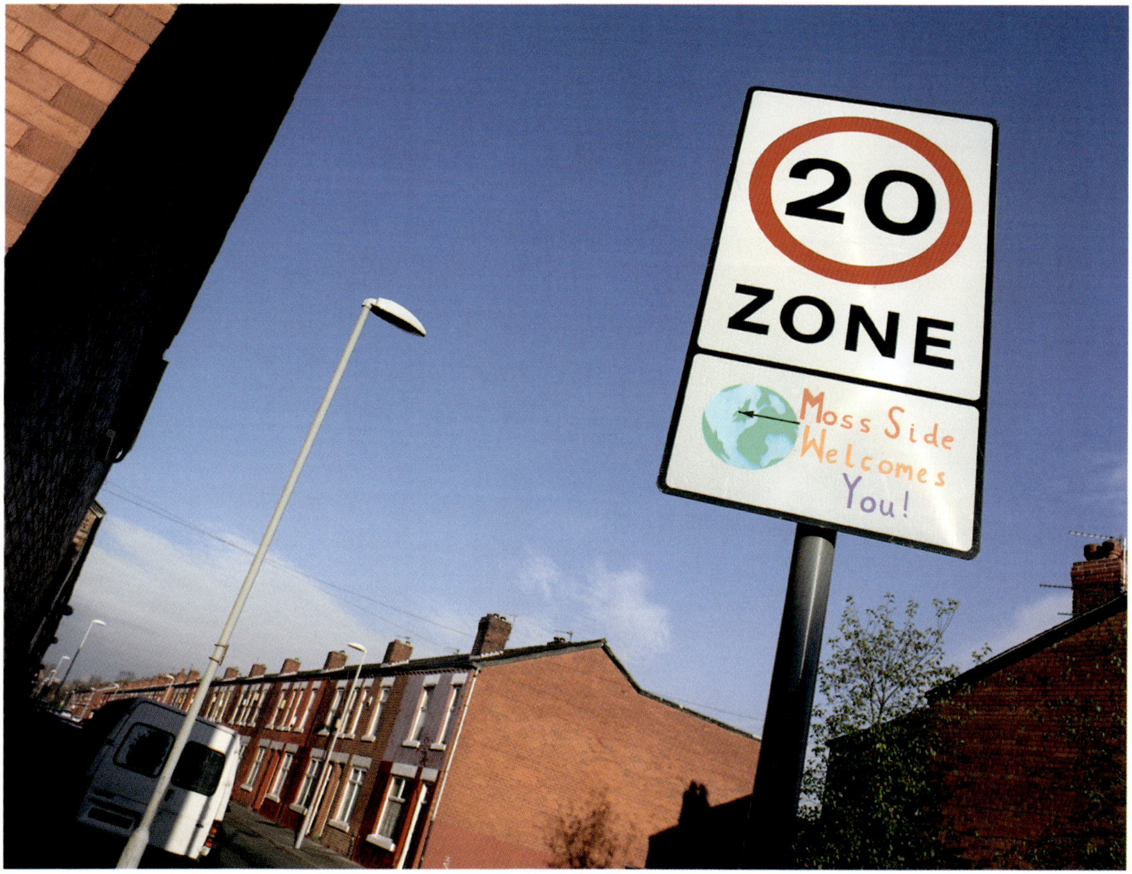

Originally built for mill workers, the terraced houses of Moss Side are now home to a diverse and welcoming local community.

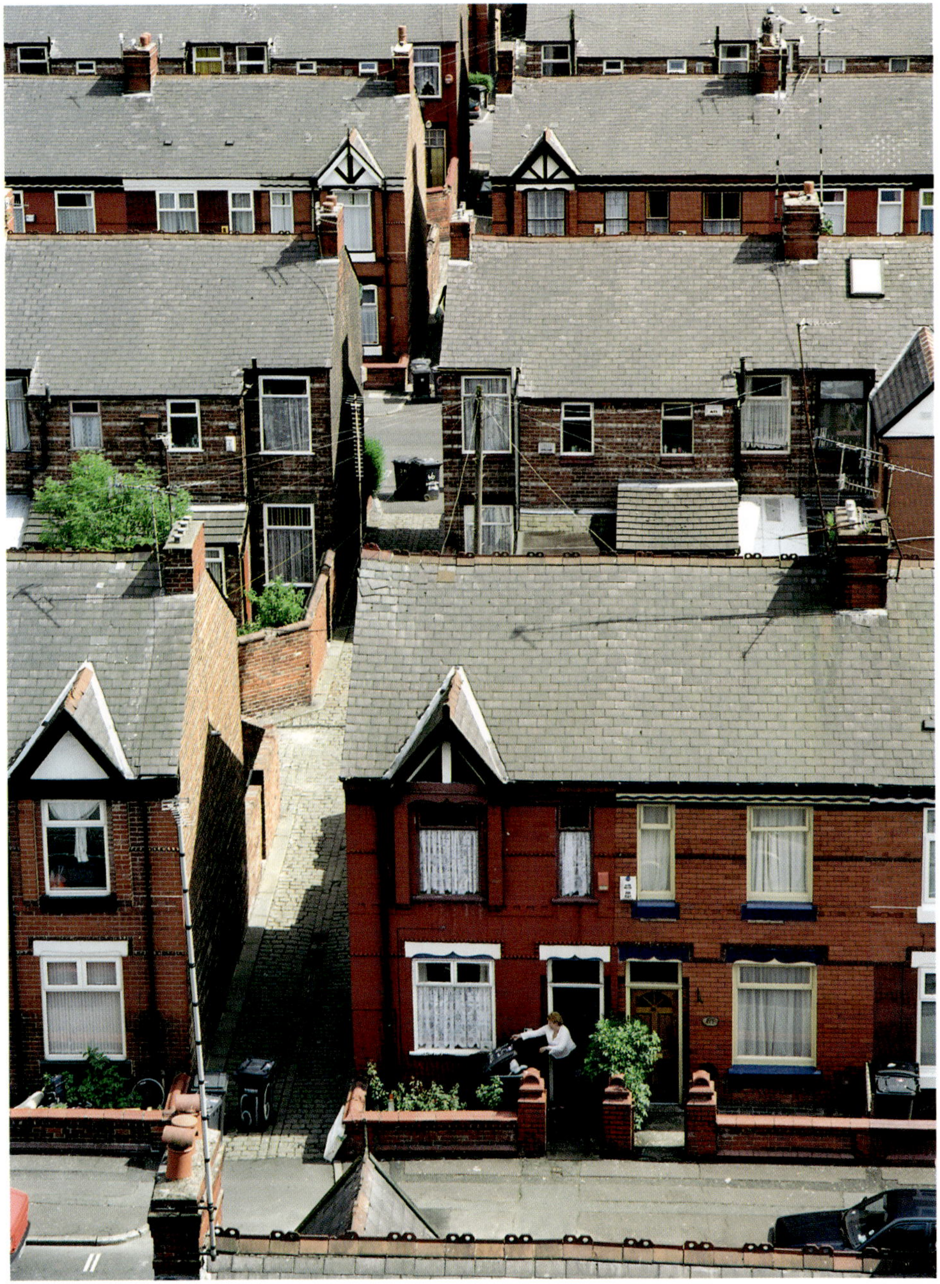

Back-to-backs in Rusholme. The street pattern reflects the field boundaries when this was agricultural land 150 years ago.

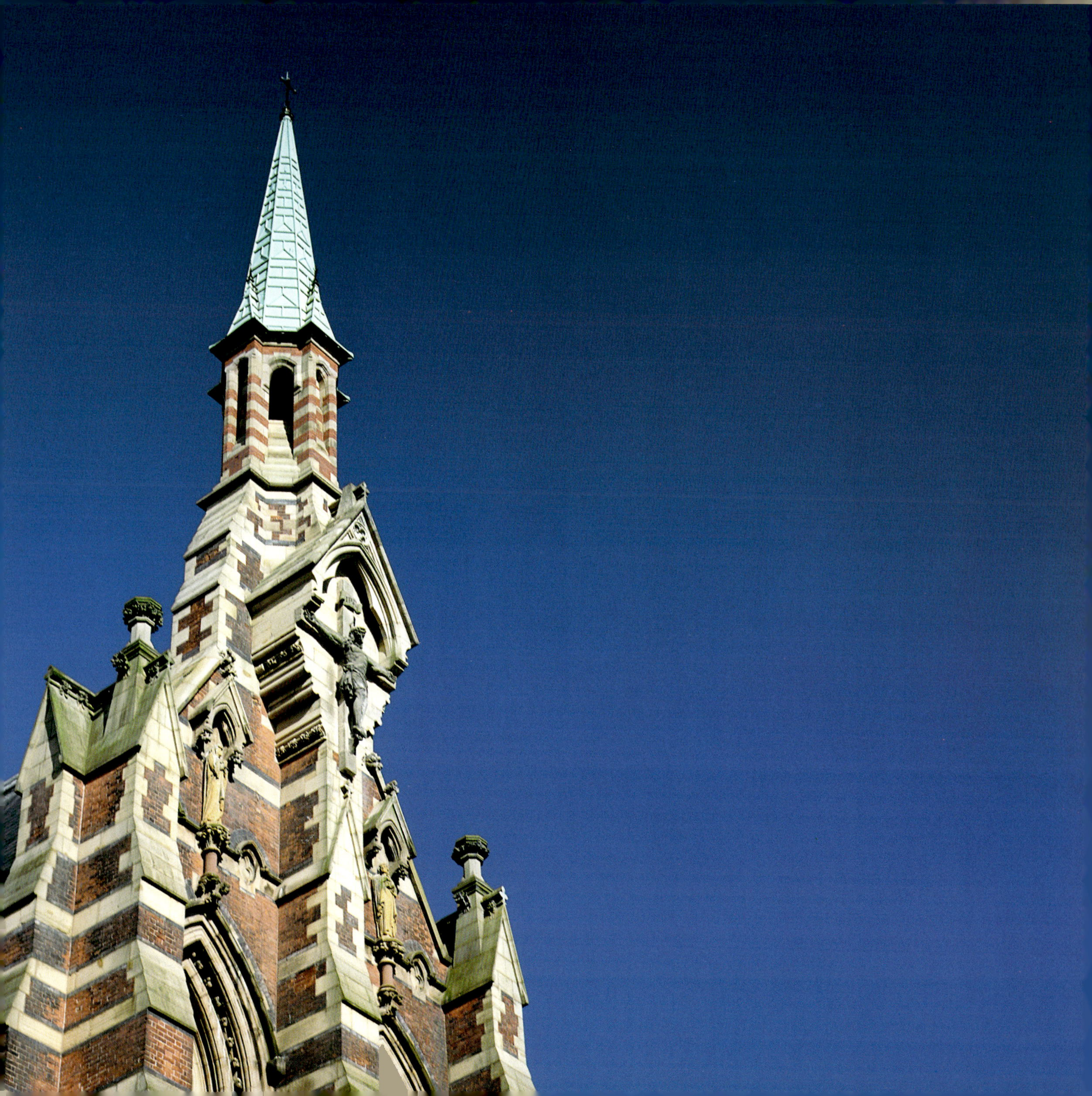

The Monastery of St Francis *(opposite)* designed by E. W. Pugin, was built by Franciscan friars in Gorton where they served the Roman Catholic population. After years of decay, considerable funding has been secured to restore the Gothic masterpiece and return it to community use.

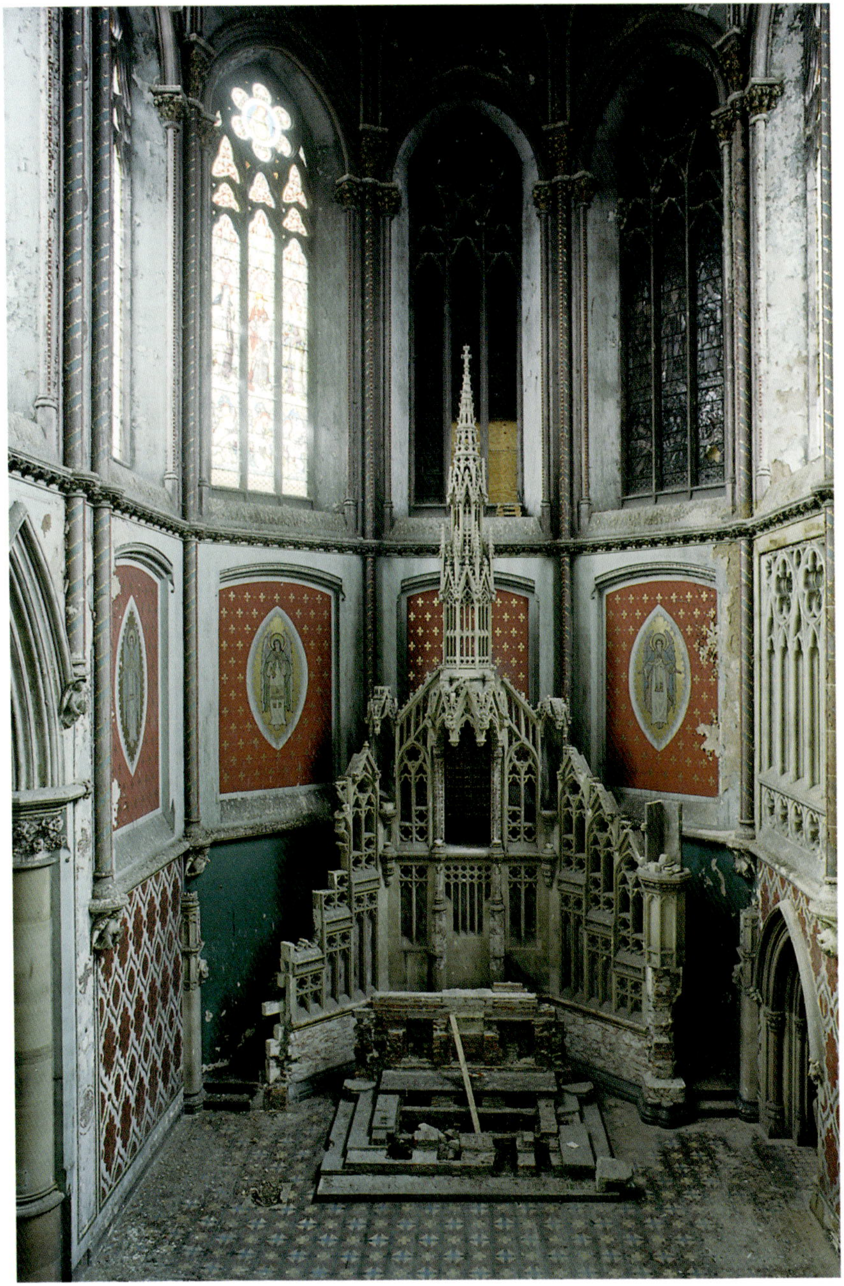

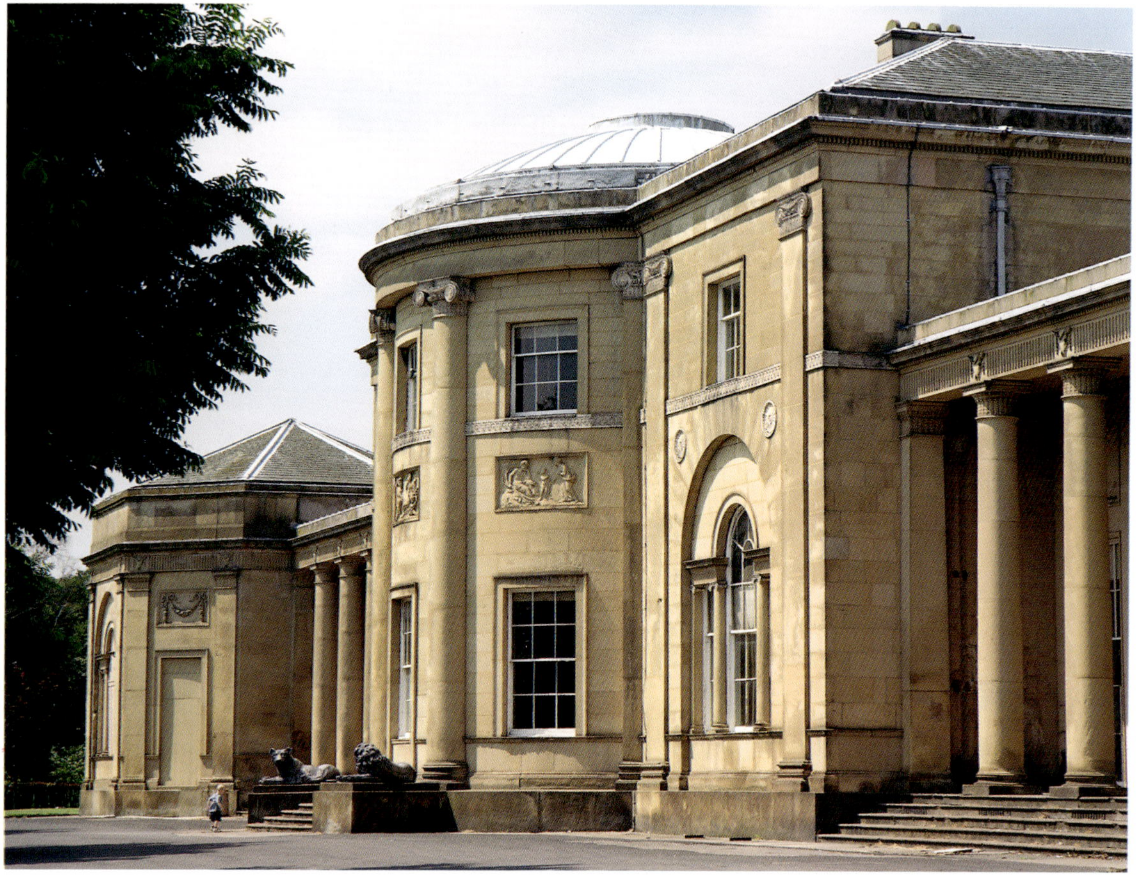

Heaton Hall stands in 650 acres of parkland to the north of the city. This neoclassical country house has been gradually restored to its eighteenth-century former glory.

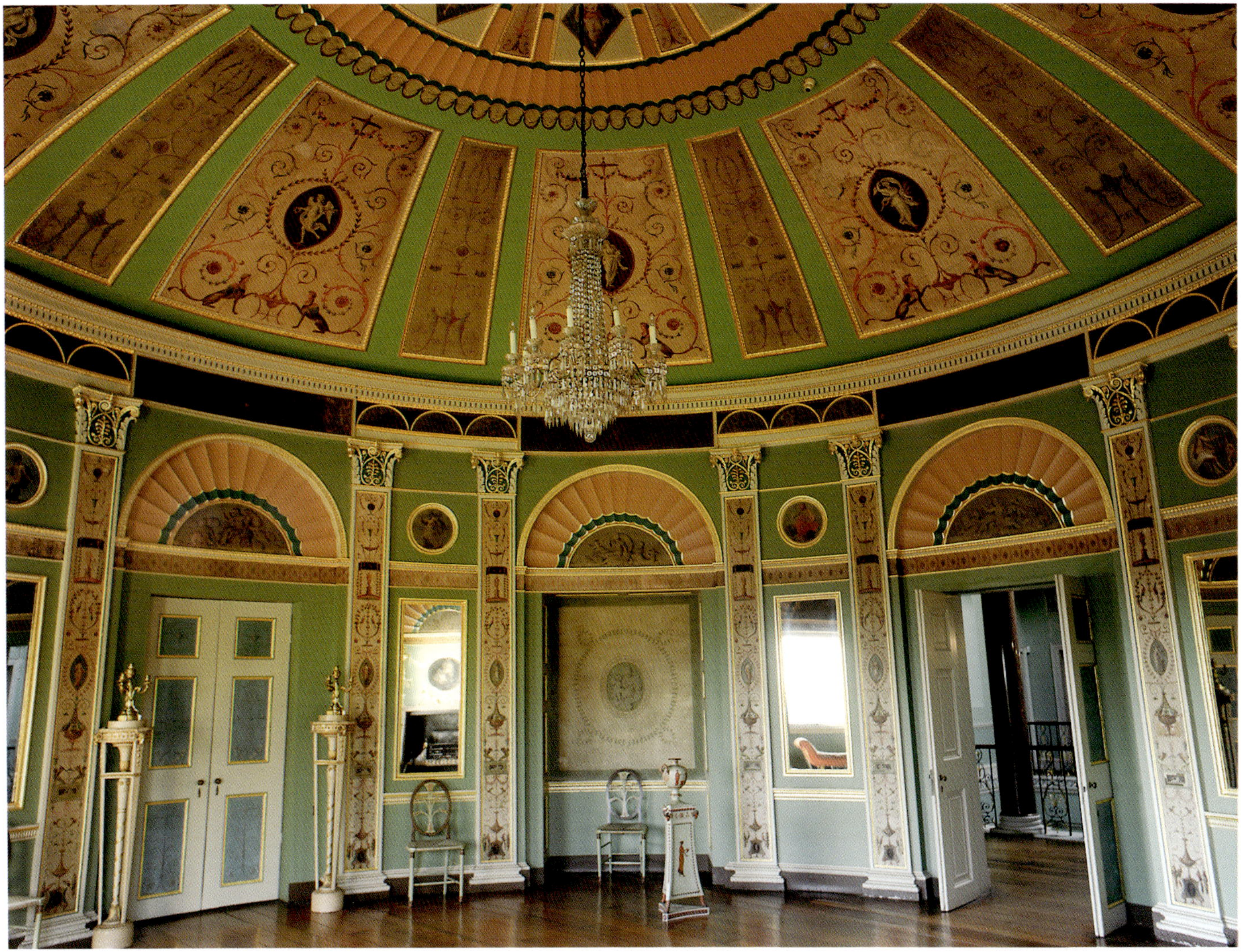

The Cupola Room, designed by Italian artist Biagio Rebecca in the Pompeiian style.

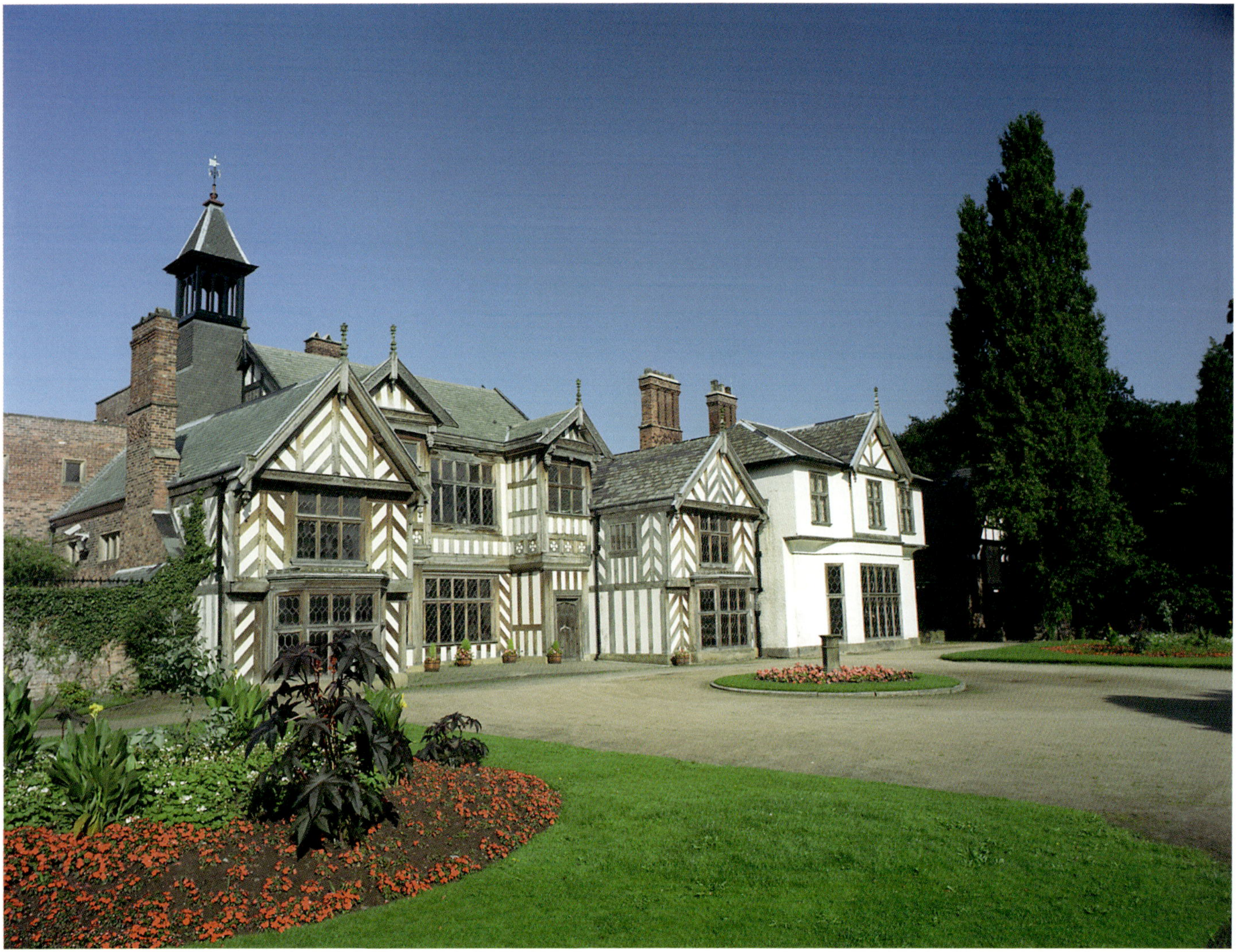

The half-timbered Wythenshawe Hall was home to fourteen generations of the Tatton family until 1926.

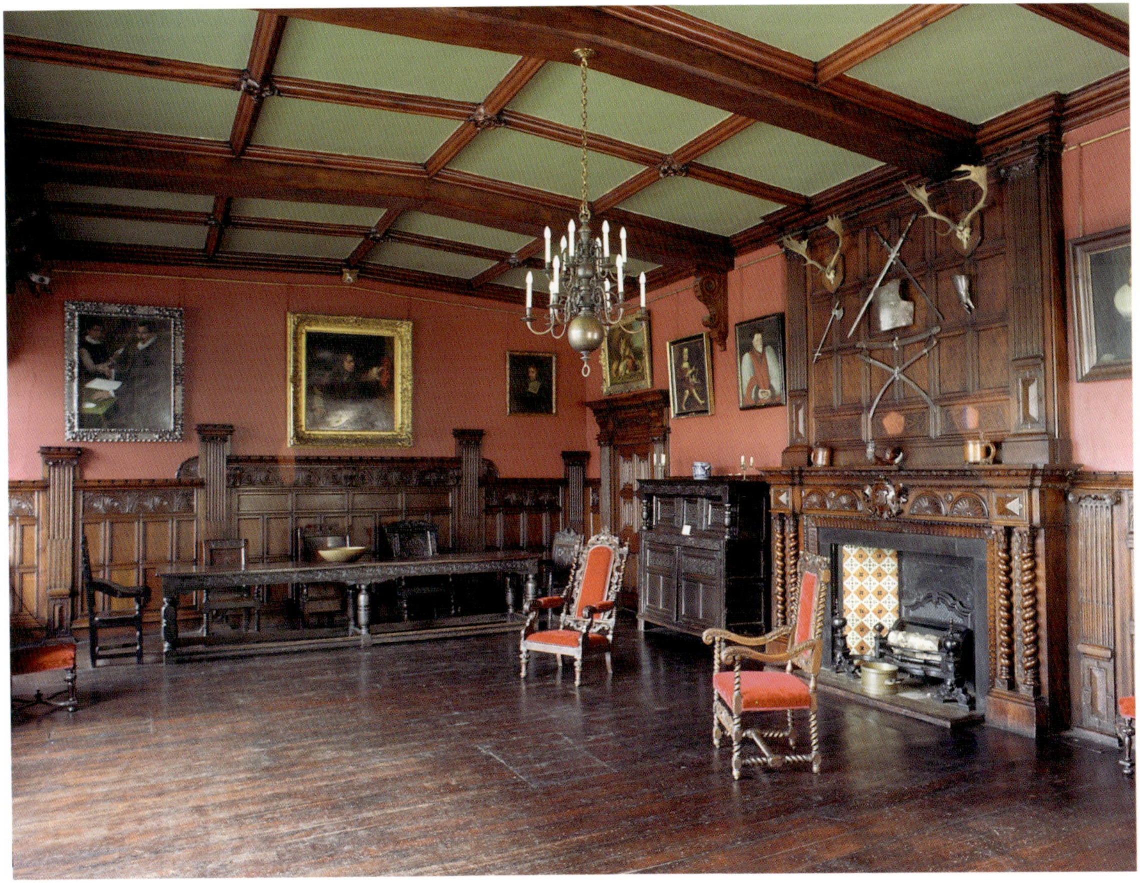

The Dining Room has been furnished to reflect life during the English Civil War, when the hall was besieged by Cromwell's Roundheads.

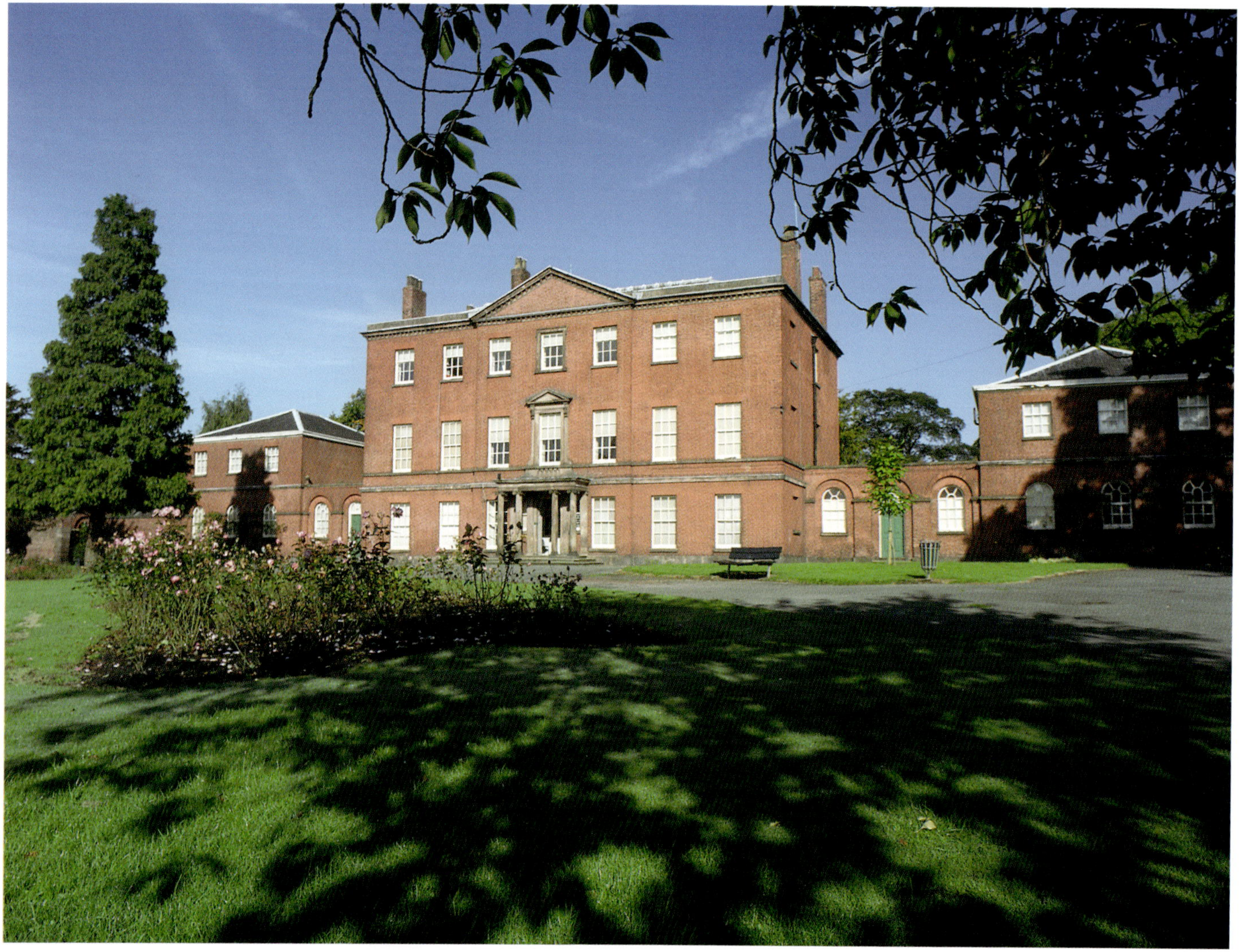

With over 23,000 items of clothing and accessories, the Gallery of Costume at Platt Hall has everything from Lancashire weavers' shawls to modern-day trainers.

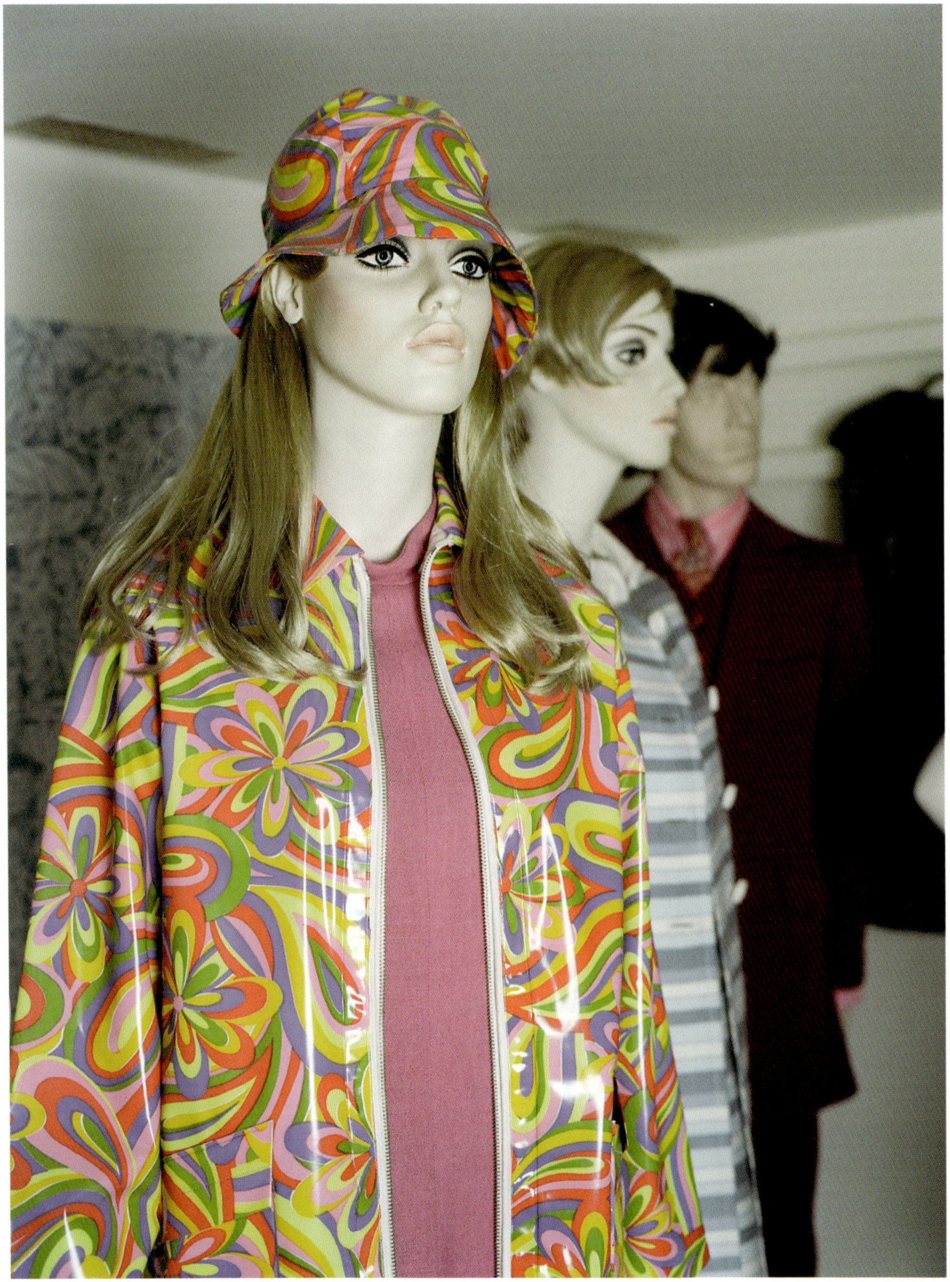

From the permanent display, 'Fashion through the Sixties'.

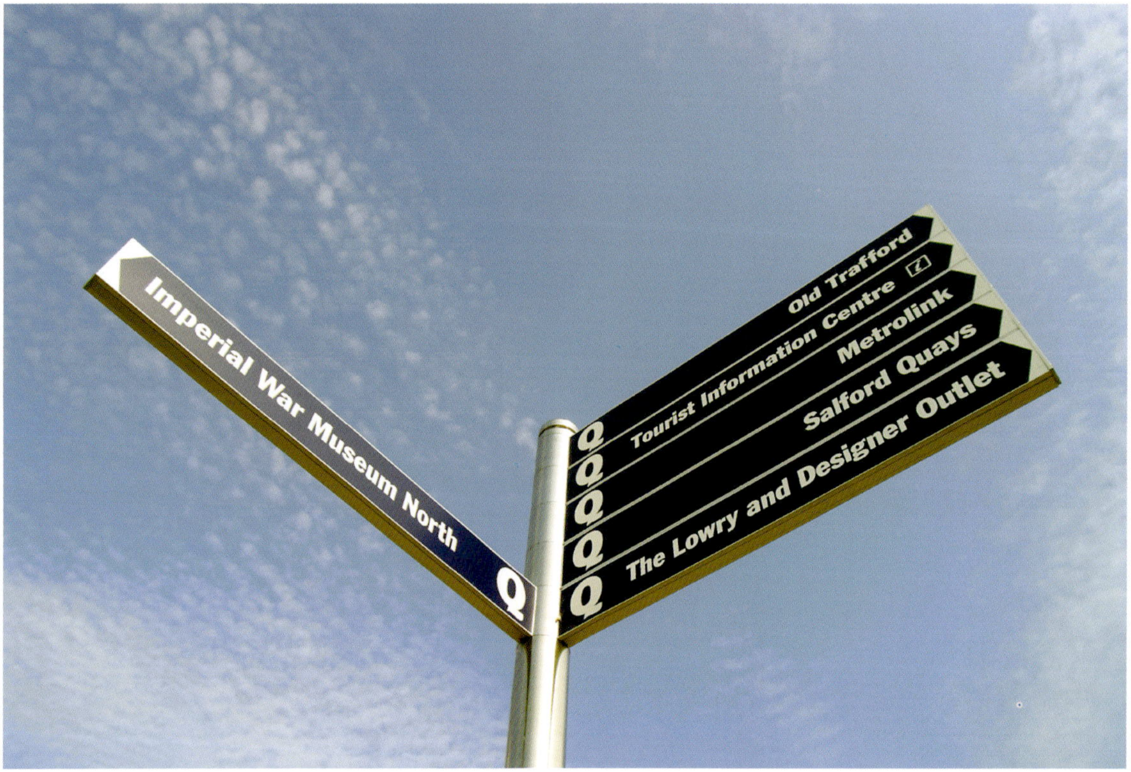

As recently as the late 1980s, Salford docks were a rundown wasteland. After fifteen years of regeneration, The Quays, as they are now known, are a hugely successful cultural and tourist attraction.

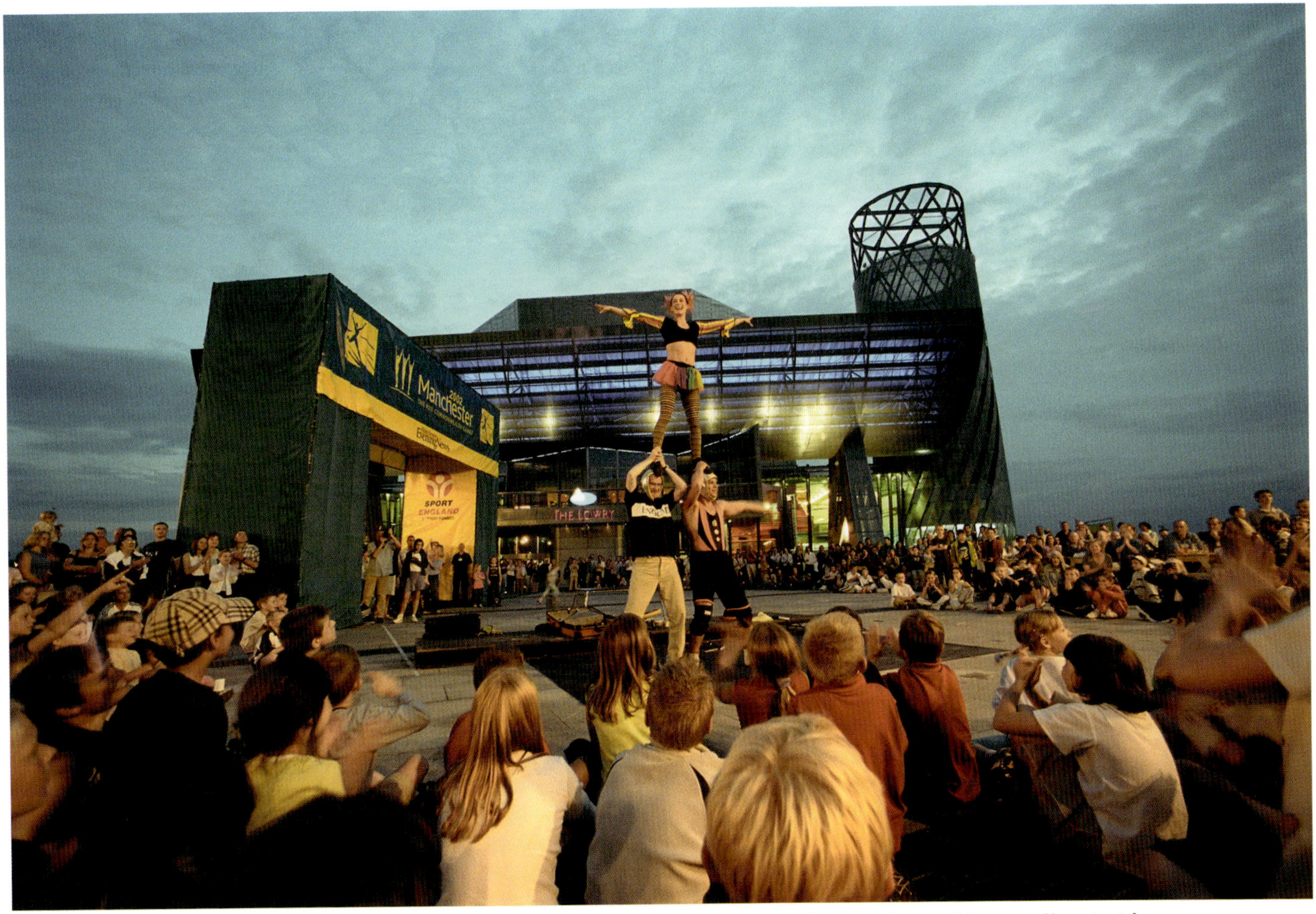

The Lowry, the centrepiece of the docks regeneration, attracts the crowds outside as well as inside.

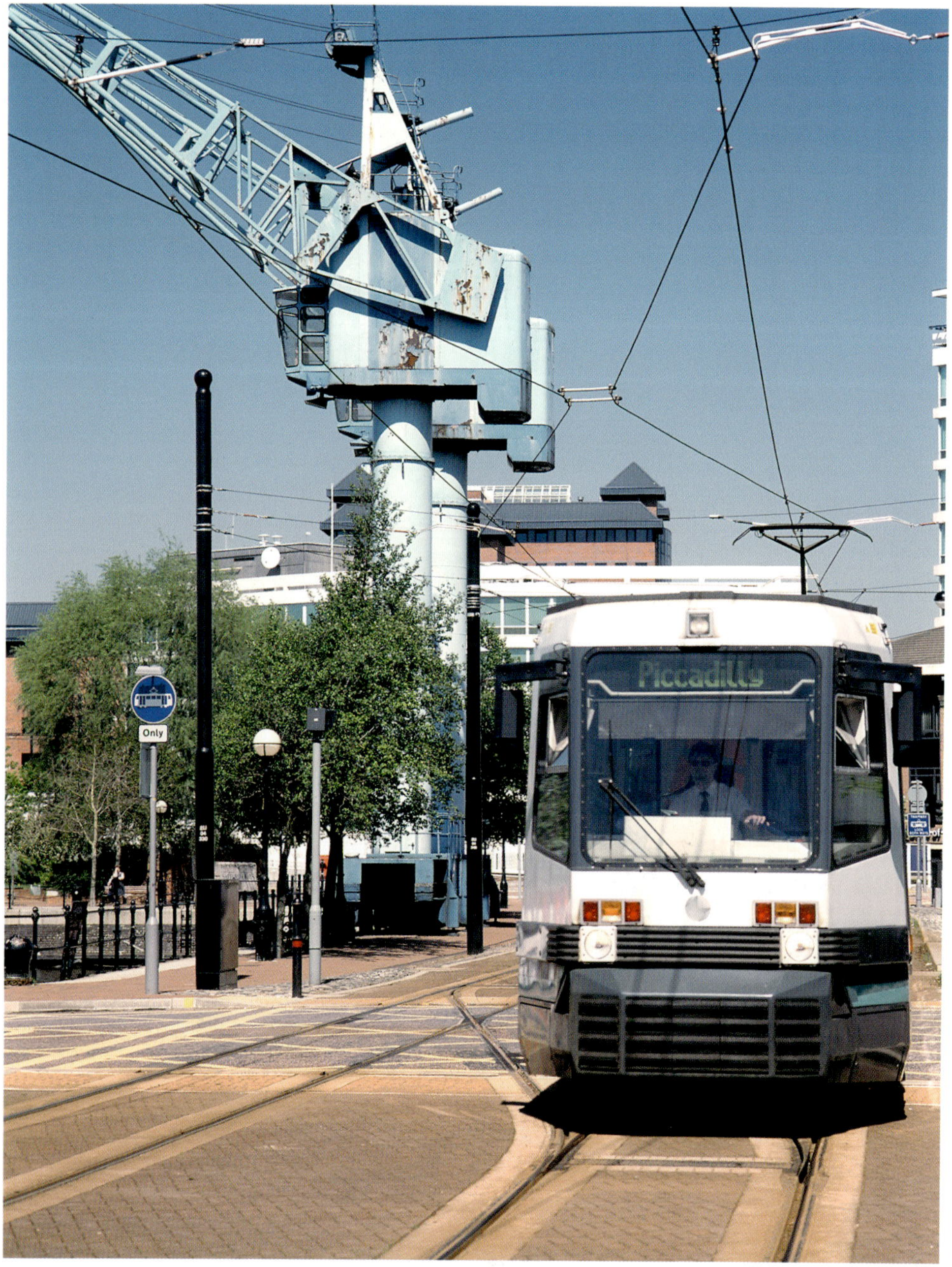

The Lowry footbridge *(opposite)* links Salford to Trafford across the Manchester Ship Canal, while Metrolink *(left)* runs through The Quays on its journey from Eccles to the city centre.

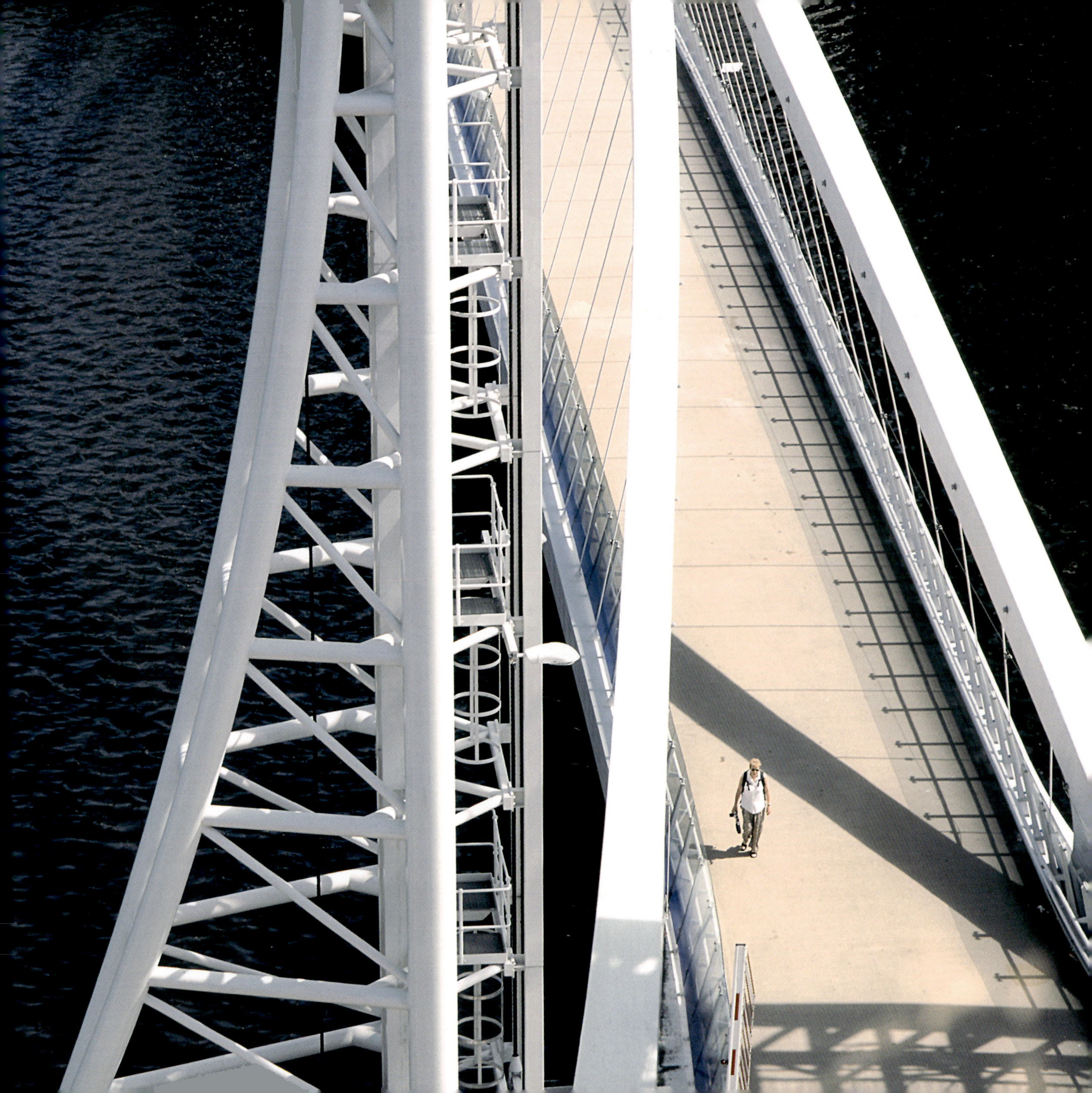

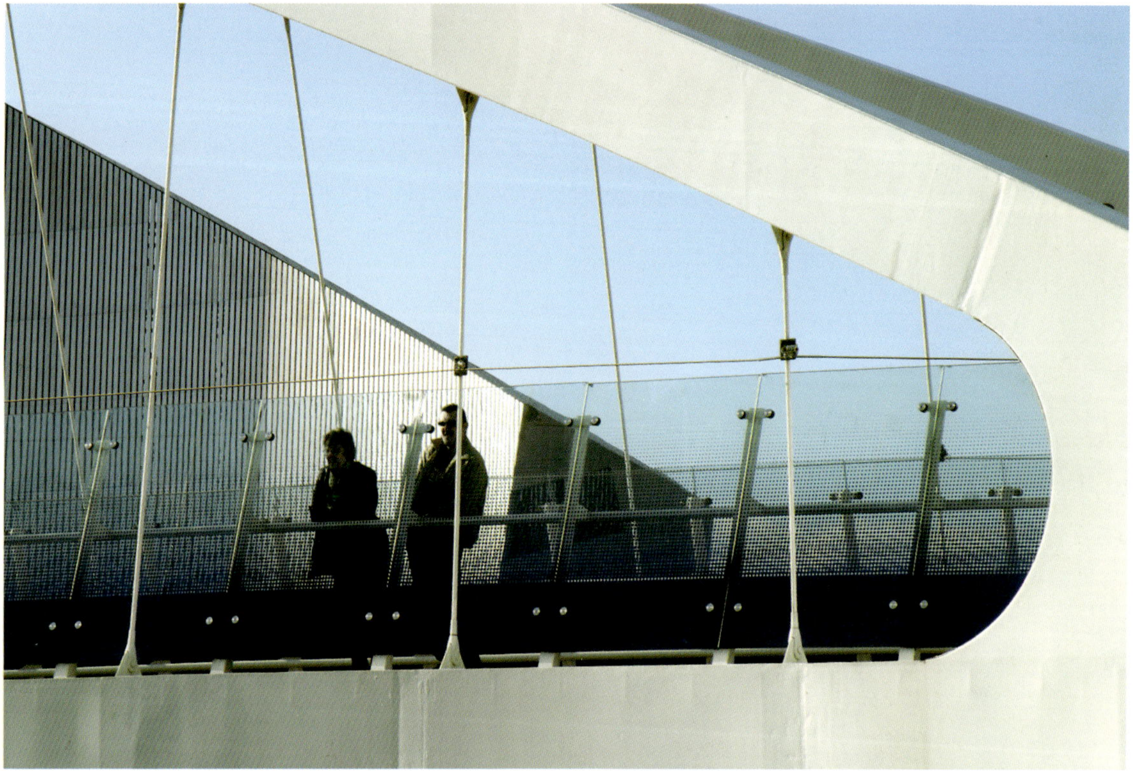

Checking out the view from the Lowry footbridge.

After extensive water treatment, the old docks have become a magnet for water sports enthusiasts.

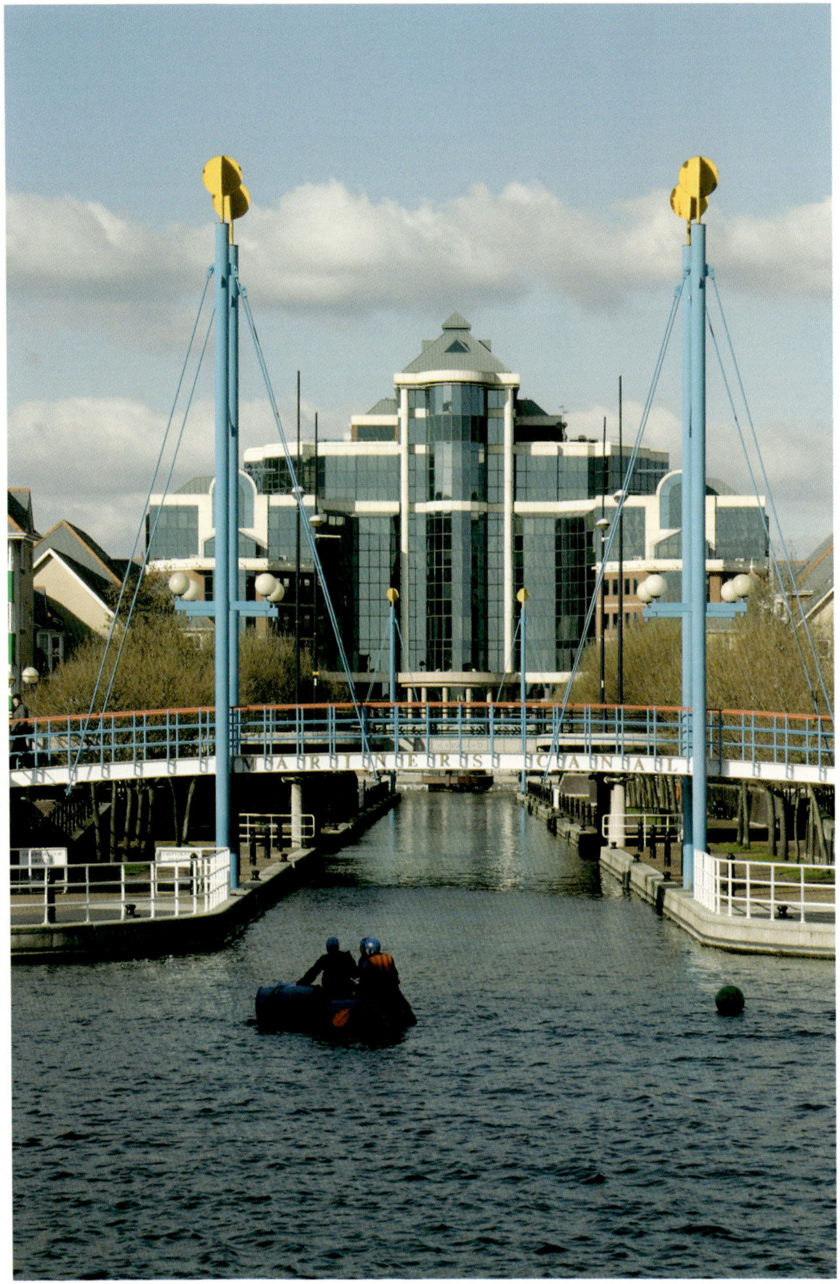

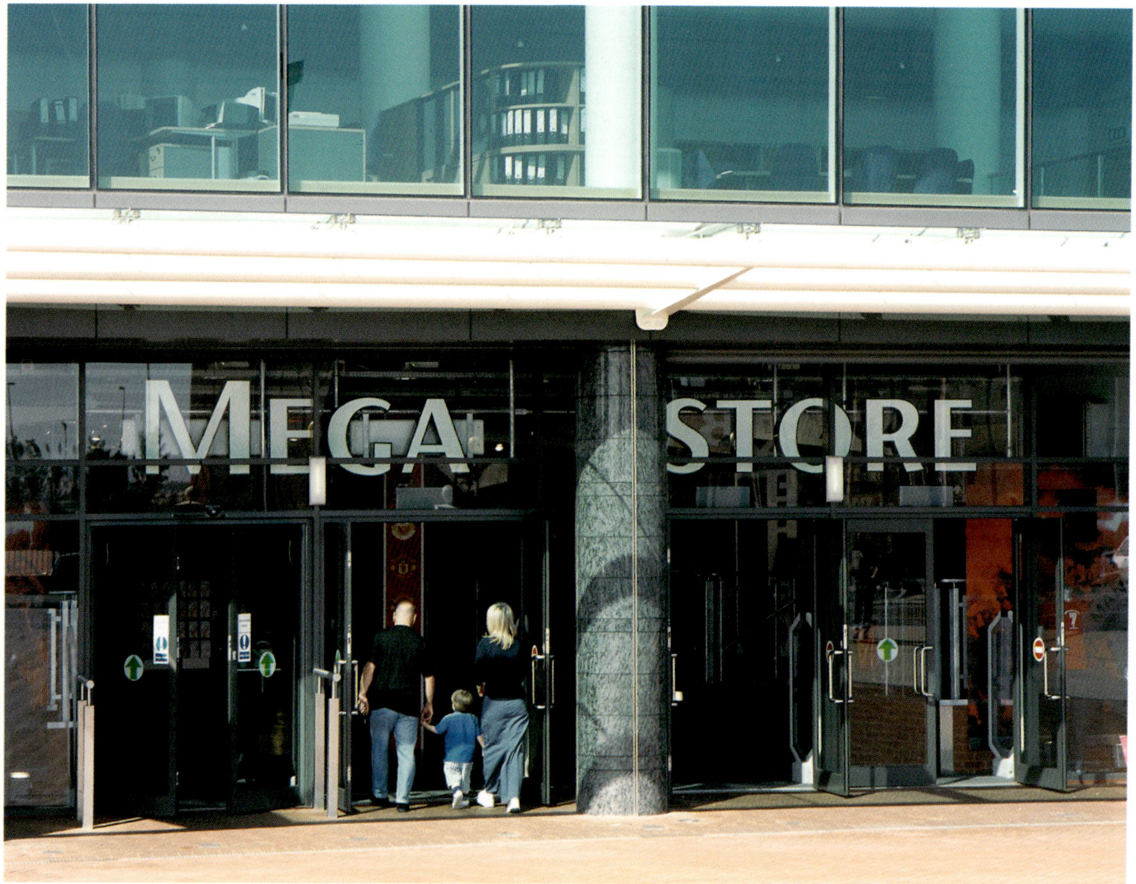

Adjacent to The Quays is the 'Theatre of Dreams' where Manchester United's Megastore catches them young.

Sir Matt Busby's bronze statue stands in front of Old Trafford's West Stand.

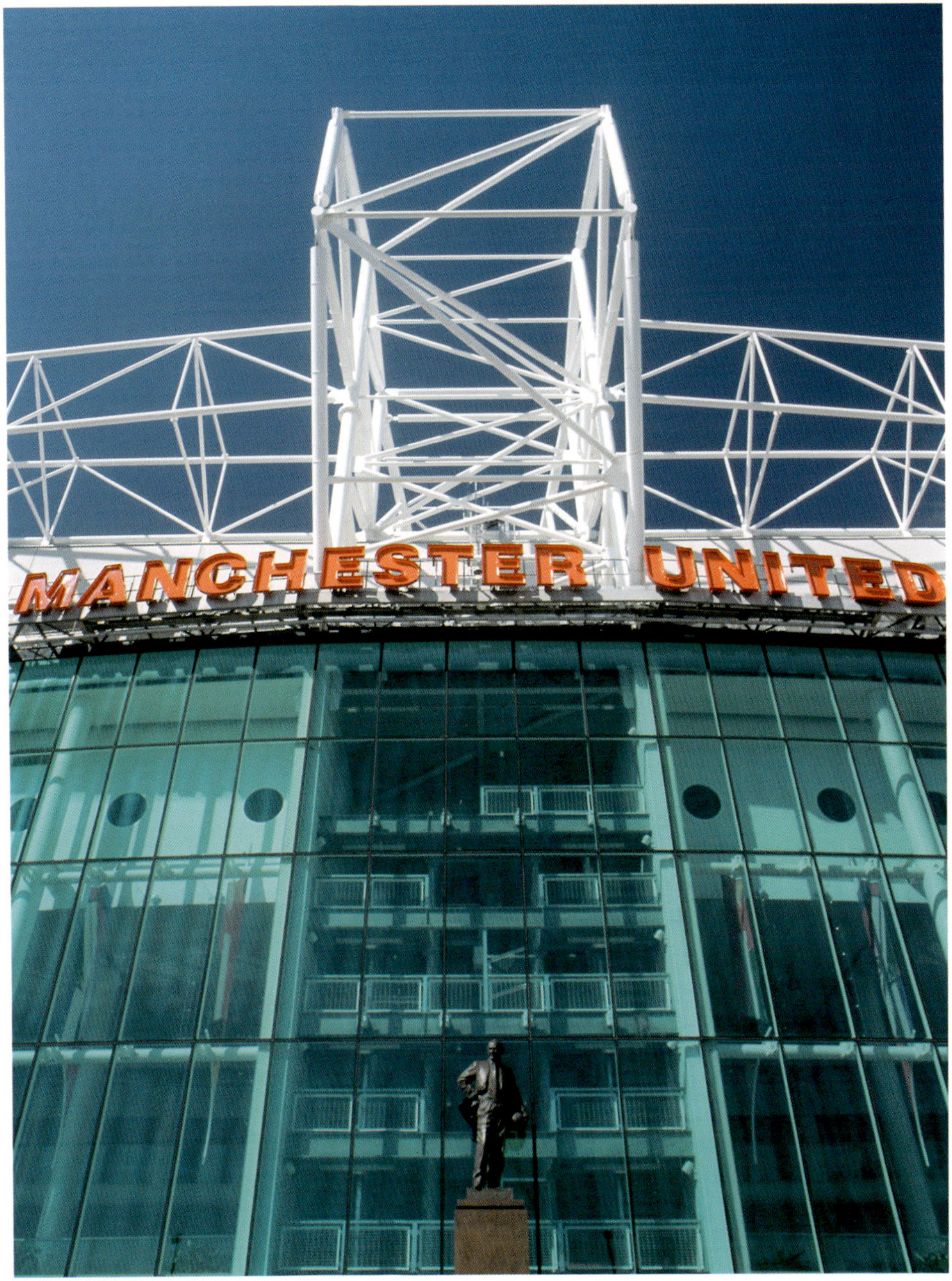

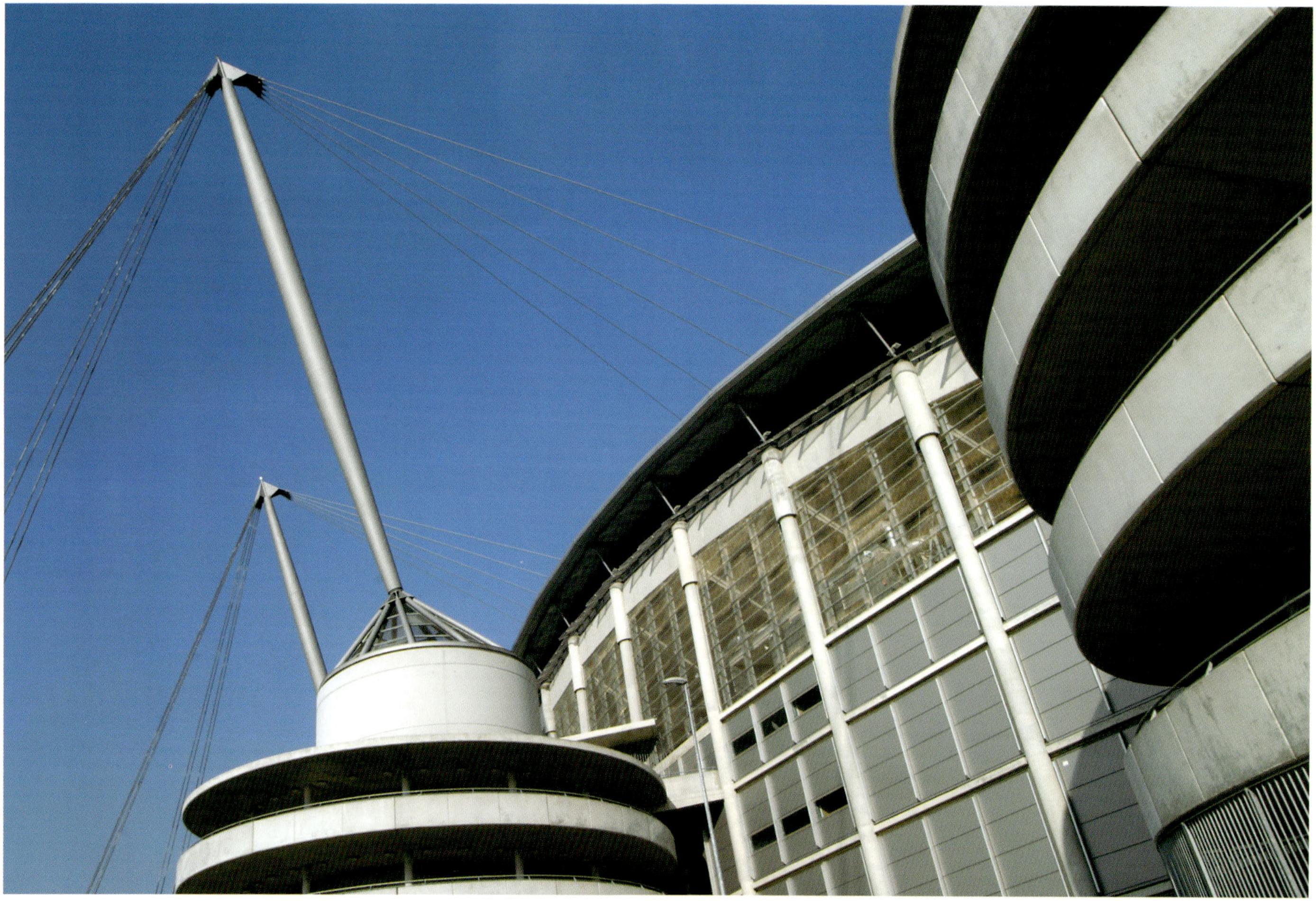

Across the city at Sportcity is the new home for rivals Manchester City Football Club, the impressive City of Manchester Stadium.

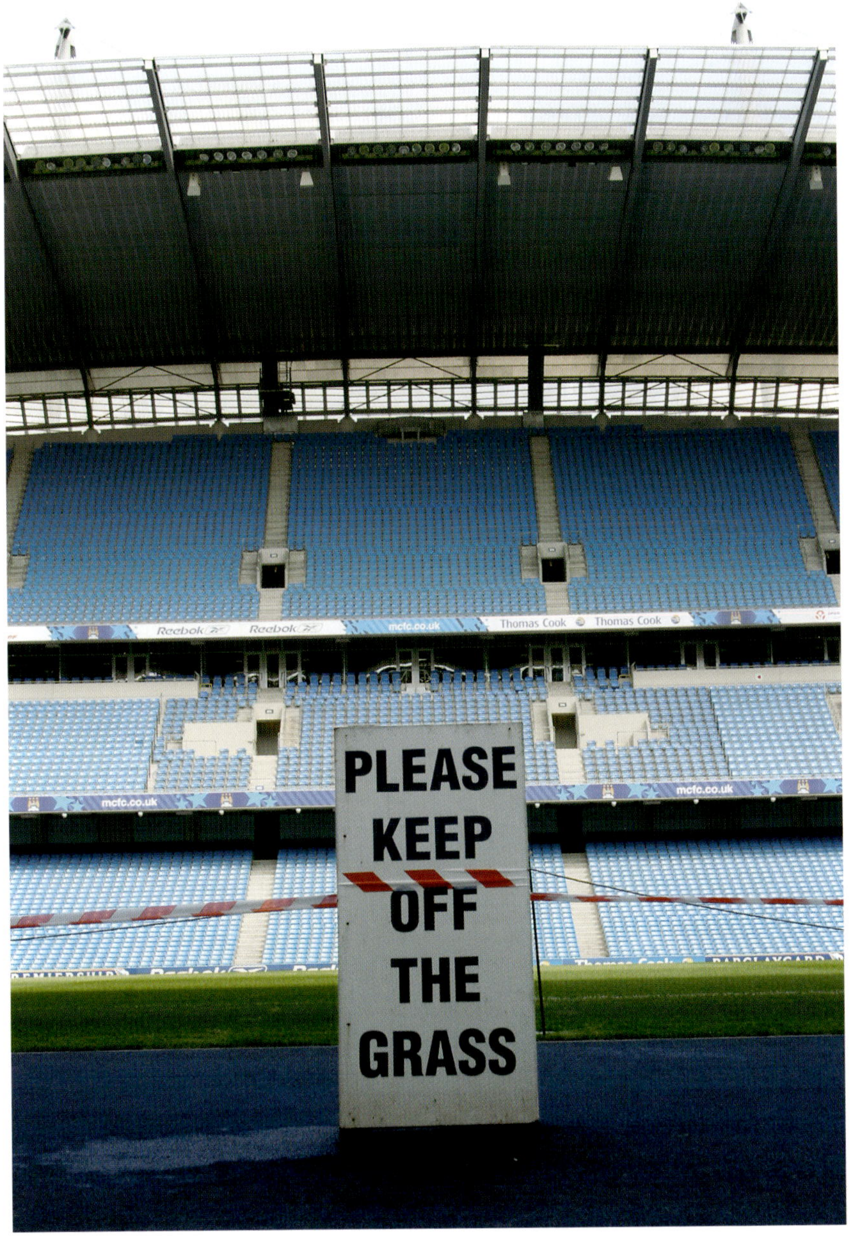

The stadium was originally built for the 2002 Commonwealth Games, but later adapted for City's use with an extended seating capacity of 48,000.

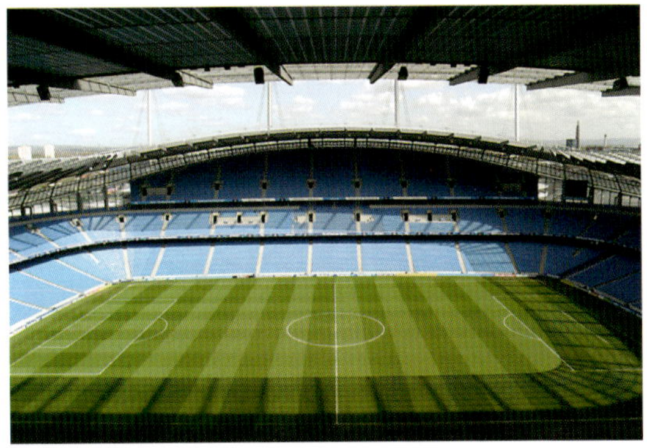

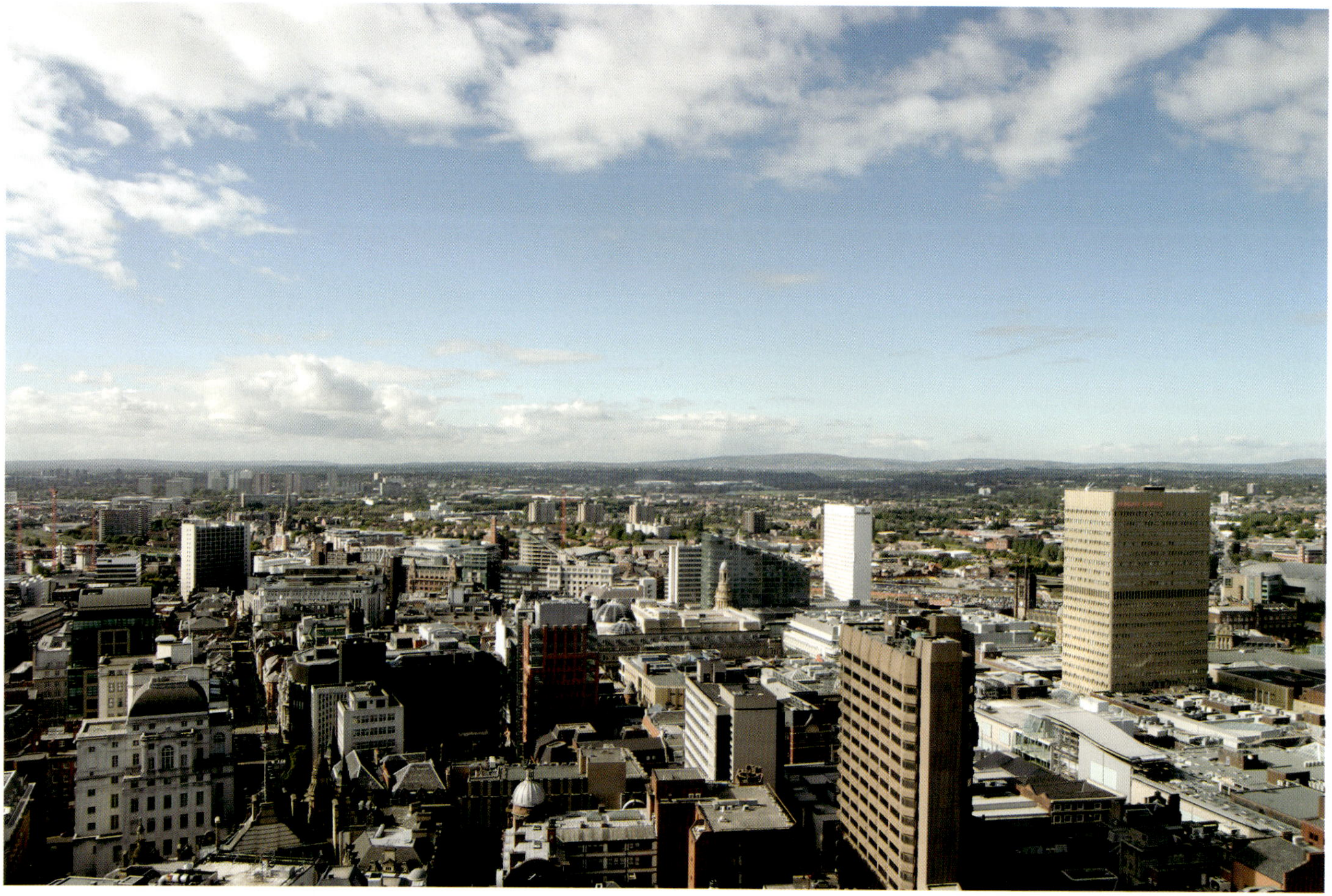

Recently described as 'Britain's Barcelona', the vibrant metropolis of Manchester has a bright future.